BAKE THE VERY BEST™

Nestlé®

Year-Round Recipes

Publications International, Ltd.

Microwave Cooking: Microwave ovens vary in wattage. Use the cooking times as guidelines and check for doneness before adding more time.

CONTENTS

Autumn

Winter

Introduction

In 1930, Kenneth and Ruth Wakefield purchased a Cape Cod-style Toll House located on the outskirts of Whitman, Massachusetts. The house served as a haven for road-weary travelers, and was over 200 years old when the Wakefields decided to open it as the Toll House Inn.

In keeping with the tradition of creating delicious homemade meals, Ruth baked for the guests. One day while preparing a batch of Butter Drop Do cookies, a favorite recipe dating back to Colonial days, Ruth cut a bar of Nestlé® Semi-Sweet Chocolate into tiny bits and added them to her dough expecting them to melt. Instead, the chocolate held its shape and softened to a delicately creamy texture. The Toll House® cookie was born!

Since they were first used by Ruth Wakefield in what would become an extremely popular cookie, Nestlé® Toll House® Semi-Sweet Morsels have satisfied the chocolate cravings of millions. Today, they're used to make many of the hundreds of delectable chocolate desserts all around the globe.

There are a million reasons to bake™ with Nestlé® Toll House®. For these recipes, and others featuring Nestlé® Carnation® Milks and Libby's® Pumpkin, visit VeryBestBaking.com.

OUR LETTER TO YOU

Here at Nestlé® Baking Kitchens, we develop recipes all year-round for you. We know from your letters and postings at VeryBestBaking.com that you and other homes find our ideas useful not only during that super-busy time of baking from late fall through the holidays, but throughout the year. That's why we decided to put together this cookbook, *Year-Round Recipes*, to share these great baking and meal solutions.

Year-Round Recipes is organized by the seasons. Within the sections for Spring, Summer, Autumn, and Winter you'll find individual chapters with recipes selected to meet the needs you'll encounter with the changing of the calendar.

Pg. 223

Pg. 281

In Autumn we offer a chapter on "After-School Snacks," while Winter brings you timely recipes for that time of year, with chapters on "Giftable Goodies"—because what expresses your love and appreciation for family and friends better than home-baked treats?—as well as sweets and dessert ideas such as Mocha Dream Cake or Nutty Dark Hot

OUR LETTER TO YOU

Pg. 70

Chocolate, which will warm your heart in the cold months.

Spring delivers a chapter full of recipes that are perfect for "Brunch with Friends," while the Summer section has plenty of ideas for desserts and treats that don't require you to turn on the oven—you can enjoy No Bake Dark Chocolate & Mint Cheesecake or Frozen Lemonade Pie and refreshing beverages, such as Cappuccino Smoothie and Toll House® Chocolate Chip Cookie Milkshake.

The recipes we've selected make sense for life in each season. We hope you find new ideas and soon-to-be family favorites as you try all of these recipes. Let us know how it goes by visiting VeryBestBaking. com and posting a message in one of the forums or visiting us on Facebook and posting on our wall.

Pg. 50

Wishing you fun baking,
Your friends in the Nestlé® Baking Kitchens

Spring

Blueberry White Chip Muffins

Jump into spring with these delicious brunch recipes! From waffles and pancakes to eggs, sausage, muffins, and more, you'll find a fantastic menu to please both family and friends. So gather around the table for great food with great company.

- 2 cups all-purpose flour
- ½ cup granulated sugar
- ¼ cup packed brown sugar
- 2½ teaspoons baking powder
- ½ teaspoon salt
- ¾ cup milk
- 1 large egg, lightly beaten
- ¼ cup butter or margarine, melted
- ½ teaspoon grated lemon peel
- 2 cups (12-ounce package) NESTLÉ® TOLL HOUSE® Premier White Morsels, *divided*
- 1½ cups fresh or frozen blueberries

  Streusel Topping (recipe follows)

PREHEAT oven to 375°F. Paper-line 18 muffin cups.

COMBINE flour, granulated sugar, brown sugar, baking powder and salt in large bowl. Stir in milk, egg, butter and lemon peel. Stir in *1½ cups* morsels and blueberries. Spoon into prepared muffin cups, filling almost full. Sprinkle with Streusel Topping.

BAKE for 22 to 25 minutes or until wooden pick inserted into centers comes out clean. Cool in pans for 5 minutes; remove to wire racks to cool slightly.

PLACE *remaining* morsels in small, *heavy-duty* resealable plastic food storage bag. Microwave on MEDIUM–HIGH (70%) power for 30 seconds; knead. Microwave at additional 10- to 15-second intervals, kneading until smooth. Cut tiny corner from bag; squeeze to drizzle over muffins. Serve warm.

Makes 18 muffins

Streusel Topping

COMBINE ⅓ cup granulated sugar, ¼ cup all-purpose flour and ¼ teaspoon ground cinnamon in small bowl. Cut in 3 tablespoons butter or margarine with pastry blender or two knives until mixture resembles coarse crumbs.

Donna's Heavenly Orange Chip Scones

4   cups all-purpose flour

1   cup granulated sugar

4   teaspoons baking powder

½   teaspoon baking soda

½   teaspoon salt

1   cup (6 ounces) NESTLÉ®
     TOLL HOUSE® Semi-Sweet
     Chocolate Mini Morsels

1   cup golden raisins

1   tablespoon grated orange peel

1   cup (2 sticks) unsalted butter,
     cut into pieces and softened

1   cup buttermilk

3   large eggs, *divided*

1   teaspoon orange extract

1   tablespoon milk

    Icing (recipe follows)

PREHEAT oven to 350°F. Lightly grease baking sheets.

COMBINE flour, granulated sugar, baking powder, baking soda and salt in large bowl. Add morsels, raisins and orange peel; mix well. Cut in butter with pastry blender or two knives until mixture resembles coarse crumbs. Combine buttermilk, *2 eggs* and orange extract in small bowl. Pour buttermilk mixture into flour mixture; mix just until a sticky dough is formed. Do not overmix. Drop by level ¼-cup measure onto prepared baking sheets. Combine *remaining* egg and milk in small bowl. Brush egg mixture over top of dough.

BAKE for 18 to 22 minutes or until wooden pick inserted in center comes out clean. For best results, bake one baking sheet at a time. Cool on wire racks for 10 minutes. Drizzle scones with icing. Serve warm.

Makes 2 dozen scones

Icing

COMBINE 2 cups powdered sugar, ¼ cup orange juice, 1 tablespoon grated orange peel and 1 teaspoon orange extract in medium bowl. Mix until smooth.

BRUNCH WITH FRIENDS AND FAMILY

Ham and Swiss Quiche

- **1 cup (4 ounces) shredded Swiss cheese,** *divided*
- **1 cup finely chopped cooked ham**
- **2 green onions, sliced**
- **1** *unbaked* **9-inch (4-cup volume) deep-dish pie shell**
- **1 can (12 fluid ounces) NESTLÉ® CARNATION® Evaporated Milk**
- **3 large eggs**
- **¼ cup all-purpose flour**
- **¼ teaspoon salt**
- **⅛ teaspoon ground black pepper**

PREHEAT oven to 350°F.

SPRINKLE ½ cup cheese, ham and green onions into pie crust. Whisk together evaporated milk, eggs, flour, salt and pepper in large bowl. Pour mixture into pie shell; sprinkle with *remaining* cheese.

BAKE for 45 to 50 minutes or until knife inserted near center comes out clean. Cool on wire rack for 10 minutes before serving.

Makes 8 servings

For Lattice-Top Quiche: *Use ready-made pie pastry for single crust pie. Cut pastry into ½-inch-wide strips. Lay pastry strips over filling in lattice-fashion, turning pastry over outside edge of dish. Bake as directed above.*

TOLL HOUSE® Mini Morsel Pancakes

2½ cups all-purpose flour

1 cup (6 ounces) NESTLÉ® TOLL HOUSE® Semi-Sweet Chocolate Mini Morsels

1 tablespoon baking powder

½ teaspoon salt

1¾ cups milk

2 large eggs

⅓ cup vegetable oil

⅓ cup packed brown sugar

Powdered sugar

Fresh sliced strawberries (optional)

Maple syrup

COMBINE flour, morsels, baking powder and salt in large bowl. Combine milk, eggs, vegetable oil and brown sugar in medium bowl; add to flour mixture. Stir just until moistened (batter may be lumpy).

HEAT griddle or skillet over medium heat; brush lightly with vegetable oil. Pour ¼ *cup* of batter onto hot griddle; cook until bubbles begin to burst. Turn; continue to cook for about 1 minute longer or until golden. Repeat with *remaining* batter.

SPRINKLE with powdered sugar; top with strawberries. Serve with maple syrup.

Makes about 18 pancakes

BRUNCH WITH FRIENDS AND FAMILY

Waffles Benedict

1 can (12 fluid ounces) NESTLÉ® CARNATION® Evaporated Milk

1½ cups (6 ounces) shredded cheddar cheese

1 teaspoon all-purpose flour

8 frozen toaster waffles

8 large eggs, well-beaten

½ teaspoon salt

¼ teaspoon ground black pepper

Nonstick cooking spray

8 slices bacon, cooked and crumbled

Chopped chives (optional)

COMBINE ¾ *cup* evaporated milk, cheese and flour in small saucepan. Cook over medium heat, stirring constantly, for about 3 minutes or until cheese is melted and sauce has slightly thickened to a creamy consistency. Remove from heat; cover.

TOAST waffles according to package directions. Keep warm.

WHISK together *remaining* evaporated milk, eggs, salt and pepper in medium bowl. Spray large skillet with nonstick cooking spray; heat over medium heat. Pour egg mixture into skillet. Cook, stirring frequently, until eggs are cooked.

TO ASSEMBLE:

TOP each waffle with eggs, cheese sauce, bacon and chives.

Makes 8 servings

Hash Brown Casserole

2 cups (8 ounces) shredded cheddar cheese

3 cartons (4 ounces *each*) cholesterol-free egg product or 6 large eggs, well beaten

1 can (12 fluid ounces) NESTLÉ® CARNATION® Evaporated Fat Free Milk

1 teaspoon salt (optional)

½ teaspoon ground black pepper

1 package (30 ounces) frozen shredded hash brown potatoes

1 medium onion, chopped

1 small green bell pepper, chopped

1 cup diced ham or 10 slices turkey bacon, cooked and chopped

Note: Substitute 6 large eggs, well beaten, for the cholesterol-free egg product.

PREHEAT oven to 350°F. Grease 13×9-inch baking dish.

COMBINE cheese, egg product, evaporated milk, salt and black pepper in large bowl. Add potatoes, onion, bell pepper and ham, if desired; mix well. Pour mixture into prepared baking dish.

BAKE for 60 to 65 minutes or until set.

Makes 12 servings

Stuffed French Toast with Fresh Berry Topping

2 **cups mixed fresh berries
(strawberries, raspberries,
blueberries and/or
blackberries)**

2 **tablespoons granulated sugar**

⅔ **cup lowfat ricotta cheese**

¼ **cup strawberry preserves**

3 **large eggs**

⅔ **cup (5-fluid-ounce can)
NESTLÉ® CARNATION®
Fat Free Evaporated Milk**

2 **tablespoons packed brown sugar**

2 **teaspoons vanilla extract**

12 **slices (about
¾-inch-thick)
French bread**

1 **tablespoon
vegetable
oil, butter or
margarine**

**Powdered sugar
(optional)**

**Maple syrup,
heated
(optional)**

COMBINE berries and granulated sugar in small bowl. Combine ricotta cheese and strawberry preserves in another small bowl; mix well. Combine eggs, evaporated milk, brown sugar and vanilla extract in pie plate or shallow bowl; mix well.

SPREAD ricotta-preserves mixture evenly over *6 slices* of bread. Top with *remaining* slices of bread to form sandwiches.

HEAT vegetable oil or butter in large, nonstick skillet or griddle over medium heat. Dip sandwiches in egg mixture, coating both sides. Cook on each side for about 2 minutes or until golden brown.

SPRINKLE with powdered sugar; top with berries. Serve with maple syrup, if desired.

Makes 6 servings

Cranberry Chocolate Panini

- ¼ **cup warm water (105°F to 115°F)**
- 1 **package (¼ ounce) active-dry yeast or fast-rising yeast**
- 1 **cup NESTLÉ® CARNATION® Evaporated Milk**
- 2 **tablespoons honey**
- 2 **tablespoons butter, melted, *divided***
- 1¼ **teaspoons salt**
- 3 **to 3½ cups bread flour**
- ¼ **cup NESTLÉ® TOLL HOUSE® Milk Chocolate Morsels (optional)**
- 4 **bars (8-ounce box) NESTLÉ® TOLL HOUSE® Semi-Sweet Chocolate Baking Bars, broken into pieces**
- ¼ **cup dried sweetened cranberries or cherries, coarsely chopped**

COMBINE water and yeast in large mixer bowl. Let stand for 5 minutes or until mixture looks creamy. Add evaporated milk, honey, *1 tablespoon* butter and salt. With mixer on medium speed, gradually add 2 cups flour, ½ cup at a time, scraping bowl often. Using wooden spoon, stir in morsels and cranberries. Stir in up to 1 cup of remaining flour. Dough should stick to spoon and clean itself from side of bowl.

TURN dough out onto slightly floured surface. Knead in additional flour to make a slightly stiff dough that is smooth and elastic (6 to 8 minutes). Place in greased bowl; turn to grease surface. Cover; let rise in warm place for about 1 hour or until double in size.

PUNCH dough down. Divide dough into 8 pieces. Flatten each piece into 6×4-inch rectangle. Place

one square chocolate in center and roll up. Fold ends under. Place on greased baking sheet(s). Cover; let rise in warm place for 15 minutes or until double in size.

PREHEAT oven to 375°F. Brush rolls with *remaining* butter.

BAKE for 18 to 22 minutes or until rolls are golden brown and sound hollow when tapped on bottom. Remove to wire rack to cool completely.

Makes 8 rolls

Iced Café Latte

- 1 **can (12 fluid ounces) NESTLÉ® CARNATION® Evaporated Lowfat 2% Milk**
- 4 **to 5 teaspoons NESCAFÉ® CLASICO™ 100% Pure Instant Coffee Granules**
- 3 **teaspoons granulated sugar**
  Ice cubes

COMBINE evaporated milk, coffee granules and sugar in 2-cup glass measure. Microwave on HIGH (100%) power for 1 minute; stir well. Pour over ice cubes.

Makes 2 servings

Classic CARNATION® Coffeecake

2½ **cups all-purpose baking mix**

½ **cup dry NESTLÉ® CARNATION® Instant Nonfat Dry Milk**

⅓ **cup plus 1 tablespoon butter, softened**

½ **cup packed brown sugar, *divided***

¼ **cup plus 2 tablespoons granulated sugar, *divided***

3 **large eggs**

½ **cup water**

1 **teaspoon ground cinnamon**

PREHEAT oven to 350°F. Grease 9-inch-square baking pan.

COMBINE baking mix and dry milk in small bowl. Beat ⅓ *cup* butter, ¼ *cup* brown sugar and ¼ *cup* granulated sugar in large mixer bowl until creamy. Add eggs and water; beat on medium speed for 2 minutes until blended. Gradually beat in baking mix mixture just until blended.

COMBINE *remaining* ¼ *cup* brown sugar, 2 *tablespoons* granulated sugar, 1 *tablespoon* butter and cinnamon in small bowl.

SPREAD batter into prepared pan. Sprinkle cinnamon-sugar mixture over batter. Poke round end of wooden spoon randomly into batter to form streusel ribbons in cake.

BAKE for 30 to 35 minutes or until wooden pick inserted in center comes out clean. Cool in pan on wire rack. Serve warm. Store any remaining cake tightly covered.

Makes 12 servings

Orange Brunch Muffins

3 cups all-purpose baking mix

¾ cup all-purpose flour

⅔ cup granulated sugar

2 large eggs, lightly beaten

½ cup plain yogurt

½ cup orange juice

1 tablespoon grated orange peel

2 cups (12-ounce package) **NESTLÉ® TOLL HOUSE® Premier White Morsels,** *divided*

½ cup chopped macadamia nuts or walnuts

PREHEAT oven to 375°F. Grease or paper-line 18 muffin cups.

COMBINE baking mix, flour and sugar in large bowl. Add eggs, yogurt, orange juice and orange peel; stir just until blended. Stir in 1⅓ cups morsels. Spoon into prepared muffin cups, filling ¾ full. Sprinkle with nuts.

BAKE for 18 to 22 minutes or until wooden pick inserted in center comes out clean. Cool in pans for 10 minutes; remove to wire racks to cool slightly.

MICROWAVE *remaining* morsels in small, *heavy-duty* resealable plastic food storage bag on MEDIUM-HIGH (70%) power for 1 minute; knead bag. Microwave at additional 10- to 15-second intervals, kneading until smooth. Cut tiny corner from bag; squeeze to drizzle over muffins. Serve warm.

Makes 18 muffins

BRUNCH WITH FRIENDS AND FAMILY

Brunch Sausage Casserole

1 package (16 ounces) fresh breakfast sausage, cooked, drained and crumbled

4 cups cubed day-old bread

2 cups (8 ounces) shredded sharp cheddar cheese

2 cans (12 fluid ounces *each*) NESTLÉ® CARNATION® Evaporated Milk

10 large eggs, lightly beaten

1 teaspoon dry mustard

¼ teaspoon onion powder

Ground black pepper to taste

GREASE 13×9-inch baking dish. Place bread in prepared baking dish. Sprinkle with cheese.

COMBINE evaporated milk, eggs, dry mustard and onion powder in medium bowl. Pour evenly over bread and cheese. Sprinkle with sausage. Cover; refrigerate overnight.

PREHEAT oven to 325°F.

BAKE for 55 to 60 minutes or until cheese is golden brown. Cover with foil if top browns too quickly. Season with ground black pepper.

Makes 8 to 10 servings

NESTLÉ® TOLL HOUSE® Hot Cocoa

½ **cup granulated sugar**

⅓ **cup NESTLÉ® TOLL HOUSE® Baking Cocoa**

4 **cups milk,** *divided*

1 **teaspoon vanilla extract**

Whipped cream or miniature marshmallows (optional)

COMBINE sugar and cocoa in medium saucepan; stir. Gradually stir in ⅓ *cup* milk to make a smooth paste; stir in *remaining* milk.

WARM over medium heat, stirring constantly, until hot. Do not boil. Remove from heat; stir in vanilla extract. Top with whipped cream or marshmallows, if desired, before serving.

Makes 4 servings

Butterscotch Sticky Buns

5 **tablespoons butter or margarine,** *divided*

2 **packages (8 ounces** *each***) refrigerated crescent dinner rolls**

1⅔ **cups (11-ounce package) NESTLÉ® TOLL HOUSE® Butterscotch Flavored Morsels,** *divided*

½ **cup chopped pecans**

¼ **cup granulated sugar**

1½ **teaspoons lemon juice**

1½ **teaspoons water**

1 **teaspoon ground cinnamon**

PREHEAT oven to 375°F.

PLACE 2 *tablespoons* butter in 13×9-inch baking pan; melt in oven for 2 to 4 minutes or until butter sizzles. Unroll dinner rolls; separate into 16 triangles. Sprinkle triangles with 1⅓ *cups* morsels. Starting at shortest side, roll up each triangle; arrange in prepared baking pan.

BAKE for 15 to 20 minutes or until lightly browned.

MICROWAVE *remaining* morsels and *remaining* butter in medium, uncovered, microwave-safe bowl on MEDIUM-HIGH (70%) power for 30 seconds. STIR. Morsels may retain some of their original shape. If necessary, microwave at additional 10- to 15-second intervals, stirring just until morsels are melted. Stir in nuts, sugar, lemon juice, water and cinnamon. Pour over hot rolls.

BAKE for 5 minutes or until bubbly. Immediately loosen buns from pan. Cool in pan on wire rack for 10 minutes; serve warm.

Makes 16 buns

Pear Oven Pancake

- **2 tablespoons butter, melted**
- **½ cup all-purpose flour**
- **¼ cup *plus* 2 tablespoons granulated sugar, *divided***
- **¼ teaspoon salt**
- **1 can (12 fluid ounces) NESTLÉ® CARNATION® Evaporated Milk**
- **3 large eggs**
- **1 ripe pear, cored and thinly sliced**
- **½ teaspoon ground cinnamon**

PREHEAT oven to 450°F.

POUR melted butter into 9-inch deep-dish pie plate or cake pan. Swirl to coat bottom and sides of plate.

COMBINE flour, ¼ cup sugar and salt in medium bowl. Whisk evaporated milk and eggs in another medium bowl until blended. Add to flour mixture; whisk for 30 seconds or until smooth. Pour batter into prepared pie plate. Arrange pear slices on top of batter in pinwheel design, pushing down slightly. Combine *remaining 2 tablespoons* sugar and cinnamon in small bowl. Sprinkle top with sugar mixture.

BAKE for 15 to 20 minutes or until puffed and golden brown. Serve warm.

Makes 6 servings

Tip: *For a harvest twist on this fabulous recipe, substitute sautéed apples for pears.*

Strawberry Swirl Smoothie

**1 can (12 fluid ounces) NESTLÉ®
CARNATION® Evaporated Lowfat
2% Milk, *chilled***

**1½ cups (to 2 cups) whole strawberries, frozen
or fresh**

**1 container (6 ounces) light strawberry
yogurt**

PLACE evaporated milk, strawberries and yogurt in
blender; cover. Blend until smooth.

Makes 4 servings (8 ounces each)

Chocolate Brunch Waffles

2¼ cups all-purpose flour

½ cup granulated sugar

1 tablespoon baking powder

¾ teaspoon salt

**1 cup (6 ounces) NESTLÉ® TOLL HOUSE®
Semi-Sweet Chocolate Morsels**

¾ cup (1½ sticks) butter or margarine

1½ cups milk

3 large eggs, lightly beaten

1 tablespoon vanilla extract

**Toppings (whipped cream, chocolate
shavings, sifted powdered sugar, fresh
fruit, ice cream)**

COMBINE flour, sugar, baking powder and salt in
large bowl.

MICROWAVE morsels and butter in medium,
uncovered, microwave-safe bowl on HIGH (100%)
power for 1 minute. STIR. Morsels may retain some
of their original shape. If necessary, microwave at
additional 10- to 15-second intervals, stirring just
until morsels are melted. Cool to room temperature.
Stir in milk, eggs and vanilla extract. Add chocolate
mixture to flour mixture; stir (batter will be thick).

COOK in Belgian waffle maker* according to
manufacturer's directions. Serve warm with your
choice of toppings.

Makes 10 Belgian waffle squares

**Can also be cooked in standard waffle maker (makes about
20 standard-size waffle squares).*

Sunrise Sausage Bake

- **2 cans (12 fluid ounces *each*) NESTLÉ® CARNATION® Evaporated Milk**
- **8 large eggs, beaten**
- **1 pound precooked sausage links, cut into ¼-inch slices**
- **2 cups (8-ounce package) shredded cheddar cheese**
- **1 cup chopped red and/or green bell pepper**
- **2 green onions (green parts only), sliced**
- **½ teaspoon onion powder**
- **¼ teaspoon garlic powder**
- **8 cups ½-inch cubed Italian or French bread (about 9 slices)**

PREHEAT oven to 350°F. Grease 13×9-inch baking dish.

COMBINE milk, eggs, sausage, cheese, red pepper, green onions, onion powder and garlic powder in large bowl. Add bread cubes, stirring gently to moisten bread. Pour mixture into baking dish.

BAKE for 45 minutes or until set. Serve warm.

Makes 12 servings

Tip: *This bake can be assembled ahead of time and refrigerated. Let stand at room temperature for 30 minutes before baking.*

Tip: *Substitute multi-grain bread for Italian or French bread.*

Premier White Morsel & Cranberry Cinnamon Rolls

- **2** loaves (1 pound *each*) frozen white yeast bread dough, thawed, *divided*
- **2** tablespoons butter, softened, *divided*
- **¼** cup granulated sugar
- **1** tablespoon ground cinnamon
- **2** cups (12-ounce package) NESTLÉ® TOLL HOUSE® Premier White Morsels, *divided*
- **1** cup sweetened dried cranberries, coarsely chopped, *divided*
- **1** cup powdered sugar, sifted
- **3** tablespoons milk

GREASE two 9-inch-round baking pans.

ROLL 1 bread loaf into 16×10-inch rectangle on lightly floured surface.

SPREAD 1 *tablespoon* softened butter over dough. Combine sugar and cinnamon in small bowl; sprinkle 2 *tablespoons* over dough leaving ½-inch border around sides. Sprinkle with ¾ *cup* morsels and ½ *cup* cranberries, firmly pressing morsels and cranberries into dough.

ROLL up dough tightly, starting at short end; seal edges with water. Cut into 6 slices; place cut side up in prepared baking pan. Repeat with *remaining* bread loaf, butter, sugar mixture, morsels and cranberries; place in second prepared baking pan. Cover; let rise in warm place until dough almost fills pans, about 30 minutes

PREHEAT oven to 350°F.

BAKE for 25 to 30 minutes or until golden brown. Cool for 15 minutes in pans on wire racks.

MELT *remaining* morsels in small, uncovered, microwave-safe bowl on MEDIUM-HIGH (70%) power for 30 seconds; STIR. Morsels may retain some of their original shape. If necessary, microwave at additional 10- to 15-second intervals, stirring just until morsels are melted. Stir in powdered sugar and milk to make a stiff glaze. Drizzle over cinnamon rolls.

Makes 12 servings

Quiche Lorraine

1 *unbaked* 9-inch (4-cup volume) deep-dish pie shell

6 slices bacon, chopped

½ cup chopped onion

1½ cups (6 ounces) shredded Swiss cheese

1 can (12 fluid ounces) NESTLÉ® CARNATION® Evaporated Milk

3 large eggs, well beaten

¼ teaspoon salt

⅛ teaspoon ground black pepper

⅛ teaspoon ground nutmeg

PREHEAT oven to 350°F.

COOK bacon in large skillet over medium heat. When bacon starts to turn brown, add onion. Cook until bacon is crisp; drain. Sprinkle cheese into bottom of pie shell. Top with bacon mixture. Combine evaporated milk, eggs, salt, pepper and nutmeg in small bowl until blended. Pour into pie shell.

BAKE for 30 to 35 minutes or until knife inserted halfway between center and edge comes out clean. Cool for 5 minutes on wire rack before serving.

Makes 8 servings

Notes: *Quiche fits a variety of meal occasions from brunch to dinner and also makes an outstanding appetizer. If using metal or foil pans, bake on preheated heavy-duty baking sheet.*

Puffy Baked Apple Pancake

Nonstick cooking spray

½ cup NESTLÉ® CARNATION® Evaporated Milk

⅓ cup all-purpose baking mix

2 tablespoons granulated sugar, *divided*

3 large eggs, separated

2 tablespoons orange juice

¼ teaspoon ground cinnamon

1 medium apple, cored, quartered and cut into thin slices

1 tablespoon cinnamon-sugar mixture

PREHEAT oven to 375°F. Spray 10-inch ovenproof skillet lightly with nonstick cooking spray. Place in oven for 10 minutes.

PLACE evaporated milk, baking mix, 1 tablespoon sugar, egg yolks, orange juice and cinnamon in blender; blend until smooth. Beat egg whites in large mixer bowl until soft peaks form; gradually add *remaining* sugar. Beat until stiff peaks form. Fold milk mixture into egg whites.

POUR batter into hot skillet. Gently push each apple slice about ½ inch into batter, peel side up, to form spoke-like pattern around batter. Sprinkle with cinnamon-sugar.

BAKE for 10 to 15 minutes or until set. Serve immediately.

Makes 6 to 8 servings

Down-Home Sausage Gravy over Biscuits

1 package (16 ounces) fresh breakfast sausage

2 tablespoons finely chopped onion

6 tablespoons all-purpose flour

2 cans (12 fluid ounces *each*) NESTLÉ® CARNATION® Evaporated Milk

1 cup water

¼ teaspoon salt

Hot pepper sauce to taste

Hot biscuits

COMBINE sausage and onion in large skillet. Cook over medium-low heat, stirring occasionally, until sausage is no longer pink. Stir in flour; mix well. Stir in evaporated milk, water, salt and hot pepper sauce. Cook, stirring occasionally, until mixture comes to a boil. Cook for 1 to 2 minutes.

SERVE immediately over biscuits.

Makes 10 servings

Petit Pain au Chocolate

1 **package (17.25 ounces) frozen puff pastry sheets, thawed**

1 **cup (6 ounces) NESTLÉ® TOLL HOUSE® Milk Chocolate Morsels, *divided***

1 **large egg, beaten**

1 **bar (2 ounces *total*) NESTLÉ® TOLL HOUSE® Semi-Sweet Chocolate Baking Bars, broken into pieces**

2 **tablespoons butter or margarine**

1 **cup powdered sugar**

2 **tablespoons hot water**

PREHEAT oven to 350°F. Grease 2 baking sheets.

UNFOLD 1 pastry sheet on lightly floured surface. Roll out to make 10-inch square. Cut into 4 squares. Place 2 *tablespoons* morsels in center of each square. Brush edges lightly with beaten egg and fold squares to form triangles. Press edges to seal. Place on prepared baking sheet about 2 inches apart. Repeat with *remaining* pastry sheet. Brush top of each pastry with beaten egg.

BAKE for 15 to 17 minutes or until puffed and golden. Cool on baking sheets for 2 minutes; remove to wire racks to cool completely.

MELT baking bar and butter in small, uncovered, microwave-safe bowl on HIGH (100%) power for 30 seconds. STIR. If pieces retain some of their original shape, microwave at additional 10- to 15-second intervals, stirring just until melted. Stir in sugar. Add water, stirring until icing is smooth, adding additional water, if necessary. Drizzle icing over pastries.

Makes 8 pastries

Puffy Pumpkin Pancakes

2 cups complete pancake mix

1½ cups water

⅔ cup LIBBY'S® 100% Pure Pumpkin

Nonstick cooking spray

Pancake syrup (optional)

COMBINE pancake mix, water and pumpkin in medium bowl. Stir just until moistened. Batter may be lumpy.

HEAT griddle or large skillet over medium heat; spray with nonstick cooking spray. Pour ¼ cup batter onto hot griddle; cook until batter bubbles begin to burst. Turn and continue cooking for 1 to 2 minutes or until golden. Repeat with remaining batter. Serve with syrup.

Makes 6 servings (12 pancakes total)

CARNATION®
Scrambled Eggs

8 large eggs

½ cup NESTLÉ® CARNATION® Evaporated Milk

Nonstick cooking spray

Salt and ground black pepper to taste

WHISK together eggs and evaporated milk in medium bowl. Spray large skillet with nonstick cooking spray; heat over medium-low heat. Pour egg mixture into skillet. Cook, without stirring, until egg mixture begins to set on bottom and around edges. With a spatula or spoon, lift cooked egg mixture so uncooked egg mixture flows underneath. Continue cooking, stirring gently, until egg mixture is cooked through and still moist. Remove from heat. Season with salt and pepper.

Makes 4 servings (¾ cup each)

TOLL HOUSE® Crumbcake

TOPPING:

- ⅓ **cup packed brown sugar**
- 1 **tablespoon all-purpose flour**
- 2 **tablespoons butter or margarine, softened**
- ½ **cup chopped nuts**
- 2 **cups (12-ounce package) NESTLÉ® TOLL HOUSE® Semi-Sweet Chocolate Mini Morsels, *divided***

CAKE:

- 1¾ **cups all-purpose flour**
- 1 **teaspoon baking powder**
- 1 **teaspoon baking soda**
- ¼ **teaspoon salt**
- ¾ **cup granulated sugar**
- ½ **cup (1 stick) butter or margarine, softened**
- 1 **teaspoon vanilla extract**
- 3 **large eggs**
- 1 **cup sour cream**

PREHEAT oven to 350°F. Grease 13×9-inch baking pan.

FOR TOPPING:

COMBINE brown sugar, flour and butter in small bowl with pastry blender or two knives until crumbly. Stir in nuts and *½ cup* morsels.

FOR CAKE:

COMBINE flour, baking powder, baking soda and salt in small bowl. Beat granulated sugar, butter and vanilla extract in large mixer bowl until creamy. Add eggs, one at a time, beating well after each addition. Gradually add flour mixture alternately with sour cream. Fold in *remaining 1½ cups* morsels. Spread into prepared baking pan; sprinkle with topping.

BAKE for 25 to 35 minutes or until wooden pick inserted in center comes out clean. Cool in pan on wire rack.

Makes 12 servings

Spring

SPRING BREAKS

Take a break this spring with fabulous sweets and treats! You'll find enticing baked goods like Layers of Love Chocolate Brownies and Gourmet Chocolate Chip Cookies as well as holiday specific recipes. There are also a handful of easy recipes that don't require heating up your kitchen.

Gourmet Chocolate Chip Cookies

- 2 **cups all-purpose flour**
- ¾ **cup ground pecans**
- 1 **teaspoon baking powder**
- ½ **teaspoon baking soda**
- ¼ **teaspoon salt**
- ½ **cup (1 stick) butter, softened**
- ½ **cup vegetable shortening**
- ¾ **cup granulated sugar**
- ¾ **cup packed brown sugar**
- 2 **large eggs**
- 1 **teaspoon vanilla extract**
- 1¾ **cups (11.5-ounce package) NESTLÉ® TOLL HOUSE® Milk Chocolate Morsels**
- 1 **cup chopped pecans**

PREHEAT oven to 375°F.

COMBINE flour, ground pecans, baking powder, baking soda and salt in medium bowl. Beat butter and vegetable shortening in large mixer bowl on medium speed for 30 seconds. Add granulated sugar, brown sugar, eggs and vanilla extract; beat until well combined. Gradually beat in as much flour mixture as possible. Stir in *remaining* flour mixture, morsels and nuts. (Recipe may be made ahead up to this point. If desired, cover and refrigerate dough for 4 hours or up to 3 days.) Drop by rounded teaspoonful onto ungreased baking sheets.

BAKE for 10 minutes or until golden brown. Cool on baking sheets for 2 minutes; remove to wire racks to cool completely.

Makes 4 dozen cookies

SPRING BREAKS

Chocolate Chip Easter Baskets

1 package (16.5 ounces) NESTLÉ® TOLL HOUSE® Refrigerated Chocolate Chip Cookie Bar Dough

1 cup prepared white frosting

Green food coloring

¼ cup sweetened flaked coconut

WONKA® SweeTARTS® or SPREE® Jelly Beans

Thin-string licorice, various colors, cut into 3-inch pieces for basket handles (optional)

PREHEAT oven to 350°F. Grease and flour 24 mini-muffin cups. Place one square of cookie dough into each cup.

BAKE for 14 to 17 minutes or until golden brown. Remove pans to wire rack. If licorice handles are to be added, with tip of wooden pick, make two holes opposite each other on top edge of cup. Make sure holes are the same size as the width of the licorice. This is best done when cups are very warm. Cool cups completely in pans on wire rack. With tip of butter knife, remove cookie cups from muffin pans. Arrange on serving platter.

COMBINE frosting and a few drops of food coloring in small bowl, adding additional food coloring until desired shade is reached.

DISSOLVE a few drops of food coloring in ¼ teaspoon water in small, resealable food storage plastic bag. Add coconut. Seal bag and shake to evenly coat coconut.

SPOON a small amount of frosting onto the top of each cup. Add a pinch of tinted coconut. Top grass with SweeTarts Jelly Beans. Insert ends of licorice into small holes in cups for handles.

Makes 2 dozen baskets

SPRING BREAKS

Berry Springtime Parfaits

½ **cup quartered fresh strawberries**

½ **cup fresh raspberries**

½ **cup fresh blackberries**

½ **cup fresh blueberries**

¼ **cup raspberry or blackberry liqueur**

1 **container (8 ounces) mascarpone cheese (plain or coffee flavor)**

1 **cup heavy whipping cream**

¼ **cup powdered sugar**

1 **tablespoon vanilla extract**

20 **NESTLÉ CRUNCH® or Milk Chocolate NestEggs™, unwrapped, chopped**

6 **wrapped NESTLÉ CRUNCH® or Milk Chocolate NestEggs™, for garnish**

COMBINE strawberries, raspberries, blackberries, blueberries and liqueur in medium bowl. Refrigerate for 30 minutes.

COMBINE cheese, cream, sugar and vanilla extract in small mixer bowl. Beat on high speed until thick; fold in chopped NESTLÉ® NestEggs. Refrigerate for 30 minutes.

LAYER 6 parfait glasses with alternating berries and cream mixture, ending with cream mixture. Top each parfait with 1 wrapped NESTLÉ® NestEgg.

Makes 6 servings

SPRING BREAKS

NESTLÉ® TOLL HOUSE®
Stars and Stripes Cookies

- **1** **package (16.5 ounces) NESTLÉ® TOLL HOUSE® Refrigerated Chocolate Chip Cookie Bar Dough**

- **1** **package (8 ounces) light cream cheese (Neufchâtel), at room temperature**

- **⅓** **cup granulated sugar**

- **24** **fresh, medium strawberries, sliced**

- **¾** **cup fresh blueberries**

- **2** **tablespoons NESTLÉ® TOLL HOUSE® Semi-Sweet Chocolate Mini Morsels**

PREHEAT oven to 350°F.

ROLL cookie dough to ¼-inch thickness between two pieces of wax paper. Remove top piece of paper. Cut cookie dough into stars with 3-inch star cookie cutter. Transfer cookies to ungreased baking sheet(s). (If stars are too hard to remove from wax paper, refrigerate rolled dough for 10 minutes.) Roll remaining dough to ¼-inch thickness; cut out additional stars.

BAKE for 10 to 12 minutes or until light golden brown. While hot, reshape and pat edges of each star back into shape with knife. Cool on baking sheet(s) for 2 minutes; remove to wire rack(s) to cool completely.

BEAT cream cheese and sugar in small mixer bowl until fluffy. Spread onto cooled cookies. Place strawberry slices onto each cookie pointing outward. Place 5 to 6 blueberries in center of each cookie. Top each cookie with morsels.

Makes 20 cookies

SPRING BREAKS

Layers of Love Chocolate Brownies

¾ cup all-purpose flour

¾ cup NESTLÉ® TOLL HOUSE® Baking Cocoa

¼ teaspoon salt

½ cup (1 stick) butter, cut into pieces

½ cup granulated sugar

½ cup packed brown sugar

3 large eggs, *divided*

2 teaspoons vanilla extract

1 cup chopped pecans

¾ cup NESTLÉ® TOLL HOUSE® Premier White Morsels

½ cup caramel ice cream topping

¾ cup NESTLÉ® TOLL HOUSE® Semi-Sweet Chocolate Morsels

PREHEAT oven to 350°F. Grease 8-inch-square baking pan.

COMBINE flour, cocoa and salt in small bowl. Beat butter, granulated sugar and brown sugar in large mixer bowl until creamy. Add 2 *eggs*, one at a time, beating well after each addition. Add vanilla extract; mix well. Gradually beat in flour mixture. Reserve ¾ *cup* batter. Spread *remaining* batter into prepared baking pan. Sprinkle pecans and white morsels over batter. Drizzle caramel topping over top. Beat *remaining* egg and *reserved* batter in same large bowl until light in color. Stir in semi-sweet morsels. Spread evenly over caramel topping.

BAKE for 30 to 35 minutes or until center is set. Cool completely in pan on wire rack. Cut into squares.

Makes 16 brownies

Soft Cinnamon and Sugar Pretzels

¼ cup *plus* 3 tablespoons granulated sugar, *divided*

½ teaspoon ground cinnamon

1 packet (0.25 ounce) rapid-rising yeast

1¼ cups (110° to 115°F) warm water

4½ cups *plus* extra for kneading all-purpose flour

¾ cup *dry* NESTLÉ® CARNATION® Instant Nonfat Dry Milk

¾ teaspoon salt

¾ cup (1½ sticks) butter, melted, *divided*

GREASE 2 large baking sheets. Combine ¼ *cup* granulated sugar and cinnamon in small bowl; set aside.

STIR yeast into warm water in small bowl. Combine flour, dry milk, *remaining 3 tablespoons* sugar and salt in large bowl. Add ½ *cup* butter and yeast mixture into flour mixture. Stir until blended and sticky dough is formed.

PLACE dough on lightly floured surface; knead for 6 to 8 minutes, until dough is smooth and elastic, adding additional flour as necessary. Cut into 24 pieces. While working with dough, keep covered with plastic wrap. Roll each piece into a 16-inch long rope. To form pretzels, make a U-shape with the rope. Holding the ends of the rope, cross them over each other and press onto the bottom of the U and place on prepared baking sheets. Press ends of pretzel into pretzel dough. Brush with *remaining ¼ cup* butter. Sprinkle with cinnamon-sugar mixture. Allow to rise in warm place for 15 minutes or until risen slightly.

PREHEAT oven to 375°F.

BAKE for 18 to 20 minutes or until golden brown. Remove from baking sheets to wire racks. Serve warm. Store remaining tightly covered.

Makes 2 dozen pretzels

SPRING BREAKS

Premier White Lemony Cheesecake

CRUST:

- 6 tablespoons butter or margarine, softened
- ¼ cup granulated sugar
- 1¼ cups all-purpose flour
- 1 large egg yolk
- ⅛ teaspoon salt

FILLING:

- 3 bars (12 ounces) NESTLÉ® TOLL HOUSE® Premier White Baking Bars, broken into pieces
- ½ cup heavy whipping cream
- 2 packages (8 ounces each) cream cheese, softened
- 1 tablespoon lemon juice
- 2 teaspoons grated lemon peel
- ¼ teaspoon salt
- 3 large egg whites
- 1 large egg

PREHEAT oven to 350°F. Lightly grease 9-inch springform pan.

FOR CRUST:

BEAT butter and sugar in small mixer bowl until creamy. Beat in flour, egg yolk and salt. Press mixture onto bottom and 1-inch up side of prepared pan.

BAKE for 14 to 16 minutes or until crust is set.

FOR FILLING:

MICROWAVE baking bars and whipping cream in medium, uncovered, microwave-safe bowl on MEDIUM-HIGH (70%) power for 1 minute. STIR. Morsels may retain some of their original shape. If necessary, microwave at additional 10- to 15-second intervals, stirring just until morsels are melted.

BEAT cream cheese, lemon juice, lemon peel and salt in large mixer bowl until smooth. Gradually beat in melted baking bars. Beat in egg whites and egg. Pour into crust.

BAKE for 35 to 40 minutes or until edge is lightly browned. Run knife around edge of cheesecake. Cool completely in pan on wire rack. Refrigerate for several hours or overnight. Remove side of springform pan. Garnish as desired.

Makes 12 to 16 servings

SPRING BREAKS

Pumpkin Carrot Cupcakes with Orange-Cream Cheese Frosting

- **1 cup whole-wheat flour**
- **1 cup all-purpose flour**
- **2 teaspoons ground cinnamon**
- **2 teaspoons baking soda**
- **1 teaspoon salt**
- **2 cups packed brown sugar**
- **½ cup vegetable oil**
- **3 teaspoons grated orange peel, divided**
- **1 can (15 ounces) LIBBY'S® 100% Pure Pumpkin**
- **4 large eggs**
- **2 cups grated carrots**
- **¾ cup golden raisins**
- **4 ounces light cream cheese**
- **1 tablespoon butter, softened**
- **1½ cups powdered sugar, sifted**
- **Candied orange peel for garnish (optional)**

PREHEAT oven to 350°F. Paper-line 24 muffin cups.

COMBINE whole-wheat flour, all-purpose flour, cinnamon, baking soda and salt in medium bowl. Beat brown sugar, oil and 2 *teaspoons* grated orange peel in large mixer bowl until blended. Add pumpkin and eggs; beat well. Gradually beat in flour mixture. Fold in carrots and raisins. Spoon batter into prepared muffin cups, filling ⅔ full.

BAKE for 25 minutes or until wooden pick inserted in cupcake comes out almost clean. Cool in pans on wire racks for 10 minutes; remove to wire racks to cool completely.

BEAT cream cheese, butter, powdered sugar and *remaining 1 teaspoon* grated orange peel in small mixer bowl until smooth. Spread over cupcakes; garnish with candied orange peel.

Makes 2 dozen cupcakes

SPRING BREAKS

Chocolate Caliente Cookies

1¾ cups (11.5-ounce package) **NESTLÉ® TOLL HOUSE®** **Semi-Sweet Chocolate Chunks**, *divided*

1½ cups all-purpose flour

1½ teaspoons ground cinnamon

1 teaspoon baking powder

¼ teaspoon salt

¹⁄₁₆ teaspoon (pinch) ground cayenne pepper

½ cup (1 stick) butter, softened

½ cup granulated sugar

½ cup packed light brown sugar

2 large eggs

1 teaspoon vanilla extract

MICROWAVE *1 cup* chunks in medium, uncovered, microwave-safe bowl on HIGH (100%) power for 1 minute; STIR. Chunks may retain some of their original shape. If necessary, microwave at additional 10- to 15-second intervals, stirring just until chunks are melted.

COMBINE flour, cinnamon, baking powder, salt and cayenne pepper in small bowl. Beat butter, granulated sugar and brown sugar in large mixer bowl until creamy. Add eggs and vanilla extract; beat well. Add melted chocolate; stir until blended. Gradually stir in flour mixture. Refrigerate for 2 hours.

PREHEAT oven to 350°F. Line baking sheets with foil.

SHAPE dough into 1½-inch balls. Place 3 inches apart on baking sheets.

BAKE for 12 minutes or until cookies are puffed and centers are set but still soft. Immediately place *remaining* chunks, about 5 to 6 chunks per cookie, onto tops of cookies. Cool on baking sheets for 2 minutes; remove to wire racks. Allow chunks to soften and spread melted chocolate evenly over tops of cookies.

Makes 20 to 22 cookies

Chocolate-Dipped Fruit Kabobs

1 cup (6 ounces) NESTLÉ® TOLL HOUSE® Semi-Sweet Chocolate Morsels

18 pieces bite-size fresh fruit, (strawberries, apple, banana, kiwifruit)

6 (4-inch) wooden skewers

LINE baking sheet with wax paper.

MICROWAVE morsels in small, uncovered, microwave-safe bowl on HIGH (100%) power for 1 minute; STIR. Morsels may retain some of their original shape. If necessary, microwave at additional 10 to 15-second intervals, stirring just until morsels are melted.

DIP fruit about halfway into chocolate; shake off excess. Or, place melted chocolate in small, *heavy-duty* plastic bag. Cut tiny corner from bag; squeeze to drizzle over fruit. Place fruit on prepared baking sheet. Refrigerate for 5 to 10 minutes or until chocolate is set.

THREAD three pieces fruit on each skewer.

Makes 6 kabobs

Salty Peanut Butter S'more

1 package (16.5 ounces) NESTLÉ® TOLL HOUSE® Ultimates™ Peanut Butter Lovers Cookies

12 large marshmallows

1½ bars (6 ounces) NESTLÉ® TOLL HOUSE® Semi-Sweet Chocolate Baking Bar, broken in squares (optional)

⅓ cup caramel ice cream topping

¼ cup chopped peanuts

PREHEAT oven to 325°F. Cut each square of cookie dough in half (total of 24 half pieces are needed for the recipe.) Place 2 inches apart on ungreased baking sheets.

BAKE for 10 to 12 minutes or until golden brown. Cool on baking sheets for 2 minutes; remove to wire racks to cool.

TO ASSEMBLE:

SPREAD small amount of ice cream topping on flat side of 12 cookies; place on wire rack.

PLACE *remaining* 12 baked cookies flat side up on cooled baking sheet. Place 1 marshmallow on top of each cookie.

BAKE for 1 to 2 minutes or until marshmallows are soft. Immediately top each marshmallow with a square of chocolate and a reserved cookie. Gently squeeze cookies together to make a sandwich. Roll sides of sandwiches in peanuts. Cookies are best when eaten slightly warm!

Makes 12 sandwiches

SPRING BREAKS

Golden Pound Cake

3 cups cake flour

1½ teaspoons baking powder

¼ teaspoon salt

¼ teaspoon mace or ground nutmeg

1½ cups granulated sugar

1 cup (2 sticks) butter or margarine, softened

1 teaspoon vanilla extract

3 large eggs

¾ cup chopped walnuts or pecans

½ cup NESTLÉ® CARNATION® Evaporated Milk

PREHEAT oven to 350°F. Grease 9×5-inch loaf pan.

COMBINE flour, baking powder, salt and mace in medium bowl. Beat sugar, butter and vanilla extract in large mixer bowl until light and fluffy. Add eggs, one at a time, beating well after each addition. Beat in flour mixture alternately with evaporated milk. Pour into prepared loaf pan; sprinkle with nuts.

BAKE for 60 to 70 minutes or until wooden pick inserted in center comes out clean. Cool in pan for 10 minutes; remove to wire rack to cool completely.

Makes 12 servings

SPRING BREAKS

Lemon Cheesecake Bars

- 2 **cups all-purpose flour**
- ½ **cup powdered sugar**
- 1 **cup (2 sticks) butter, softened**
- 1 **package (8 ounces) cream cheese, softened**
- 2 **large eggs**
- ⅔ **cup (5 fluid-ounce can) NESTLÉ® CARNATION® Evaporated Milk**
- ½ **cup granulated sugar**
- 1 **tablespoon all-purpose flour**
- 1 **tablespoon lemon juice**
- 2 **teaspoons grated lemon peel**
- 1 **teaspoon yellow food coloring (optional)**
- 1 **cup sour cream**

PREHEAT oven to 350°F.

COMBINE flour and powdered sugar in medium bowl. Cut in butter with pastry blender or two knives until crumbly. Press onto bottom and 1-inch up sides of ungreased 13×9-inch baking pan.

BAKE for 25 minutes.

PLACE cream cheese, eggs, evaporated milk, granulated sugar, flour, lemon juice, lemon peel and food coloring in blender container; cover. Blend until smooth. Pour into partially baked crust.

BAKE for additional 15 minutes or until set. Cool in pan on wire rack. Spread sour cream over top; refrigerate. Cut into bars. Garnish as desired.

Makes 2 dozen bars

Spring S'more Bars

- ½ **cup heavy whipping cream**
- 1¾ **cups (11.5-ounce package) NESTLÉ® TOLL HOUSE® Milk Chocolate Morsels**
- 3½ **cups miniature colored marshmallows**
- 7½ **ounces chocolate-covered graham crackers, broken into bite-size pieces**

LINE 9-inch-square baking pan with heavy-duty foil.

HEAT cream in a medium saucepan over medium-high heat for 1 to 2 minutes or until bubbles appear around edges. Remove from heat. Add morsels; stir until smooth. Cool, stirring occasionally, for 10 to 12 minutes. Add marshmallows; stir to coat. Gently stir in graham cracker pieces until combined.

SPREAD mixture into prepared pan; press down lightly. Refrigerate for 2 hours or until firm. Cut into bars.

Makes 16 bars

SPRING BREAKS

Cheesecake Cookie Cups

1 package (16.5 ounces) NESTLÉ® TOLL HOUSE® Refrigerated Chocolate Chip Cookie Bar Dough

2 packages (8 ounces *each*) cream cheese, at room temperature

1 can (14 ounces) NESTLÉ® CARNATION® Sweetened Condensed Milk

2 large eggs

2 teaspoons vanilla extract

1 can (21 ounces) cherry pie filling

PREHEAT oven to 325°F. Paper-line 24 muffin cups. Place one piece of cookie dough in each muffin cup.

BAKE for 10 to 12 minutes or until cookie has spread to edge of cup.

BEAT cream cheese, sweetened condensed milk, eggs and vanilla extract in medium bowl until smooth. Pour about 3 tablespoons cream cheese mixture over each cookie in cup.

BAKE for additional 15 to 18 minutes or until set. Cool completely in pan on wire rack. Top each with level tablespoon of pie filling. Refrigerate for 1 hour.

Makes 2 dozen cookie cups

SPRING BREAKS

Deep-Dish Peach Custard Pie

1 *unbaked* 9-inch (4-cup volume) deep-dish pie shell

3½ cups (about 7 medium) peeled, pitted and sliced peaches

1 can (14 ounces) NESTLÉ® CARNATION® Sweetened Condensed Milk

2 large eggs

¼ cup (½ stick) butter or margarine, melted

1 to 3 teaspoons lemon juice

½ teaspoon ground cinnamon

Dash ground nutmeg

Streusel Topping (recipe follows)

PREHEAT oven to 425°F.

ARRANGE peaches in pie shell. Combine sweetened condensed milk, eggs, butter, lemon juice, cinnamon and nutmeg in large mixer bowl; beat until smooth. Pour over peaches.

BAKE for 10 minutes. Sprinkle with Streusel Topping. Reduce oven temperature to 350°F; bake for additional 55 to 60 minutes or until knife inserted near center comes out clean. Cool on wire rack.

Makes 8 servings

Streusel Topping

COMBINE ⅓ cup all-purpose flour, ⅓ cup packed brown sugar and ⅓ cup chopped walnuts in medium bowl. Cut in 2 tablespoons butter or margarine with pastry blender or two knives until mixture resembles coarse crumbs.

SPRING BREAKS

Oh-So-Refreshing Pumpkin-Orange Granita

1 can (15 ounces) LIBBY'S® 100% Pure Pumpkin

1¼ cups water

½ cup frozen orange juice concentrate

½ cup granulated sugar

Pinch of salt

Pinch of ground cinnamon

COMBINE pumpkin, water, concentrate, sugar, salt and cinnamon in large bowl; whisk until smooth. Pour into 8-inch-square baking pan; cover with plastic wrap. Freeze, stirring every 30 minutes to break up ice crystals, for 3 hours, or until slushy, more uniform in texture and firm enough to scrape or scoop. Using metal spoon or ice cream scoop, scrape into chilled serving dishes. Serve immediately. Freeze any remaining granita for up to 1 week. Let stand at room temperature for about 15 to 20 minutes before serving.

Makes 16 servings (about ½ cup each)

Tip: *Broken up pieces of the frozen granita can be placed in a food processor to break up before serving.*

Jelly Bean Easter Bark

2 cups (12-ounce package) NESTLÉ® TOLL HOUSE® Premier White Morsels

2 teaspoons vegetable shortening

½ cup WONKA® SweeTARTS® Jelly Beans, *divided*

LINE baking sheet with wax paper.

MICROWAVE morsels and vegetable shortening in medium, uncovered, microwave-safe bowl on MEDIUM-HIGH (70%) power for 1 minute; STIR. Morsels may retain some of their original shape. If necessary, microwave at additional 10- to 15-second intervals, stirring just until morsels are melted. Stir in ¼ cup SweeTarts Jelly Beans.

SPREAD mixture to ¼-inch thickness on prepared baking sheet. Sprinkle with *remaining* ¼ cup SweeTarts Jelly Beans. Refrigerate for about 15 minutes or until firm. Break into pieces. Store in airtight container at room temperature.

Makes 11 servings (1 pound)

Mmmmm ... Pumpkin Mousse

1 **box (3.4 ounces) vanilla instant pudding and pie filling mix**

¼ **teaspoon pumpkin pie spice or ground cinnamon**

⅔ **cup (5 fluid-ounce can) NESTLÉ® CARNATION® Evaporated Fat Free Milk**

1 **cup LIBBY'S® 100% Pure Pumpkin**

1½ **cups thawed fat-free frozen whipped topping**

COMBINE pudding mix and pie spice in medium bowl. With whisk, add evaporated milk; mix until well blended. Add pumpkin; mix well. Gently fold whipped topping into pudding mixture. Spoon into serving dishes. Top with additional whipped topping and pie spice, if desired. Serve immediately or cover and refrigerate.

Makes about 6 servings (½ cup each)

Chocolate Shamrock Bread Pudding

10 **slices bread, cubed (6 cups)**

2 **cans (12 ounces each) NESTLÉ® CARNATION® Evaporated Lowfat 2% Milk**

2 **cups (12-ounce package) NESTLÉ® TOLL HOUSE® Semi-Sweet Chocolate Morsels, *divided***

8 **large egg yolks, beaten**

¾ **cup granulated sugar**

½ **cup Irish cream liqueur**

¼ **teaspoon salt**

Whipped cream (optional)

NESTLÉ® TOLL HOUSE® Baking Cocoa (optional)

PREHEAT oven to 350°F. Grease 13×9-inch baking dish. Place bread cubes in prepared baking dish.

HEAT evaporated milk in medium saucepan over MEDIUM-HIGH heat; bring just to a boil. Remove from heat. Add 1½ cups morsels; whisk until smooth.

COMBINE egg yolks, sugar, liqueur and salt in large bowl. Slowly add milk mixture; whisk until smooth. Pour over bread; pressing bread into milk mixture.

BAKE for 35 to 40 minutes or until knife inserted in center comes out clean. Top with *remaining ½ cup* morsels. Serve warm with a dollop of whipped cream and dusting of cocoa, if desired.

Makes 12 servings

SPRING BREAKS

Margarita Pie

CRUST:

- 1 **cup crushed mini pretzels**
- 6 **tablespoons melted butter**
- 1 **tablespoon granulated sugar**

FILLING:

- 2 **tablespoons boiling water**
- 1 **envelope (7 grams) unflavored gelatin**
- 1 **can (12 fluid ounces) NESTLÉ® CARNATION® Evaporated Milk**
- 1 **cup granulated sugar**
- 2 **teaspoons grated lime peel**
- ½ **cup (4 to 5 medium limes) lime juice**
- 1 **teaspoon grated orange peel**
- 2 **tablespoons orange juice or orange-flavored liqueur**
- 1 **tablespoon tequila (optional)**
- 2 **cups frozen whipped topping, thawed,** *divided*

  Coarse sanding sugar, fresh limes slices (optional)

FOR CRUST:

PREHEAT oven to 375°F. Combine pretzel crumbs, butter and sugar in 9-inch deep-dish (4-cup volume) pie plate. Press crumb mixture onto bottom and upsides of pie plate.

BAKE for 5 to 7 minutes or until lightly browned. Cool completely on wire rack.

FOR FILLING:

PLACE gelatin in small bowl; stir in water. Let stand for 1 minute. Heat evaporated milk, sugar and softened gelatin in small saucepan over medium heat, stirring until sugar is dissolved and mixture is hot. Do not boil. Pour into medium bowl. Refrigerate uncovered for 30 minutes until cool to touch. Add lime peel, lime juice, orange peel, orange juice and tequila; mix well. Gently whisk in *1 cup* whipped topping. Pour into prepared pie crust.

REFRIGERATE for 2 hours or until set. Pipe *remaining 1 cup* whipped topping around edge of pie. Sprinkle whipped topping border with coarse sugar. Garnish with lime slices.

Makes 8 servings

Tip: *3 cups (4 ounces) mini pretzels will be needed to get 1 cup crushed.*

Tip: *To save time, you may substitute a store-bought 10-inch (9 ounces) graham cracker crumb crust for pretzel pie shell.*

Tip: *If you do not own a pastry bag, a resealable heavy-duty plastic bag can be used. Cut corner of bag and pipe out whipped topping as desired.*

Spring

Brownie Fruit Pizza

Explore lunchtime recipes for your spring entertaining! Serve cool drinks, salads, dressings, chilled soups, tasty pasta dishes, dazzling desserts, and more! This fun collection makes it easy to be the best host or hostess on your block.

1 package (18.3 ounces) traditional 13×9 chewy fudge brownie mix

⅔ cup vegetable oil

2 large eggs

¼ cup water

1 cup (6 ounces) NESTLÉ® TOLL HOUSE® Semi-Sweet Chocolate Morsels, *divided*

2 cups thawed fat-free whipped topping

3 cups fresh fruit and berries of choice (blueberries, sliced grapes, kiwifruit, pineapple, strawberries)

¼ cup sweetened flaked coconut (optional)

PREHEAT oven to 350° F. Grease and flour 15-inch-round pizza pan or 15×10-inch jelly-roll pan.

COMBINE brownie mix, oil, eggs and water in medium bowl until blended. Stir in ¾ *cup* morsels. Spread onto prepared pizza pan.

BAKE for 20 to 22 minutes or until edges are set. Remove to wire rack and cool for 3 minutes; loosen edge of brownie crust from pan with knife. Cool for 1 hour on wire rack.

SPREAD whipped topping over brownie crust. Top with fruit. Sprinkle with *remaining ¼ cup* morsels and coconut. Serve immediately or refrigerate up to 1 hour before serving.

Makes 12 servings

Tip: *⅓ cup unsweetened applesauce can be substituted for the vegetable oil. Bake at 350°F for 15 to 17 minutes.*

Tip: *Brownie crust may be made in advance. Allow to cool completely and cover with plastic wrap for up to 1 day.*

Oriental Ramen Salad

2 **tablespoons butter or margarine**

1 **package (3 ounces) dry oriental-flavor ramen noodle soup, noodles crumbled and seasoning packet reserved**

½ **cup sliced almonds**

⅔ **cup (5 fluid-ounce can) NESTLÉ® CARNATION® Evaporated Fat Free Milk**

⅔ **cup vegetable oil**

3 **tablespoons white vinegar**

2 **tablespoons granulated sugar**

2 **packages (10 ounces *each*) romaine-radicchio salad greens**

4 **green onions, sliced diagonally**

MELT butter in large skillet. Add crumbled ramen noodles and nuts; cook, stirring constantly, until noodles are golden. Remove from pan; cool.

PLACE evaporated milk, oil, ramen seasoning packet, vinegar and sugar in blender; cover. Blend until smooth.

COMBINE salad greens, noodle mixture, green onions and dressing in large bowl; toss to coat well. Serve immediately.

Makes 8 servings

Creamy Pesto Garden Pasta

1 box (12 ounces) dry tri-color
    rotini or spiral shaped pasta

1 bag (16 ounces) frozen broccoli,
    cauliflower and carrot medley

1 can (12 ounces) NESTLÉ®
    CARNATION® Evaporated Milk

2 cups (8-ounce package)
    shredded Italian cheese blend
    or Monterey Jack cheese

3 tablespoons jarred or
    refrigerated pesto with basil

¼ teaspoon ground black pepper

2 cups (8 ounces) cooked ham, cut
    into ½-inch
    pieces

COOK pasta according to package directions, adding frozen vegetables to boiling pasta water for last 2 minutes of cooking time; drain. Return pasta and vegetables to cooking pot.

MEANWHILE, combine evaporated milk, cheese, pesto and black pepper in medium saucepan. Cook over medium low heat, stirring occasionally, until cheese is melted. Remove from heat.

POUR cheese sauce over pasta and vegetables. Add ham; stir until combined.

Makes 10 servings

Penne Pasta with Sun-dried Tomato Cream Sauce

- **2 cups (8 ounces) dry penne pasta**
- **8 sun-dried tomatoes, chopped (about ⅓ cup)**
- **1 can (12 fluid ounces) NESTLÉ® CARNATION® Evaporated Lowfat 2% Milk**
- **2 cups (8-ounce package) shredded Italian-style four-cheese blend**
- **1 teaspoon dried basil**
- **¼ teaspoon garlic powder**
- **¼ teaspoon ground black pepper**

PREPARE pasta according to package directions, adding sun-dried tomatoes to boiling pasta water for last two minutes of cooking time; drain.

MEANWHILE, COMBINE evaporated milk, cheese, basil, garlic powder and pepper in medium saucepan. Cook over medium-low heat, stirring occasionally, until cheese is melted. Remove from heat.

ADD pasta and sun-dried tomatoes to cheese sauce; stir until combined.

Makes 7 servings (½ cup each)

Creamy Lime Dressing

- **1 can (5 fluid ounces) NESTLÉ® CARNATION® Evaporated Milk**
- **1 package (3 ounces) cream cheese, cut up**
- **Grated peel and juice of 1 fresh lime**
- **1 teaspoon granulated sugar**

PLACE evaporated milk, cream cheese, lime peel, lime juice and sugar in blender container; cover. Blend until smooth. Pour into small container. Cover; refrigerate for up to 1 week.

Makes 4 servings (¼ cup each)

Tip: *Drizzle dressing over a summer salad with mixed greens, shredded carrots, and sliced cucumbers, tomatoes and strawberries.*

LUNCH BY THE BUNCH

Chilled Pumpkin Soup

1 tablespoon olive oil

1 small onion, chopped

5 green onions, chopped (about 1 cup)

1 can (14.5 ounces) diced tomatoes with liquid or 3 fresh tomatoes, peeled, seeded and chopped

2 cans (14.5 ounces *each*) chicken broth

1 can (15 ounces) LIBBY'S® 100% Pure Pumpkin

1 can (12 fluid ounces) NESTLÉ® CARNATION® Evaporated Milk

½ teaspoon salt (optional)

¼ teaspoon ground black pepper

NESTLÉ® Media Crema (optional)

Paprika (optional)

HEAT oil in large saucepan over medium-high heat. Add onion and green onions; cook, stirring occasionally, for 5 to 7 minutes or until tender. Add tomatoes; cook for an additional minute.

ADD broth and pumpkin; bring to a boil. Reduce heat to low; cook, stirring occasionally, for 15 to 20 minutes. Stir in evaporated milk, salt and pepper. Remove soup from heat; cool for 15 minutes. Carefully transfer mixture to blender or food processor (in batches, if necessary); cover. Blend until smooth.

POUR soup into large bowl; cover. Refrigerate for at least 4 hours. Spoon into bowls. Top each with a dollop of Media Crema and sprinkle of paprika, if desired.

Makes 8 servings

Peaches & Cream Gelatin Delight

½ cup (1 stick) butter

1½ cups crushed vanilla wafers
(about 45) or Maria cookies
(about 30)

1 envelope (0.25 ounce)
unflavored gelatin

⅓ cup fresh lemon juice (about
2 lemons)

1 can (12 fluid ounces) NESTLÉ®
CARNATION® Evaporated Milk

1 can (14 ounces) NESTLÉ®
CARNATION® Sweetened
Condensed Milk

1 package (8 ounces) cream
cheese, at room temperature,
cut in cubes

1 can (8.75 ounces) sliced peaches,
drained

7 maraschino cherries, blotted dry

1 package (3 ounces) pineapple-
flavored gelatin

PREHEAT oven to 350°F.

MELT butter in small saucepan. Stir in cookie crumbs until
well blended. Press crumbs onto bottom of ungreased 9-inch
springform pan. Bake for 10 minutes.

DISSOLVE unflavored gelatin in lemon juice in small bowl. Place
evaporated and condensed milks, cream cheese and dissolved
gelatin in blender; blend until smooth. Pour mixture over crust;
refrigerate for 1 hour.

ARRANGE peaches and cherries on chilled pie. Prepare
pineapple gelatin as directed on package. To prevent fruit
from floating, pour about ¼ inch of gelatin over arranged
fruit. Refrigerate until slightly set, but not firm. Pour remaining
gelatin over the fruit. Refrigerate for several hours or until
completely firm.

TO SERVE: Dip knife in warm water and run around edge to
loosen. Remove side of pan.

Makes 10 servings

CARNATION® Green Tea Cooler

4 **cups boiling water**

6 **green tea bags**

1 **tablespoon honey or more to
taste**

1 **cup *dry* NESTLÉ® CARNATION®
Instant Nonfat Dry Milk**

Ice cubes

4 **fresh lime wedges**

POUR hot water over tea bags in glass or ceramic pitcher. Let
steep for 10 minutes; remove tea bags. Stir in honey. Cool and
refrigerate for at least 2 hours. Stir in dry milk.

TO SERVE: pour cooler over ice in glasses. Serve with lime
wedges. Coolers can be sweetened with additional honey if
desired.

Makes 4 servings (about 1 cup each)

Pacific Rim Wraps with Creamy Citrus Ginger Dressing

DRESSING:

- ⅔ **cup (5 fluid-ounce can) NESTLÉ® CARNATION® Evaporated Milk**
- 5 **tablespoons lemon juice**
- ¼ **cup vegetable oil**
- 3 **tablespoons granulated sugar**
- 2 **teaspoons ground ginger**
- 1 **teaspoon salt**
- ¼ **teaspoon ground black pepper**

SALAD:

- 1 **package (6.5 ounces) or 4 cups washed salad greens**
- 3 **cups shredded, cooked chicken (about 2 to 3 boneless chicken breast halves)**
- 1 **cup matchstick or shredded carrots**
- 1 **cup fresh sugar snap pea pods, cut in half**
- ½ **cup sweetened dried cranberries**
- ¼ **cup toasted slivered almonds (optional)**
- 6 **(8-inch) flour tortillas**

FOR DRESSING:

PLACE evaporated milk, lemon juice, oil, sugar, ginger, salt and black pepper in small jar or resealable container; cover with lid. Shake well until blended. Makes 1 cup.

FOR SALAD:

COMBINE salad greens, chicken, carrots, sugar snap peas, dried cranberries and almonds in large bowl. Add *2/3 cup* dressing; toss until evenly coated.

PLACE *1 cup* salad mixture on each tortilla. Roll up tightly. Cut in half and serve along with *remaining* dressing, if desired. Or, wrap each in wax paper, foil or plastic wrap and refrigerate to eat later.

Makes 6 servings

Tip: *Dressing can be made a day ahead and refrigerated. Shake well before using.*

Tip: *Use pre-cooked grilled chicken strips to save time.*

Tip: *Look for pre-packaged matchstick carrots in your local store's produce section.*

LUNCH BY THE BUNCH

Cucumber & Tomato Greek Salad with Roasted Red Pepper Dressing

ROASTED RED PEPPER DRESSING:

- ⅔ **cup (5 ounce can) NESTLÉ® CARNATION® Evaporated Milk**
- 1 **jar (7 ounces) roasted red peppers, drained**
- 1 **tablespoon lemon juice**
- ½ **teaspoon dried basil**
- ¼ **teaspoon dried oregano**
- ½ **clove garlic, finely chopped**
- ⅛ **teaspoon salt**
- ⅛ **teaspoon ground black pepper**

SALAD:

- 3 **medium tomatoes, cut into wedges**
- 1 **seedless cucumber, peeled and thinly sliced**
- 1 **small red onion, thinly sliced**
- ½ **cup (2 ounces) crumbled feta cheese**
- ⅓ **cup coarsely chopped Kalamata olives**

FOR ROASTED RED PEPPER DRESSING:

PLACE milk, red peppers, lemon juice, basil, oregano, garlic, salt and pepper in blender; cover. Blend until smooth. Makes 1½ cups.

FOR SALAD:

PLACE tomatoes, cucumbers and onion in large bowl. Pour ¾ *cup* dressing over salad; toss until coated. Sprinkle with cheese and olives. Serve with *remaining* dressing, if desired, or refrigerate for later use.

Makes 6 servings

Summer

No-Bake Dark Chocolate & Mint Cheesecake

Help beat the heat this summer with these cool no-bake desserts! That's right—no need to turn on the oven. Just whip up a simple recipe like Easy No-Bake Crunchy Cranberry Almond Bars for an afternoon snack or the Chocolate Mudslide Pie for a sweet ending to a nice meal. You're guaranteed to satisfy a sweet tooth or two.

1 *prepared* 9-inch (6 ounces) chocolate crumb crust

1⅔ cups (10-ounce package) NESTLÉ® TOLL HOUSE® Dark Chocolate & Mint Morsels

2 packages (8 ounces *each*) ⅓ less fat cream cheese (Neufchâtel), at room temperature

¾ cup packed brown sugar

¼ cup granulated sugar

¼ cup heavy whipping cream, *divided*

1 teaspoon vanilla extract

SET aside ½ cup morsels for ganache topping. From *remaining* morsels, sort out 1 *tablespoon* mint morsels and place in small, *heavy-duty* plastic bag for drizzle; set aside.

MELT *remaining* morsels in medium, uncovered, microwave-safe bowl on MEDIUM-HIGH (70%) power for 1 minute; STIR. Morsels may retain some of their original shape. If necessary, microwave at additional 10- to 15- second intervals, stirring just until morsels are melted. Cool slightly.

BEAT cream cheese, brown sugar, granulated sugar, *2 tablespoons* cream and vanilla extract in medium mixer bowl on medium speed for 2 minutes. Add melted chocolate; continue beating for 1 minute. Spoon into crust and smooth top.

MICROWAVE *remaining 2 tablespoons* cream in 1-cup glass measure on HIGH (100% power) for 20 seconds or until boiling. Add *reserved ½ cup* morsels to cream; let sit for 1 minute. Stir until smooth. Cool for 5 minutes. Spread ganache over cheesecake to within ¼-inch of edge.

MICROWAVE *reserved* mint morsels in bag on MEDIUM-HIGH (70%) power for 20 seconds; knead. Microwave at 10- to 15-second intervals, kneading until smooth. Cut tiny corner from bag. Drizzle over top of ganache. Refrigerate for at least 2 hours.

Makes 10 servings

SUMMER SWEETS

NESTLÉ® Very Best Fudge

3 cups granulated sugar

1 can (12 fluid ounces) NESTLÉ® CARNATION® Evaporated Milk

¼ cup (½ stick) butter or margarine

½ teaspoon salt

4 cups miniature marshmallows

4 cups (24 ounces or two 12-ounce packages) NESTLÉ® TOLL HOUSE® Semi-Sweet Chocolate Morsels

1 cup chopped pecans or walnuts (optional)

2 teaspoons vanilla extract

LINE 13×9-inch baking pan or two 8-inch-square baking pans with foil.

COMBINE sugar, evaporated milk, butter and salt in 4- to 5-quart heavy-duty saucepan. Bring to a full rolling boil over medium heat, stirring constantly. Boil, stirring constantly, for 4 to 5 minutes. Remove from heat.

STIR in marshmallows, morsels, nuts and vanilla extract. Stir vigorously for 1 minute or until marshmallows are melted. Pour into prepared pan(s). Refrigerate for 2 hours or until firm. Lift from pan; remove foil. Cut into pieces. Store tightly covered in refrigerator. Makes about 4 pounds.

Makes 48 servings (2 pieces per serving)

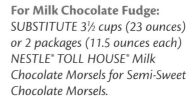

For Milk Chocolate Fudge: *SUBSTITUTE 3½ cups (23 ounces) or 2 packages (11.5 ounces each) NESTLÉ® TOLL HOUSE® Milk Chocolate Morsels for Semi-Sweet Chocolate Morsels.*

For Butterscotch Fudge: *SUBSTITUTE 3⅓ cups (22 ounces) or 2 packages (11-ounce each) NESTLÉ® TOLL HOUSE® Butterscotch Flavored Morsels for Semi-Sweet Chocolate Morsels.*

For Peanutty Fudge: *SUBSTITUTE 3⅓ cups (22 ounces) or 2 packages (11-ounce each) NESTLÉ® TOLL HOUSE® Peanut Butter & Milk Chocolate Morsels for Semi-Sweet Chocolate Morsels and 1⁄2 cup chopped peanuts for pecans or walnuts.*

SUMMER SWEETS

Dark Chocolate Truffles

⅔ **cup heavy whipping cream**

1⅔ **cups (10-ounce package) NESTLÉ® TOLL HOUSE® Dark Chocolate Morsels**

Finely chopped toasted nuts, toasted flaked coconut and/ or unsweetened cocoa powder for coating truffles

LINE baking sheet with parchment or wax paper.

HEAT cream to a gentle boil in medium, heavy-duty saucepan. Remove from heat. Add morsels. Stir until mixture is smooth and chocolate is melted. Refrigerate for 15 to 20 minutes or until slightly thickened.

DROP chocolate mixture by rounded teaspoon onto prepared baking sheet. Refrigerate for 20 minutes. Shape or roll into balls; coat with nuts, coconut or cocoa. Store in airtight container in refrigerator.

Makes about 3 to 4 dozen truffles

SUMMER SWEETS

Easy Pumpkin Cream Pie

- 1 *prepared* 9-inch (6 ounces) graham cracker crumb crust
- 1 can (15 ounces) LIBBY'S® 100% Pure Pumpkin
- 1 package (5.1 ounces) vanilla instant pudding and pie filling mix
- 1 cup NESTLÉ® CARNATION® Evaporated Milk
- 1 teaspoon pumpkin pie spice
- 2 cups (about 6 ounces) frozen whipped topping, thawed, *divided*

   Fresh raspberries (optional)

COMBINE pumpkin, pudding mix, milk and pumpkin pie spice in large mixer bowl; beat for 1 minute or until blended. Fold in *1½ cups* whipped topping. Spoon into crust. Freeze for at least 4 hours or until firm. Let stand in refrigerator 1 hour before serving. Garnish with *remaining ½ cup* whipped topping and raspberries. Serve immediately.

Makes 8 servings

Scotcheroos

   Nonstick cooking spray
- 1½ cups creamy peanut butter
- 1 cup granulated sugar
- 1 cup light corn syrup
- 6 cups toasted rice cereal
- 1⅔ cups (11-ounce package) NESTLÉ® TOLL HOUSE® Butterscotch Flavored Morsels
- 1 cup (6 ounces) NESTLÉ® TOLL HOUSE® Semi-Sweet Chocolate Morsels

COAT 13×9-inch baking pan with cooking spray.

COMBINE peanut butter, sugar and corn syrup in large saucepan. Cook over medium-low heat, stirring frequently, until melted. Remove from heat. Add cereal; stir until thoroughly coated. Press onto bottom of prepared baking pan.

MICROWAVE butterscotch morsels and semi-sweet chocolate morsels in large, uncovered, microwave-safe bowl on HIGH (100%) power for 1 minute. STIR. Morsels may retain some of their original shape. If necessary, microwave at additional 10- to 15-second intervals, stirring just until morsels are melted. Spread over cereal mixture.

REFRIGERATE for 15 to 20 minutes or until topping is firm. Cut into bars.

Makes 2½ dozen bars

SUMMER SWEETS

No-Bake Butterscotch Snack Bites

3 **cups toasted rice cereal**

1 **cup quick oats**

1 **cup coarsely chopped walnuts, pecans and/or almonds**

1⅔ **cups (11-ounce package) NESTLÉ® TOLL HOUSE® Butterscotch Flavored Morsels, *divided***

½ **teaspoon salt**

½ **cup light corn syrup**

PAPER-LINE or lightly grease 24 muffin cups.

COMBINE cereal, oats, nuts, ½ cup morsels and salt in large mixing bowl.

MELT *remaining* morsels and corn syrup in uncovered, microwave-safe bowl on MEDIUM-HIGH (70%) power for 1 minute; STIR. Morsels may retain some of their original shape. If necessary, microwave at additional 10- to 15-second intervals, stirring just until morsels are melted.

DRIZZLE melted morsel mixture over cereal mixture; stir until combined. Working quickly, press ¼ cup of mixture into each prepared cup. Let stand at room temperature for 20 minutes or until firm. Store in tightly covered container(s) at room temperature.

Makes 2 dozen snack bites

For Mini Snack Bites: *Paper-line or grease mini muffin cups. Prepare recipe as above; press about 1 tablespoon of mixture into each prepared cup. Makes about 4½ dozen mini snack bites.*

For Snack Bite Bars: *Lightly grease 13×9-inch baking pan. Prepare recipe as above and press mixture into prepared pan. Let stand at room temperature for 30 minutes or until firm. Makes 2 dozen bars.*

Tip: *Morsels can also be melted on top of a double boiler following package melting directions, adding corn syrup to melted morsels.*

SUMMER SWEETS

Easy No-Bake BUTTERFINGER® & Peanut Butter Pretzel Bars

Nonstick cooking spray

4 **cups miniature marshmallows**

¼ **cup (½ stick) butter**

¼ **teaspoon salt**

1¾ **cups (11.5-ounce package) NESTLÉ® TOLL HOUSE® Milk Chocolate Morsels, *divided***

2 **tablespoons creamy peanut butter**

4 **cups toasted rice cereal squares**

10 **(about 1½ cups) Fun Size NESTLÉ® BUTTERFINGER® Candy Bars, coarsely chopped**

1 **cup small pretzel twists, broken into ½-inch pieces**

LINE 13×9-inch baking pan with foil leaving an overhang on two sides. Spray foil with nonstick cooking spray.

HEAT marshmallows, butter and salt in large, *heavy-duty* saucepan over medium-low heat, stirring frequently, for 5 to 10 minutes, until smooth. Remove from heat. Add *1 cup* morsels and peanut butter; stir until melted.

WORKING QUICKLY, stir in cereal, chopped BUTTERFINGER® and pretzels. Stir in *remaining ¾ cup* morsels. Spread mixture into prepared baking pan with greased spatula, pressing down lightly. Cool for 2 hours or until set. Lift from pan; remove foil. Cut into bars with serrated knife.

Makes 2 dozen bars

SUMMER SWEETS

Chocolate Velvet Pie

1 *prepared* **8-inch (6 ounces) chocolate crumb crust**

1¾ **cups (11.5-ounce package) NESTLÉ® TOLL HOUSE® Milk Chocolate Morsels**

1 **package (8 ounces) cream cheese, softened**

1 **teaspoon vanilla extract**

1 **cup heavy whipping cream, whipped**

Sweetened whipped cream (optional)

Chocolate curls (optional)

Chopped nuts (optional)

MICROWAVE morsels in medium, uncovered, microwave-safe bowl on MEDIUM-HIGH (70%) power for 1 minute. STIR. Morsels may retain some of their original shape. If necessary, microwave at additional 10- to 15-second intervals, stirring just until morsels are melted. Cool to room temperature.

BEAT melted chocolate, cream cheese and vanilla extract in large mixer bowl until light in color. Fold in whipped cream. Spoon into crust. Refrigerate until firm. Top with sweetened whipped cream, chocolate curls and nuts.

Makes 8 servings

SUMMER SWEETS

No-Bake Chocolate Peanut Butter Bars

2 cups peanut butter, *divided*

¾ cup (1½ sticks) butter, softened

2 cups powdered sugar, *divided*

3 cups graham cracker crumbs

2 cups (12-ounce package) NESTLÉ® TOLL HOUSE® Semi-Sweet Chocolate Mini Morsels, *divided*

GREASE 13×9-inch baking pan.

BEAT *1¼ cups* peanut butter and butter in large mixer bowl until creamy. Gradually beat in *1 cup* powdered sugar. With hands or wooden spoon, work in *remaining 1 cup* powdered sugar, graham cracker crumbs and *½ cup* morsels. Press evenly into prepared pan. Smooth top with spatula.

MELT *remaining ¾ cup* peanut butter and *remaining 1½ cups* morsels in medium, *heavy-duty* saucepan over *lowest* possible heat, stirring constantly until smooth. Spread over graham cracker crust in pan. Refrigerate for at least 1 hour or until chocolate is firm; cut into bars. Store in refrigerator.

Makes 5 dozen bars

SUMMER SWEETS

Easy No-Bake Crunchy Cranberry Almond Bars

Nonstick cooking spray

4 **cups miniature marshmallows**

¼ **cup (½ stick) butter**

¼ **teaspoon salt**

2 **cups (12-ounce package) NESTLÉ® TOLL HOUSE® Premier White Morsels, *divided***

4 **cups toasted wheat cereal squares**

¾ **cup sweetened dried cranberries**

¾ **cup sliced almonds, toasted***

*Note: To toast almonds, bake at 350°F until light golden brown, about 8 minutes, stirring frequently.

LINE 13×9-inch baking pan with foil leaving an overhang on two sides. Spray foil with nonstick cooking spray.

HEAT marshmallows, butter and salt in large, *heavy-duty* saucepan over medium-low heat, stirring frequently, for 5 to 10 minutes, until smooth. Remove from heat. Add *1 cup* morsels; stir until melted.

WORKING QUICKLY, stir in cereal, cranberries, almonds and *remaining 1 cup* morsels. Spread mixture into prepared baking pan with greased spatula, pressing down lightly. Cool for 2 hours or until set. Lift from pan; peel off foil. Cut into bars with serrated knife.

Makes 2 dozen bars

SUMMER SWEETS

Decadent Chocolate Satin Pie

1 **prepared** 9-inch (6 ounces) graham cracker crust

1¼ **cups NESTLÉ® CARNATION® Evaporated Milk**

2 **large egg yolks**

1⅓ **cups (10-ounce package) NESTLÉ® TOLL HOUSE® Dark Chocolate Morsels**

Sweetened whipped cream

Chopped nuts (optional)

WHISK together evaporated milk and egg yolks in medium saucepan. Heat over medium-low heat, stirring constantly, until mixture is very hot and thickens slightly. Do not boil. Place chocolate in food processor fitted with metal blade. With processor running, slowly pour milk mixture into chocolate. Process 10 to 20 seconds. Scrape down sides and continue processing until smooth.

POUR into crust. Refrigerate for 3 hours or until firm. Top with sweetened whipped cream before serving; sprinkle with nuts.

Makes 8 servings

SUMMER SWEETS

Gimme S'more Pie

1 *prepared* 9-inch (6 ounces) graham cracker crumb crust

1 can (12 fluid ounces) NESTLÉ® CARNATION® Evaporated Milk, *divided*

1 package (3.9 ounces) chocolate instant pudding and pie filling mix

3 cups mini marshmallows, *divided*

2 cups frozen whipped topping, thawed

½ cup NESTLÉ® TOLL HOUSE® Milk Chocolate Morsels

WHISK 1¼ cups evaporated milk and pudding mix in medium bowl until well blended. Pour into crust.

MICROWAVE 2 cups marshmallows and *remaining ¼ cup* evaporated milk in medium, uncovered, microwave-safe bowl on HIGH (100%) power for 30 to 45 seconds; stir until smooth. Let stand for 15 minutes. Gently fold in whipped topping. Spoon marshmallow mixture over chocolate layer; smooth top with spatula.

REFRIGERATE for 2 hours or until set. Top with *remaining 1 cup* marshmallows and morsels.

Makes 8 servings

Tip: *For a gooey s'more topping, place chilled pie on a baking sheet. Preheat broiler. Place baking sheet with pie on rack 6 inches from broiler unit (pie top should be at least 4 inches from broiler unit). Broil for 30 seconds or until marshmallows are light brown and morsels are shiny. Watch carefully as browning occurs very fast! A handheld kitchen butane torch can be used as well.*

SUMMER SWEETS

CARNATION® Key Lime Pie

1 **_prepared_ 9-inch (6 ounces) graham cracker crumb crust**

1 **can (14 ounces) NESTLÉ® CARNATION® Sweetened Condensed Milk**

½ **cup (about 3 medium limes) fresh lime juice**

1 **teaspoon grated lime peel**

2 **cups frozen whipped topping, thawed**

Lime peel twists or lime slices (optional)

BEAT sweetened condensed milk and lime juice in small mixer bowl until combined; stir in lime peel. Pour into crust; spread with whipped topping. Refrigerate for 2 hours or until set. Garnish with lime peel twists.

Makes 8 servings

SUMMER SWEETS

Chocolate Mudslide Frozen Pie

1 *prepared* 9-inch (6 ounces) chocolate crumb crust

1 cup (6 ounces) NESTLÉ® TOLL HOUSE® Semi-Sweet Chocolate Morsels

1 teaspoon NESCAFÉ® TASTER'S CHOICE® 100% Pure Instant Coffee Granules

1 teaspoon hot water

¾ cup sour cream

½ cup granulated sugar

1 teaspoon vanilla extract

1½ cups heavy whipping cream

1 cup powdered sugar

¼ cup NESTLÉ® TOLL HOUSE® Baking Cocoa

2 tablespoons NESTLÉ® TOLL HOUSE® Semi-Sweet Chocolate Mini Morsels

MELT *1 cup* morsels in small, *heavy-duty* saucepan over *lowest possible* heat. When morsels begin to melt, remove from heat; stir. Return to heat for a few seconds at a time, stirring until smooth. Remove from heat; cool for 10 minutes.

COMBINE coffee granules and water in medium bowl. Add sour cream, granulated sugar and vanilla extract; stir until sugar is dissolved. Stir in melted chocolate until smooth. Spread into crust; refrigerate.

BEAT cream, powdered sugar and cocoa in small mixer bowl until stiff peaks form. Spread or pipe over chocolate layer. Sprinkle with mini morsels. Freeze for at least 6 hours or until firm.

Makes 8 servings

SUMMER SWEETS

Easy Coconut Banana Cream Pie

1 *prebaked* 9-inch (4-cup volume) deep-dish pie shell

1 can (14 ounces) NESTLÉ® CARNATION® Sweetened Condensed Milk

1 cup cold water

1 package (3.4 ounces) vanilla or banana cream instant pudding and pie filling mix

1 cup flaked coconut

1 container (8 ounces) frozen whipped topping, thawed, *divided*

2 medium bananas, sliced, dipped in lemon juice

Toasted or tinted flaked coconut (optional)

COMBINE sweetened condensed milk and water in large bowl. Add pudding mix and coconut; mix well. Fold in 1½ cups whipped topping.

ARRANGE single layer of bananas on bottom of pie crust. Pour filling into crust. Top with *remaining* whipped topping. Refrigerate for 4 hours or until well set. Top with toasted or tinted coconut.

Makes 8 servings

Note: *To make 2 pies, divide filling between 2 prebaked 9-inch (2-cup volume each) pie crusts. Top with remaining whipped topping.*

SUMMER SWEETS

Chocolate Caramels

- 1 cup (2 sticks) butter
- 1 cup granulated sugar
- 1 cup packed dark brown sugar
- 1 cup light corn syrup
- 1 can (14 ounces) NESTLÉ® CARNATION® Sweetened Condensed Milk
- 2 packets (1 ounce *each*) NESTLÉ® TOLL HOUSE® CHOCO BAKE® Pre-Melted Unsweetened Chocolate Flavor
- 1 teaspoon vanilla extract

LINE 8-inch-square baking pan with foil; grease.

COMBINE butter, granulated sugar, brown sugar and corn syrup in *heavy-duty*, medium saucepan. Cook over medium heat, stirring constantly, until mixture comes to a boil and butter is melted. Add sweetened condensed milk and Choco Bake. Cook over medium-low heat, stirring frequently, for 25 to 35 minutes or until mixture reaches 245°F on candy thermometer. Remove from heat; stir in vanilla extract. Immediately pour into prepared pan. Cool at room temperature.

LIFT from pan; remove foil. Cut into about ½-inch squares or size desired and wrap individually in plastic wrap, twisting ends. Store in refrigerator or at room temperature; use within 7 to 10 days.

Makes 36 servings (2 pieces per serving)

SUMMER SWEETS

Chocolate-Peanut Butter S'mores Fondue

½ cup milk

1⅔ cups (11-ounce package) NESTLÉ® TOLL HOUSE® Peanut Butter & Milk Chocolate Morsels

1 jar (7 ounces) marshmallow creme

1 cup graham cracker crumbs

8 Granny Smith apples, cored and sliced

HEAT milk in medium, *heavy-duty* saucepan over medium-high heat just until hot. Do not boil. Reduce heat to low. Add morsels; stir until smooth. Whisk in marshmallow creme until smooth. Remove from heat.

POUR chocolate mixture into fondue pot or serving bowl. Place graham cracker crumbs in separate serving bowl. To serve, dip apple slices into warm chocolate mixture, then dip into graham cracker crumbs.

Makes 6 servings (½ cup each)

Note: *NESTLÉ® TOLL HOUSE® Milk Chocolate Morsels (11.5-ounce package) or NESTLÉ® TOLL HOUSE® Semi-Sweet Chocolate Morsels (12-ounce package) may be used in place of NESTLÉ® TOLL HOUSE® Peanut Butter & Milk Chocolate Morsels*

Banana Pudding

60 to 70 vanilla wafers*

1 cup granulated sugar

3 tablespoons cornstarch

¼ teaspoon salt

2 cans (12 fluid ounces *each*) NESTLÉ® CARNATION® Evaporated Milk

2 eggs, lightly beaten

3 tablespoons butter, cut into pieces

1½ teaspoons vanilla extract

5 ripe but firm large bananas, cut into ¼-inch slices

1 container (8 ounces) frozen whipped topping, thawed

A 12-ounce box of vanilla wafers contains about 88 wafers.

LINE bottom and side of 2½-quart glass bowl with about 40 wafers.

COMBINE sugar, cornstarch and salt in medium saucepan. Gradually stir in evaporated milk to dissolve cornstarch. Whisk in eggs. Add butter. Cook over medium heat, stirring constantly, until the mixture begins to thicken. Reduce heat to low; bring to a simmer and cook for 1 minute, stirring constantly. Remove from heat. Stir in vanilla extract. Let cool slightly.

POUR *half* of pudding over wafers. Top with *half* of bananas. Layer *remaining* vanilla wafers over bananas. Combine *remaining* pudding and bananas; spoon over wafers. Refrigerate for at least 4 hours. Top with whipped topping.

Makes 8 servings

SUMMER SWEETS

Chocolate Raspberry Mousse Pie

- 1 *prepared* 9-inch (6 ounces) chocolate crumb crust
- 1 can (12 ounces) NESTLÉ® CARNATION® Evaporated Milk
- 2 large egg yolks
- 2 cups (12-ounce package) NESTLÉ® TOLL HOUSE® Semi-Sweet Chocolate Morsels
- 1 container (8 ounces) frozen whipped topping, thawed, *divided*
- 1 container (6 ounces) or 1⅓ cups fresh raspberries, *divided*

WHISK together evaporated milk and egg yolks in medium saucepan. Heat over medium-low heat, stirring constantly, until mixture is very hot and thickens slightly. Do not boil. Remove from heat; stir in morsels until completely melted and mixture is smooth. Pour into large bowl. Refrigerate for 30 minutes until cool. Gently stir in *2 cups* whipped topping.

REFRIGERATE for 2 hours until thickened. Sprinkle *1 cup* raspberries over crust. Spoon chilled chocolate mousse over raspberries. Dollop *remaining 1 cup* whipped topping on center of pie; top with *remaining ⅓ cup* raspberries.

Makes 8 servings

Creamy Frozen Lime Pie

- 1 *prepared* 9-inch (6 ounces) graham cracker crumb crust
- 1 package (8 ounces) cream cheese, softened
- 1 can (14 ounces) NESTLÉ® CARNATION® Sweetened Condensed Milk
- 1 cup NESTLÉ® CARNATION® Evaporated Milk
- ½ cup (about 3 medium limes) lime juice
- 1 teaspoon grated lime peel

  Lime slices, berries or mint sprigs (optional)

BEAT cream cheese in small mixer bowl until smooth. Gradually add sweetened condensed milk and evaporated milk; beat until smooth.

ADD lime juice and lime peel; beat on medium speed for 1 minute. Pour into crust; freeze for at least 2 hours or until firm.

LET stand at room temperature for 10 to 15 minutes. Garnish with lime slices, berries or mint sprigs. Serve immediately.

Makes 8 servings

SUMMER SWEETS

No-Bake Chocolate Cheesecake Pie

- **1** *prepared* **9-inch (6 ounces) chocolate crumb crust**
- **2** **bars (8 ounces) NESTLÉ® TOLL HOUSE® Semi-Sweet Chocolate Baking Bar, melted and cooled**
- **2** **packages (8 ounces *each*) cream cheese, softened**
- **¾** **cup packed brown sugar**
- **¼** **cup granulated sugar**
- **2** **tablespoons milk**
- **1** **teaspoon vanilla extract**

   Sweetened whipped cream (optional)

BEAT cream cheese, brown sugar, granulated sugar, milk and vanilla extract in small mixer bowl on high speed for 2 minutes. Add melted chocolate; beat on medium speed for 2 minutes.

SPOON into crust. Refrigerate for 1½ hours or until firm. Top with whipped cream.

Makes 10 servings

Dark Chocolate Orange Fondue

- **⅔** **cup heavy whipping cream**
- **2** **bars (8 ounces) NESTLÉ® TOLL HOUSE® Dark Chocolate Baking Bar, finely chopped**
- **1** **tablespoon orange liqueur (optional)**
- **1** **teaspoon grated orange peel**

   Marshmallows, fresh fruit (washed and patted dry), cake cubes and/or pretzels

HEAT cream in small, heavy-duty saucepan over medium-high heat; bring to a boil. Remove from heat. Add chocolate; stir until smooth. Add liqueur and orange peel; mix well.

TRANSFER fondue to fondue pot; place over low heat. To serve, dip marshmallows, fruit, cake and/or pretzels into melted chocolate. Stir often while on heat.

Makes 10 servings

SUMMER SWEETS

Double Layer Pumpkin Pie

- 1 *prepared* 9-inch (6 ounces) graham cracker pie crust
- 4 ounces cream cheese, softened
- 1 tablespoon NESTLÉ® CARNATION® Evaporated Milk, *chilled*
- 1 tablespoon granulated sugar
- 1½ cups frozen whipped topping, thawed
- 1 cup NESTLÉ® CARNATION® Evaporated Milk, *chilled*
- 1 tablespoon granulated sugar
- 2 packages (3.4 ounces *each*) vanilla instant pudding & pie filling mix
- 1 can (15 ounces) LIBBY'S® 100% Pure Pumpkin
- 2 teaspoons pumpkin pie spice*

   Whipped topping (optional)

You may substitute 1 teaspoon ground cinnamon, ½ teaspoon ground ginger and ¼ teaspoon ground cloves for pumpkin pie spice.

COMBINE cream cheese, *1 tablespoon* evaporated milk and granulated sugar in large bowl with wire whisk until smooth. Gently stir in whipped topping. Spread on bottom of pie crust.

POUR *1 cup* evaporated milk into bowl. Add pudding mixes. Beat with wire whisk for 1 minute (mixture will be thick). Stir in pumpkin and pumpkin pie spice with wire whisk until well mixed. Spread over cream cheese layer.

REFRIGERATE for 4 hours or until set. Garnish with additional whipped topping.

Makes 8 servings

Creamy Lemon Raspberry Pie

- 1 *prepared* 9-inch (6 ounces) shortbread crumb crust
- ¼ cup seedless red raspberry jam
- ½ pint (about 1 cup) fresh red raspberries, *divided*
- 4 ounces cream cheese, softened
- 1 can (12 fluid ounces) NESTLÉ® CARNATION® Evaporated Milk
- 2 packages (about 3.4 ounces *each*) lemon instant pudding and pie filling mix

   Grated peel of 1 lemon
- 1 container (8 ounces) frozen whipped topping, thawed, *divided*

   Additional grated lemon peel (optional)

SPREAD raspberry jam over bottom of crust. Sprinkle ¾ *cup* raspberries over jam.

BEAT cream cheese in large mixer bowl until creamy. Gradually add evaporated milk, pudding mixes and lemon peel. Beat for 2 minutes on medium speed until well blended. Gently stir in *half* of whipped topping. Spoon into crust; top with *remaining* whipped topping.

REFRIGERATE for 2 hours or until set. Garnish with *remaining ¼ cup* raspberries and additional lemon peel just before serving.

Makes 8 servings

Summer

Loaded Potato Potluck Favorite

It's a party! Discover travel-friendly summer foods like moist brownies, take-along casseroles, fluffy cakes, crispy pies, and more. Whether it's a backyard barbecue, a picnic in the park, or a beautiful beachfront gathering—these recipes are sure to please.

8   medium potatoes (about 2½ to 3 pounds total), peeled and cut into 1-inch chunks

1   cup NESTLÉ® CARNATION® Evaporated Milk

½   cup sour cream

1   teaspoon salt

½   teaspoon ground black pepper

2   cups (8-ounce package) shredded cheddar cheese, *divided*

6   slices bacon, cooked and crumbled, *divided*

    Sliced green onions (optional)

PLACE potatoes in large saucepan. Cover with water; bring to a boil. Cook over medium-high heat for 15 to 20 minutes or until tender; drain.

PREHEAT oven to 350°F. Grease 2½- to 3-quart casserole dish.

RETURN potatoes to saucepan; add evaporated milk, sour cream, salt and pepper. Beat with hand-held mixer until smooth. Stir in 1½ cups cheese and *half* of bacon. Spoon mixture into prepared casserole dish.

BAKE for 20 to 25 minutes or until heated through. Top with *remaining ½ cup* cheese, *remaining* half of bacon and green onions. Bake for an additional 3 minutes or until cheese is melted.

Makes 16 servings (½ cup each)

Tip: *This casserole can be assembled ahead of time and refrigerated. Cover with foil and bake at 350°F for 40 to 45 minutes or until heated. Uncover; top with cheese, bacon and green onions; bake for an additional 3 minutes or until cheese is melted.*

PORTABLE PARTY

Molten Chocolate Cakes

2 tablespoons plus ¾ cup (1½ sticks) butter, divided

2 bars (8 ounces) NESTLÉ® TOLL HOUSE® Dark Chocolate Baking Bar, broken into pieces

3 large eggs

3 large egg yolks

¼ cup *plus* 1 tablespoon granulated sugar

1 teaspoon vanilla extract

1 tablespoon all-purpose flour

Powdered sugar

PREHEAT oven to 425°F. Generously butter six (6-ounce) ramekins or custard cups with 2 *tablespoons* butter.

STIR ¾ *cup* butter and chocolate in medium, heavy-duty saucepan over low heat until chocolate is melted and mixture is smooth. Remove from heat. Beat eggs, egg yolks, sugar and vanilla extract in large mixer bowl until thick and pale yellow, about 8 minutes. Fold one-third of chocolate mixture into egg mixture. Fold in remaining chocolate mixture and flour until well blended. Divide batter evenly among prepared ramekins. Place on baking sheet.

BAKE for 12 to 13 minutes or until sides are set and 1-inch centers move slightly when shaken. Remove from oven to wire rack.

TO SERVE: Run a thin knife around top edge of cakes to loosen slightly; carefully invert onto serving plates. Lift ramekins off of cakes. Sprinkle with powdered sugar. Serve immediately.

Makes 6 servings

PORTABLE PARTY

Italian-Style Mac & Cheese with Chicken Sausage

2 cups (8 ounces) dry elbow macaroni (regular or whole wheat)

1 can (12 fluid ounces) NESTLÉ® CARNATION® Evaporated Lowfat 2% Milk

2 cups (8-ounce package) shredded Italian-style 4- or 5-cheese blend

2 links (6 ounces) fully-cooked Italian-seasoned chicken sausage,* cut into ¼-inch slices

½ teaspoon garlic powder

½ teaspoon ground black pepper

1 cup cherry tomatoes, cut in half

2 tablespoons finely sliced fresh basil leaves

*Different flavors of chicken sausage can be substituted.

PREPARE pasta according to package directions; drain.

MEANWHILE, COMBINE evaporated milk, cheese, sausage, garlic powder and black pepper in medium saucepan. Cook over medium-low heat, stirring occasionally, until cheese is melted. Remove from heat.

ADD pasta to cheese sauce; stir until combined. Add tomatoes and basil; stir gently until mixed in.

Makes 6 servings (1 cup each)

PORTABLE PARTY

Party Potatoes Italiano

Nonstick cooking spray

1 can (14.5 ounces) Italian-style diced tomatoes

1 cup panko (Japanese bread crumbs)

1 package (30 ounces) frozen hash brown potatoes, thawed

1½ cups sour cream

1¼ cups (3.75 ounces) BUITONI Refrigerated Freshly Shredded Parmesan Cheese

1 can (10.75 ounces) reduced-fat cream of chicken soup

⅔ cup (5 fluid-ounce can) NESTLÉ® CARNATION® Evaporated Milk

2 tablespoons olive oil

1 teaspoon onion powder

1 teaspoon Italian herb seasoning

½ teaspoon salt

½ teaspoon freshly ground black pepper

2 tablespoons chopped fresh basil or parsley

PREHEAT oven to 350°F. Spray 13×9-inch baking dish with nonstick cooking spray.

PLACE tomatoes in a strainer set over a bowl. Let juice drain for 15 minutes; reserve juice. Toss drained tomatoes with bread crumbs in medium bowl; set aside for later use.

COMBINE hash browns, sour cream, cheese, soup, evaporated milk, oil, onion powder, Italian seasoning, salt, pepper and reserved juice from tomatoes in large bowl. Spread potato mixture evenly into prepared dish. Sprinkle tomato mixture over top.

BAKE for 1 hour or until bubbly at the edges. Sprinkle with fresh basil or parsley before serving.

Makes 12 servings

PORTABLE PARTY

Chocolate Caramel Brownies

1 package (18.25 ounces) chocolate cake mix

1 cup chopped nuts

½ cup (1 stick) butter or margarine, melted

1 cup NESTLÉ® CARNATION® Evaporated Milk, *divided*

35 (10-ounce package) caramels, unwrapped

2 cups (12-ounce package) NESTLÉ® TOLL HOUSE® Semi-Sweet Chocolate Morsels

PREHEAT oven to 350°F.

COMBINE cake mix and nuts in large bowl. Stir in butter and ⅔ *cup* evaporated milk (batter will be thick). Spread *half* of batter into greased 13×9-inch baking pan.

BAKE for 15 minutes.

HEAT caramels and *remaining* evaporated milk in small saucepan over low heat, stirring constantly, until caramels are melted. Sprinkle morsels over brownie; drizzle with caramel mixture.

DROP *remaining* batter by heaping teaspoonfuls over caramel mixture.

BAKE for 25 to 30 minutes or until center is set. Cool in pan on wire rack.

Makes 2 dozen brownies

Golden Corn Soup

- **1 package (16 ounces) fresh corn with husks removed (4 medium ears)**
- **2 cans (12 fluid ounces *each*) NESTLÉ® CARNATION® Evaporated Lowfat 2% Milk or Evaporated Fat Free Milk**
- **1 tablespoon extra-virgin olive oil**
- **1 small yellow onion, chopped**
- **1 carrot, peeled and sliced**
- **1 celery stalk, sliced**
- **2 large cloves garlic, chopped**
- **Kosher salt and ground black pepper for seasoning**
- **1 cup water**
- **2 large fresh thyme sprigs**
- **Light sour cream or crème fraîche (optional)**
- **Chopped fresh chives (optional)**

CUT kernels from the cobs; reserve kernels and cobs. Place evaporated milk and corncobs in large saucepan; bring to a boil over medium-high heat. Reduce heat to low; cover. Cook for 8 minutes.

MEANWHILE, heat oil in large skillet over medium-high heat. Add onion; cook, stirring frequently, for 3 to 4 minutes or until translucent. Stir in carrot, celery, garlic and reserved corn kernels. Season with salt and ground black pepper. Cook, stirring frequently, for 5 minutes or until vegetables are tender.

ADD vegetable mixture, water and thyme in saucepan; cover. Cook over medium heat, stirring occasionally, for 20 minutes. Discard corncobs and thyme. Cool mixture for about 10 minutes.

POUR soup into blender until it is half full; cover. Blend until smooth. Pour through a medium sieve into clean saucepan (discard contents of sieve). Repeat process with remaining soup. Reheat soup until heated through. Serve topped with swirl of sour cream and chives.

Makes 4 to 5 servings

Cook's Tip: *Soup is also great served chilled.*

Chewy Butterscotch Brownies

- **2½ cups all-purpose flour**
- **1 teaspoon baking powder**
- **½ teaspoon salt**
- **1 cup (2 sticks) butter or margarine, softened**
- **1¾ cups packed brown sugar**
- **1 tablespoon vanilla extract**
- **2 large eggs**
- **1⅔ cups (11-ounce package) NESTLÉ® TOLL HOUSE® Butterscotch Flavored Morsels, *divided***
- **1 cup chopped nuts**

PREHEAT oven to 350°F.

COMBINE flour, baking powder and salt in medium bowl. Beat butter, sugar and vanilla extract in large mixer bowl until creamy. Beat in eggs. Gradually beat in flour mixture. Stir in *1 cup* morsels and nuts. Spread into ungreased 13×9-inch baking pan. Sprinkle with *remaining ⅔ cup* morsels.

BAKE for 30 to 40 minutes or until wooden pick inserted in center comes out clean. Cool in pan on wire rack.

Makes about 4 dozen brownies

PORTABLE PARTY

Incredible Banana Split Cake

½ **cup (1 stick) butter**

2 **large eggs**

2¾ **cups all-purpose flour**

2½ **teaspoons baking powder**

1 **teaspoon salt**

1 **can (15¼ ounces) pineapple tidbits in juice, undrained**

½ **cup buttermilk**

1¼ **cups (7.5 ounces) granulated sugar**

⅔ **cup mashed banana**

1 **teaspoon vanilla extract**

1¼ **cups NESTLÉ® TOLL HOUSE® Semi-Sweet Chocolate Morsels**

½ **cup chopped walnuts, toasted, divided**

1½ **cups chopped fresh strawberries**

1 **cup chopped banana**

Chocolate Glaze (recipe follows)

ALLOW butter and eggs to stand at room temperature for 30 minutes. Grease and lightly flour a 12-cup Bundt pan.

PREHEAT oven to 350°F.

BEAT butter in large mixer bowl on medium to high speed for 30 seconds. Gradually add sugar, ¼ cup at a time, beating on medium speed until well combined. Add eggs, mashed banana and vanilla extract; beat well. Alternately add flour mixture and buttermilk mixture, beating on low speed after each addition just until combined. Stir in morsels and ¼ *cup* walnuts. Gently fold in drained pineapple tidbits, strawberries and banana. Spread batter into prepared pan.

BAKE for 60 to 65 minutes or until a wooden pick inserted near center comes out clean. Cool cake in pan on wire rack for 20 minutes. Remove from pan; cool completely on wire rack. Drizzle cake with Chocolate Glaze and sprinkle with *remaining* ¼ *cup* walnuts. Cover; refrigerate at least 2 hours before serving.

Makes 12 to 16 servings

Chocolate Glaze

HEAT ¾ cup NESTLÉ® TOLL HOUSE® Semi-Sweet Chocolate Morsels, 3 tablespoons butter and 3 tablespoons light corn syrup in small saucepan over low heat, stirring until chocolate melts and mixture is smooth. Use immediately.

PORTABLE PARTY

Strawberry Cheesecake Pie

- 1 *prepared* 9-inch (6 ounces) graham cracker crumb crust
- ⅔ cup (5 fluid-ounce can) NESTLÉ® CARNATION® Fat Free Evaporated Milk
- 1 package (8 ounces) fat free cream cheese, softened
- 1 large egg
- ½ cup granulated sugar
- 2 tablespoons all-purpose flour
- 1 teaspoon grated lemon peel
- 1½ to 2 cups halved fresh strawberries
- 3 tablespoons strawberry jelly, warmed

PREHEAT oven to 325°F.

PLACE evaporated milk, cream cheese, egg, sugar, flour and lemon peel in blender; cover. Blend until smooth. Pour into crust.

BAKE for 35 to 40 minutes or until center is set. Cool completely in pan on wire rack. Arrange strawberries on top of pie; drizzle with jelly. Refrigerate well before serving.

Makes 8 servings

100-Calorie Pumpkin Pie Tartlets

- 16 (2½-inch) foil baking cups
  Nonstick cooking spray
- ¾ cup granulated sugar
- 1 tablespoon cornstarch
- 1 teaspoon ground cinnamon
- ½ teaspoon ground ginger
- ½ teaspoon salt
- 2 large egg whites
- 1 can (15 ounces) LIBBY'S® 100% Pure Pumpkin
- 1 can (12 fluid ounces) NESTLÉ® CARNATION® Evaporated Fat Free Milk
- 1 cup fat free whipped topping
- 12 small gingersnap cookies, broken into ¼-inch pieces

PREHEAT oven to 350°F. Place baking cups on baking sheet with sides. Spray each cup with cooking spray.

COMBINE sugar, cornstarch, cinnamon, ginger and salt in small bowl. Beat egg whites in large bowl. Stir in pumpkin and sugar mixture. Gradually stir in evaporated milk. Spoon ¼ *to* ⅓ *cup* of mixture into each prepared cup.

BAKE for 25 to 28 minutes or until knife inserted near centers comes out clean. Cool on baking sheet for 20 minutes. Refrigerate for at least 1 hour. Top each with whipped topping and gingersnap crumbs.

Makes
16 servings

PORTABLE PARTY

Butterscotch Banana Cake

1⅔ cups (11-ounce package) **NESTLÉ® TOLL HOUSE® Butterscotch Flavored Morsels**, *divided*

1 package (18.5 ounces) yellow cake mix

4 large eggs

¾ cup (2 medium) mashed ripe bananas

½ cup vegetable oil

¼ cup water

¼ cup granulated sugar

PREHEAT oven to 375°F. Grease 10-cup Bundt or round tube pan.

MICROWAVE *1⅓ cups* morsels in medium, uncovered, microwave-safe bowl on MEDIUM-HIGH (70%) power for 1 minute. STIR. Morsels may retain some of their original shape. If necessary, microwave at additional 10- to 15-second intervals, stirring just until morsels are melted. Combine cake mix, eggs, bananas, vegetable oil, water and granulated sugar in large mixer bowl. Beat on low speed until moistened. Beat on high speed for 2 minutes. Stir 2 cups batter into melted morsels. Alternately spoon batters into prepared baking pan.

BAKE for 35 to 45 minutes or until wooden pick inserted in cake comes out clean. Cool in pan for 20 minutes; invert onto wire rack to cool completely.

PLACE *remaining* morsels in small, *heavy-duty* plastic bag. Microwave on MEDIUM-HIGH (70%) power for 30 seconds; knead. Microwave at additional 10- to 15-second intervals, kneading until smooth. Cut tiny corner from bag; squeeze to drizzle over cake.

Makes 12 to 16 servings

PORTABLE PARTY

Red, White and Blueberry Torte

TORTE:

- ¾ **cup granulated sugar**
- 6 **tablespoons butter or margarine**
- 1 **tablespoon water**
- 1½ **cups (9 ounces) NESTLÉ® TOLL HOUSE® Semi-Sweet Chocolate Morsels,** *divided*
- 1 **teaspoon vanilla extract,** *divided*
- 2 **large eggs**
- ⅔ **cup all-purpose flour**
- ¼ **teaspoon baking soda**
- ¼ **teaspoon salt**

TOPPING:

- 1 **package (8 ounces) cream cheese, at room temperature**
- 2 **tablespoons granulated sugar**
- ½ **of an 8-ounce container frozen light whipped topping, thawed**
- 2 **cups sliced strawberries**
- ¼ **cup fresh blueberries**

FOR TORTE:

PREHEAT oven to 350°F. Line 9-inch-round cake pan with wax paper; grease paper.

COMBINE *¾ cup* sugar, butter and water in small, *heavy-duty* saucepan. Bring to a boil, stirring constantly; remove from heat. Add ¾ *cup* morsels; stir until smooth. Stir in *½ teaspoon* vanilla extract. Add eggs, one at a time, stirring well after each addition. Add flour, baking soda and salt; stir until well blended. Stir in *remaining ¾ cup* morsels. Pour into prepared cake pan.

BAKE for 20 to 25 minutes or until wooden pick inserted in center comes out slightly sticky. Cool in pan for 15 minutes. Invert torte onto wire rack; remove wax paper. Turn right side up; cool completely.

FOR TOPPING:

BEAT cream cheese, 2 *tablespoons* sugar and *remaining ½ teaspoon* vanilla extract in small mixer bowl until creamy. Stir in whipped topping. Spread over torte; top with berries. Refrigerate until ready to serve.

Makes 8 to 10 servings

PORTABLE PARTY

Pepperoni Pizza Quiche

1 *unbaked* 9-inch (4-cup volume) frozen pie shell

1 package (8 ounces) shredded Italian blend cheese, divided

2 ounces thinly sliced pepperoni (about 20 to 30, 1½ to 2-inch diameter slices), cut into quarters, *divided*

1 can (12 ounces) NESTLÉ® CARNATION® Evaporated Milk

3 large eggs, beaten

2 tablespoons all-purpose flour

1 teaspoon dried basil leaves

⅛ teaspoon garlic powder

PREHEAT oven to 350°F.

SPRINKLE *1 cup* cheese and *half* of pepperoni pieces onto bottom of pie shell.

WHISK evaporated milk, eggs, flour, basil and garlic powder in medium bowl until blended. Pour mixture into pie shell. Sprinkle with remaining cheese. Decorate top with remaining pepperoni pieces and any other topping you like. Place quiche on baking sheet (if pie pan is made of aluminum foil).

BAKE for 40 to 45 minutes or until knife inserted near center comes out clean. Cool for 5 minutes before serving.

Makes 8 servings

Tip: *Choose ¼ cup of any of your favorite toppings (such as chopped onions, red or green peppers or sliced black olives) and add as topping with the remaining pepperoni pieces.*

PORTABLE PARTY

"Best"-over Ham & Pesto Pasta

1   box (12 ounces) dry tri-color rotini or spiral shaped pasta (about 3½ cups)

1   bag (16 ounces) frozen broccoli, cauliflower and carrot medley

1   can (12 fluid ounces) NESTLÉ® CARNATION® Evaporated Milk

2   cups (8-ounce package) shredded Italian cheese blend or Monterey Jack cheese

3   tablespoons jarred or refrigerated pesto with basil

¼   teaspoon ground black pepper

2   cups (8 ounces) cooked ham, cut into ½-inch pieces

COOK pasta according to package directions, adding frozen vegetables to boiling pasta water for last 2 minutes of cooking time; drain. Return pasta and vegetables to cooking pot.

MEANWHILE, COMBINE evaporated milk, cheese, pesto and black pepper in medium saucepan. Cook over medium low heat, stirring occasionally, until cheese is melted. Remove from heat.

POUR cheese sauce over pasta and vegetables. Add ham; stir until combined.

Makes 10 servings

Milk Chocolate Banana Brownies

1¾ cups (11.5-ounce package) NESTLÉ® TOLL HOUSE® Milk Chocolate Morsels, *divided*

½   cup all-purpose flour

½   cup whole-wheat flour

¾   teaspoon baking powder

½   teaspoon salt

1   cup packed light brown sugar

½   cup (1 stick) butter, *softened*

2   large eggs

1   teaspoon vanilla extract

2   medium ripe bananas, quartered lengthwise and chopped

PREHEAT oven to 350°F. Grease 9-inch-square baking pan.

MICROWAVE *1 cup* morsels in small, uncovered, microwave-safe bowl on MEDIUM-HIGH (70%) power for 45 seconds; STIR. If necessary, microwave at additional 10- to 15-second intervals, stirring just until morsels are smooth. Cool to room temperature.

COMBINE flour, whole-wheat flour, baking powder and salt in small bowl. Beat brown sugar and butter in medium mixer bowl until creamy. Add eggs and vanilla extract; beat well. Beat in melted chocolate. Gradually beat in flour mixture. Stir in bananas and *remaining ¾ cup* morsels. Spread into prepared baking pan.

BAKE for 40 to 45 minutes or until wooden pick inserted in center comes out clean. Cool completely in pan on wire rack. Cut into bars. Store in covered container in refrigerator.

Makes 16 brownies

PORTABLE PARTY

Sensational S'more Torte

TORTE:

- 1¾ cups all-purpose flour
- 1¾ cups granulated sugar
- ¾ cup NESTLÉ® TOLL HOUSE® Baking Cocoa
- 1½ teaspoons baking soda
- 1 teaspoon salt
- 1½ cups sour cream
- ⅔ cup butter, softened
- 2 large eggs
- 1½ teaspoons vanilla extract

FILLING:

- 2 cups (12-ounce package) NESTLÉ® TOLL HOUSE® Semi-Sweet Chocolate Mini Morsels
- 1 package (3.5 ounces) vanilla instant pudding and pie filling mix
- 1 cup cold milk
- 1 package (8 ounces) cream cheese, softened
- 1 container (12 ounces) frozen whipped topping, thawed
- 4 cups miniature marshmallows, *divided*
- 16 whole graham crackers
- 10 fudge-covered graham crackers or 5 squares chocolate graham crackers

FOR TORTE:

PREHEAT oven to 350°F. Grease and line bottom of two 8-inch-square cake pans with parchment paper.

COMBINE flour, sugar, baking cocoa, baking soda and salt in large mixer bowl. Beat in sour cream, butter, eggs and vanilla extract until just moistened. Beat on medium speed for 3 to 4 minutes or until light in color. Spoon into prepared pans.

BAKE for 40 to 45 minutes or until wooden pick inserted in center comes out clean. Cool in pans on wire racks for 10 minutes; remove to wire racks to cool completely.

FOR FILLING:

MICROWAVE morsels in microwave-safe bowl on HIGH (100%) power for 1 minute; STIR. Morsels may retain some of their original shape. If necessary, microwave at additional 10- to 15-second intervals, stirring until morsels are smooth.

COMBINE pudding mix and milk in large mixer bowl. Beat for 2 minutes or until thickened. Beat in cream cheese. Fold in whipped topping. Fold in *3 cups* marshmallows.

SLICE each cake layer in half horizontally. Place two layers, side-by-side, cut-side-down on large serving platter. Spread *half* the melted chocolate over the cake layers. Lightly press *half* the graham crackers into melted chocolate, cutting crackers to fit. Spread *half* the filling over graham crackers. Repeat with *remaining* cake layers, melted chocolate, graham crackers and filling, covering tops only, not sides of cake.

COARSELY chop chocolate covered graham crackers. Sprinkle over top of torte. Sprinkle with *remaining* marshmallows. Refrigerate for at least 5 hours or overnight.

Makes 16 servings

PORTABLE PARTY

Marshmallow Sandwich Cookies

1 package (16.5 ounces) NESTLÉ® TOLL HOUSE® Refrigerated Chocolate Chip Cookie Dough*

8 large marshmallows

*Or substitute dough from one batch Original NESTLÉ® TOLL HOUSE® Chocolate Chip Cookies (NESTLÉ® TOLL HOUSE® Semi-Sweet Chocolate Morsels 6-ounce package recipe).

PREPARE refrigerated cookie dough according to package directions. (If using dough from one batch Original cookie dough, make 16 cookies, baked 9 to 11 minutes.) Cool on baking sheets on wire racks for 1 minute; remove to wire racks to cool completely.

PLACE marshmallow on bottom side of one cookie. Microwave on medium (50%) power for 10 to 20 seconds or until marshmallow expands. Top with second cookie. Cool for 1 to 2 minutes. Repeat with remaining cookies and marshmallows.

Makes 8 sandwich cookies

Potato Bacon Casserole

4 cups frozen shredded hash brown potatoes

½ cup finely chopped onion

8 ounces bacon or turkey bacon, cooked and crumbled*

1 cup (4 ounces) shredded cheddar cheese

1 can (12 fluid ounces) NESTLÉ® CARNATION® Evaporated Milk or NESTLÉ® CARNATION® Evaporated Lowfat 2% Milk

1 large egg, lightly beaten or ¼ cup egg substitute

1½ teaspoons seasoned salt

*May substitute with 1 package (2.1 ounces) precooked bacon slices, cut into small pieces.

PREHEAT oven to 350°F. Grease 8-inch-square baking dish.

LAYER ½ potatoes, ½ of onion, ½ of bacon and ½ of cheese in prepared baking dish; repeat layers. Combine evaporated milk, egg and seasoned salt in small bowl. Pour evenly over potato mixture; cover.

BAKE for 55 to 60 minutes. Uncover; bake for an additional 5 minutes. Let stand for 10 to 15 minutes before serving.

Makes 6 servings

PORTABLE PARTY

Summer Berry Brownie Torte

BROWNIE:

- **1 cup granulated sugar,** *divided*
- **6 tablespoons butter or margarine**
- **1 tablespoon water**
- **1½ cups (9 ounces) NESTLÉ® TOLL HOUSE® Semi-Sweet Chocolate Morsels,** *divided*
- **½ teaspoon vanilla extract**
- **2 large eggs**
- **⅔ cup all-purpose flour**
- **¼ teaspoon baking soda**
- **¼ teaspoon salt**

FILLING:

- **½ cup heavy whipping cream**
- **2 cups sliced strawberries or other fresh berries**

FOR BROWNIE:

PREHEAT oven to 350°F. Grease and wax paper-line 9-inch-round cake pan.

COMBINE ¾ cup sugar, butter and water in small, *heavy-duty* saucepan. Bring to a boil, stirring constantly; remove from heat. Add ¾ cup morsels; stir until smooth. Stir in vanilla extract. Add eggs, one at a time, stirring well after each addition. Add flour, baking soda and salt; stir until well blended. Stir in *remaining* ¾ *cup* morsels. Pour into prepared cake pan.

BAKE for 20 to 25 minutes or until wooden pick inserted in center comes out slightly sticky. Cool for 15 minutes in pan. Invert onto wire rack; remove wax paper. Turn right side up; cool completely.

FOR FILLING:

BEAT cream and *remaining* sugar in small mixer bowl until stiff peaks form.

SPREAD filling over brownie; top with berries.

Makes 8 to 10 servings

PORTABLE PARTY

Tropical Sunshine Cake

- **1 package (18.25 ounces) yellow cake mix**
- **1 can (12 fluid ounces) NESTLÉ® CARNATION® Evaporated Milk**
- **2 large eggs**
- **1 can (20 ounces) crushed pineapple in juice, drained (juice reserved), *divided***
- **½ cup chopped almonds**
- **¾ cup sifted powdered sugar**
- **1 cup flaked coconut, toasted**
- **Whipped cream**

PREHEAT oven to 350°F. Grease 13×9-inch baking pan.

COMBINE cake mix, evaporated milk and eggs in large mixer bowl. Beat on low speed for 2 minutes. Stir in *1 cup* pineapple. Pour batter into prepared baking pan. Sprinkle with almonds.

BAKE for 30 to 35 minutes or until wooden pick inserted in center comes out clean. Cool in pan on wire rack for 15 minutes.

COMBINE sugar and 2 tablespoons *reserved* pineapple juice in small bowl; mix until smooth. Spread over warm cake; sprinkle with coconut and *remaining* pineapple. Cool completely before serving. Top with whipped cream.

Makes 12 servings

Chocolate Banana Cream Pie

- **1 package (16.5 ounces) NESTLÉ® TOLL HOUSE® Refrigerated Chocolate Chip Cookie Bar Dough, softened**
- **1 can (12 fluid ounces) NESTLÉ® CARNATION® Evaporated Milk***
- **1 package (about 3.4 ounces) banana cream or vanilla instant pudding and pie filling mix**
- **2 medium bananas, peeled and sliced**
- **1½ cups frozen whipped topping, thawed**
- **NESTLÉ® NESQUIK® Chocolate Flavor Syrup, (optional)**
- **NESTLÉ® TOLL HOUSE® Semi-Sweet Chocolate Mini Morsels, (optional)**

PREHEAT oven to 350°F. Grease 9-inch pie plate.

PRESS 20 *squares* of cookie dough* onto bottom and up side of prepared pie plate.

BAKE for 18 to 22 minutes or until golden brown; flatten down with back of spoon to form pie shell. Cool completely on wire rack.

BEAT milk and pudding mix according to package directions in small bowl; refrigerate for 5 minutes. Spread *1 cup* pudding over cookie crust (save *remaining* pudding for later use). Top pudding with bananas; spread with whipped topping. Refrigerate for at least 1 hour or until set. Drizzle with Nesquik; top with morsels. Cut into wedges.

Makes 8 servings

*You will have 4 squares left. Refrigerate for future use or bake and enjoy!

Savory Parmesan Bread Sticks

⅓ **cup grated Parmesan cheese**

½ **teaspoon dried Italian herbs**

¼ **teaspoon garlic powder**

1 **packet (0.25 ounce) rapid-rising yeast**

1¼ **cups (110° to 115°F) warm water**

4½ **cups all-purpose flour *plus* extra for kneading**

¾ **cup dry NESTLÉ® CARNATION® Instant Nonfat Dry Milk**

3 **tablespoons granulated sugar**

¾ **teaspoon salt**

½ **cup (1 stick) plus 2 tablespoons butter, melted, *divided***

GREASE 2 large baking sheets. Combine cheese, herbs and garlic powder in small bowl; set aside.

STIR yeast into warm water in small bowl. Combine flour, dry milk, sugar and salt in large bowl. Add ½ *cup* butter and yeast mixture to flour mixture. Stir until blended and sticky dough is formed.

PLACE dough on lightly floured surface; knead for 6 to 8 minutes, until dough is smooth and elastic, adding additional flour as necessary. Cut into 24 pieces. While working with dough, keep covered with plastic wrap. Roll each piece into a 10-inch long rope. Flatten rope slightly; holding ends, twist and place on prepared baking sheet. Press down ends. Brush dough with *remaining 2 tablespoons* butter. Sprinkle with cheese mixture. Allow to rise in warm place for 15 minutes or until risen slightly.

PREHEAT oven to 375°F.

BAKE for 15 to 20 minutes until golden brown. Remove from baking sheets to wire racks. Serve warm. Store remaining tightly covered.

Makes 2 dozen bread sticks

PORTABLE PARTY

Cherry Berry Cheesecake Pie

CRUST:

- 1½ **cups finely ground gingersnap cookie crumbs (about 30 (2-inch) cookies)**
- 2 **tablespoons granulated sugar**
- ⅓ **cup melted butter**

FILLING:

- 1 **can (12 fluid ounces) NESTLÉ® CARNATION® Evaporated Milk**
- 1½ **packages (12 ounces) cream cheese, at room temperature**
- 2 **large eggs**
- ¾ **cup granulated sugar**
- ¼ **cup all-purpose flour**
- 1 **tablespoon grated lemon peel**
- 2 **cups pitted fresh cherries* and mixed berries (such as blueberries, raspberries and/or sliced strawberries)**
- 3 **tablespoons cherry, raspberry or strawberry jam, warmed**

*1 can (15 ounces) pitted, dark sweet bing cherries, drained (about 1 cup) can be used instead of fresh cherries.

PREHEAT oven to 350°F. Grease 9-inch deep-dish pie dish.

FOR CRUST:

COMBINE crumbs and sugar in pie dish. Stir in butter. Press crumb mixture onto bottom and up sides of prepared pie plate.

BAKE for 8 minutes. Cool completely on wire rack.

FOR FILLING:

PLACE evaporated milk, cream cheese, eggs, sugar, flour and lemon peel in blender; cover. Blend until smooth. Pour into prepared pie crust.

BAKE for 30 to 35 minutes or until center is set. Cool completely on wire rack. Refrigerate for at least 3 hours. Arrange cherries and berries on top of pie; drizzle with warmed jam.

Makes 8 servings

PORTABLE PARTY

Creamy Vegetable Lasagna

- **1 tablespoon olive oil**
- **2 medium zucchini, cut lengthwise into quarters, then into ½-inch pieces**
- **2 medium bell peppers (red, green or yellow), chopped into ½-inch pieces**
- **2 garlic cloves, finely chopped**
- **½ teaspoon salt, *divided***
- **½ teaspoon ground black pepper, *divided***
- **⅓ cup all-purpose flour**
- **2 cans (12 fluid ounces *each*) NESTLÉ® CARNATION® Evaporated Lowfat 2% Milk, *divided***
- **1 jar (26 ounces) prepared marinara sauce, *divided***
- **1 package (8 ounces) or 12 sheets no-boil lasagna noodles, *divided***
- **1½ cups (6 ounces) shredded part-skim mozzarella cheese, *divided***
- **½ cup grated Parmesan cheese (optional)**

PREHEAT oven to 375°F. Grease 13×9-inch baking dish.

HEAT oil in large skillet over medium-high heat. Add zucchini and peppers; cook, stirring frequently, until soft, for about 8 minutes. Add garlic; cook for an additional 2 minutes. Season with ¼ *teaspoon* each salt and pepper. Remove from heat.

MEANWHILE, WHISK together flour, ¼ *cup* evaporated milk and *remaining* ¼ *teaspoon* each of salt and black pepper in medium saucepan until smooth. Whisk in *remaining* evaporated milk. Heat over medium heat, stirring frequently, until mixture comes to a boil. Reduce heat; simmer for 3 minutes or until thickened. Stir 2 *cups* of milk mixture into cooked vegetables; reserve *remaining* milk mixture.

SPREAD ½ *cup* marinara sauce over bottom of the prepared baking dish. Top with 3 noodles. Top with *half* of the vegetable mixture. Top with 3 noodles. Spread *1 cup* marinara sauce and sprinkle with ¾ *cup* mozzarella cheese. Layer 3 noodles, *remaining* vegetables and *remaining* 3 noodles. Top with *remaining* marinara sauce, reserved milk mixture, *remaining* ¾ *cup* mozzarella cheese and Parmesan cheese.

BAKE for 35 to 40 minutes until golden and bubbly on the edges. Let stand for 10 minutes before serving.

Makes 12 servings

Tip: *For extra flavor, add a bay leaf to the white sauce while cooking.*

Summer

Dive into summer with a refreshing selection of recipes! Check out the cool beverages like the Orange Cream Milkshake or the Guava Smoothie. Or perk up your taste buds with an ice cream-packed dessert like Swirled Mint Ice Cream Bars or the Cookie and Ice Cream Dessert. What a delicious way to enjoy the summer!

TOLL HOUSE® Chocolate Chip Cookie Milkshake

1   pint (2 cups) vanilla ice cream

2   cups (about 8) freshly baked and crumbled NESTLÉ® TOLL HOUSE® Refrigerated Chocolate Chip Cookies

1   cup milk *or* ⅔ cup (5-ounce can) NESTLÉ® CARNATION® Evaporated Milk, chilled

PLACE ice cream, cookies and 1 cup milk *or* ⅔ cup (5-ounce can) NESTLÉ® CARNATION® Evaporated Milk in blender; cover. Blend until smooth. If a smoother shake is desired, add some additional milk.

Makes 3 servings

Guanábana Shake

1   package (14 ounces) frozen guanábana pulp

1   can (12 fluid ounces) NESTLÉ® CARNATION® Evaporated Milk

1   cup water

¼   cup granulated sugar

PLACE frozen pulp, evaporated milk, water and sugar in blender container; cover. Blend until smooth.

Makes 6 servings

Note: *Frozen mango, guava, papaya, coconut, passion fruit, tamarind or pineapple may be substituted for guanábana pulp.*

TOLL HOUSE® Chocolate Chip Cookie Milkshake

REFRESHING TREATS

Pineapple Pecan Cup

1   can (12 fluid ounces) NESTLÉ®
    CARNATION® Evaporated Milk

1   cup chopped pecans

1   package (8 ounces) cream cheese, cut up

1   jar (12 ounces) pineapple preserves

    Fresh pineapple wedges and mint leaves
    (optional)

PLACE evaporated milk, pecans, cream cheese and
preserves in blender container; cover. Blend until
smooth. Place ½ *cup* mixture into each of 8 dessert
cups or ramekins. Refrigerate for 2 hours or until
chilled. Garnish with pineapple wedges and mint
leaves, if desired.

Makes 8 servings

Tropical Avocado Smoothie

    Pulp of 1 medium avocado

2   cans (12 fluid ounce *each*) NESTLÉ®
    CARNATION® Evaporated Lowfat
    2% Milk, *chilled**

¼   cup granulated sugar or to taste

1   teaspoon grated lime peel (optional)

    Crushed ice (optional)

*May use 2 cans (12 fluid ounces each) CARNATION® Evaporated Fat
Free Milk.*

PLACE avocado, evaporated milk, sugar and lime
peel in blender container; cover. Blend for 30 to
45 seconds until smooth.

SERVE in tall glasses. Top with crushed ice, if desired.

Makes 4 to 5 servings

Note: *If a thinner drink is desired, blend in 1 cup ice
cubes with drink ingredients.*

REFRESHING TREATS

Yummy Fruit Smoothie

3 cups assorted fresh fruit (such as bananas, strawberries, mango, papaya, pineapple)

1 can (12 fluid ounces) NESTLÉ® CARNATION® Evaporated Milk, *chilled*

½ cup crushed ice

1 to 2 tablespoons sugar (optional)

PLACE fruit, evaporated milk and ice in blender; cover. Blend until smooth. Taste; add sugar if needed.

Makes 4 servings

Variation: *May substitute 3 cups cut-up frozen, unsweetened fruit or canned fruit for the fresh fruit. If using frozen fruit, thaw slightly and cut into smaller pieces. Crushed ice may not be needed. For canned fruit, drain and reserve juice or syrup. Substitute juice or syrup for sugar, if needed.*

Orange Cream Milkshake

1 can (12 fluid ounces) NESTLÉ® CARNATION® Evaporated Milk

1 pint (4 large scoops) vanilla ice cream

1 can (6 ounces) orange juice concentrate

PLACE evaporated milk, ice cream and concentrate in blender; cover. Blend until smooth.

Makes 4 servings

Note: *For a thinner shake, decrease amount of ice cream.*

REFRESHING TREATS

Mini Lemon Lime Tartlets

1 **package (16.5 ounces) NESTLÉ®
TOLL HOUSE® Refrigerated
Sugar Cookie Bar Dough**

1 **can (14 ounces) NESTLÉ®
CARNATION® Sweetened
Condensed Milk**

1 **package (8 ounces) ⅓ less fat
cream cheese (Neufchâtel) or
regular cream cheese, at room
temperature**

2 **cups thawed fat free, reduced
fat or regular frozen whipped
topping**

¼ **cup lemon juice**

2 **teaspoons grated lemon peel**

¼ **cup lime juice**

2 **teaspoons grated lime peel**

**Additional lemon and lime
quarter slices, peel curls or
grated peel (optional)**

PREHEAT oven to 325°F. Paper-line 24 muffin cups.

CUT dough along pre-scored lines; place one piece of cookie dough in each muffin cup.

BAKE for 13 to 15 minutes or until golden brown. Cookies will be puffy. Cool completely in pan on wire rack.

BEAT sweetened condensed milk and cream cheese in large mixer bowl until smooth. Gently fold in whipped topping. Divide mixture into two medium bowls. Stir lemon juice and lemon peel into one bowl and lime juice and lime peel into other bowl.

POUR about 3 tablespoons lemon-cream cheese mixture, followed by the lime-cream cheese mixture, over 24 cookie cups. Refrigerate for 2 hours or overnight. Decorate with lemon and lime quarter slices, curls or peel, if desired.

Makes 2 dozen tartlets

Tip: *Using low and reduced fat cream cheese and whipped topping helps to make these treats lower in fat.*

Tip: *Love lemon but not crazy about lime? Simply double the lemon juice and grated lemon peel in the recipe and leave out the lime, and make 24 lemon tartlets. Tartlets may be frozen in an airtight container for up to 2 weeks. Allow to thaw at room temperature for 30 minutes before serving.*

REFRESHING TREATS

Swirled Mint Ice Cream Bars

2½ cups (about 22) finely ground creme-filled chocolate sandwich cookies

3 tablespoons butter or margarine, melted

1⅔ cups (10-ounce package) NESTLÉ® TOLL HOUSE® SWIRLED™ Semi-Sweet & Premier White Morsels, *divided*

1 container (1.5 quarts) mint chocolate chip DREYER'S® or EDY'S® SLOW CHURNED™ Light Ice Cream, slightly softened

NESTLÉ® NESQUIK® Chocolate Flavor Syrup

LINE 13×9-inch baking pan with plastic wrap or foil with edges hanging over sides.

MIX cookie crumbs and butter in small bowl. Press onto bottom of prepared pan. Sprinkle *1 cup* morsels over crumb crust. Scoop ice cream over morsels; spread evenly with knife or small spatula.

SPRINKLE with *remaining ⅔ cup* morsels and press down lightly. Freeze for about 2 hours.

TO SERVE: Let stand for 5 minutes. Lift dessert out of pan; remove plastic wrap. Cut into bars. Drizzle with NESQUIK®.

Makes 15 servings

REFRESHING TREATS

Zesty Lemon Mini Pound Cakes

1 cup (6 ounces) NESTLÉ® TOLL HOUSE® Premier White Morsels*

2½ cups all-purpose flour

1 teaspoon baking powder

½ teaspoon salt

1 cup (2 sticks) butter, softened

1½ cups granulated sugar

2 teaspoons vanilla extract

3 large eggs

3 to 4 tablespoons (about 3 medium lemons) grated lemon peel

1⅓ cups buttermilk

1½ cups powdered sugar

¼ cup fresh lemon juice

*May substitute 6 ounces of NESTLÉ® TOLL HOUSE® Premier White Baking Bars, broken into pieces for the morsels.

PREHEAT oven to 350°F. Grease and flour *two* 6-cake mini Bundt pans.

MELT morsels in medium, uncovered, microwave-safe bowl on MEDIUM-HIGH (70%) power for 1 minute; STIR. Morsels may retain some of their original shape. If necessary, microwave at additional 10- to 15-second intervals, stirring just until morsels are melted. Cool slightly.

COMBINE flour, baking powder and salt in small bowl. Beat butter, sugar and vanilla extract in large mixer bowl until creamy. Beat in eggs, one at a time, beating well after each addition. Beat in lemon peel and melted morsels. Gradually beat in flour mixture alternately with buttermilk. Pour into prepared pans.

BAKE for 20 to 25 minutes or until wooden pick inserted in cakes comes out clean. Cool in pan on wire racks for 10 minutes. Combine powdered sugar and lemon juice in small bowl. Make holes in cakes with wooden pick; pour *half* of lemon glaze over cakes. Let stand for 5 minutes. Invert onto serving platter. Make holes in top of cakes; pour *remaining* glaze over cakes. Cool completely before serving.

Makes 12 mini cakes

REFRESHING TREATS

Mom's Special Occasion Ice Cream Cookie Dessert

COOKIES:

- **1 package (16.5 ounces) NESTLÉ® TOLL HOUSE® Refrigerated Chocolate Chip Cookie Bar Dough**

WALNUT MIX:

- **1 cup chopped walnuts**
- **1½ tablespoons butter or margarine, melted**
- **1 tablespoon packed brown sugar**

CHOCOLATE SAUCE:

- **1 can (12 fluid ounces) NESTLÉ® CARNATION® Evaporated Lowfat 2% Milk**
- **1 cup (6 ounces) NESTLÉ® TOLL HOUSE® Semi-Sweet Chocolate Morsels**
- **1 cup powdered sugar**
- **2 packets (1 ounce *each*) NESTLÉ® TOLL HOUSE® CHOCO BAKE® Pre-Melted Unsweetened Chocolate Flavor**
- **2 tablespoons butter or margarine**
- **1 tablespoon vanilla extract**
- **½ gallon vanilla DREYER'S® or EDY'S® SLOW CHURNED™ Light Ice Cream, softened**

FOR COOKIES:

BAKE cookies according to package directions; remove to wire racks to cool completely. Chop cooled cookies into small pieces.

FOR WALNUT MIX:

PREHEAT oven to 375°F. Grease 8-inch-square baking pan.

COMBINE walnuts, butter and brown sugar in small bowl. Pour into prepared pan. Bake for 8 to 10 minutes; stir well. Cool completely in pan on wire rack.

FOR CHOCOLATE SAUCE:

COMBINE evaporated milk, morsels, powdered sugar, Choco Bake and butter in medium, *heavy-duty* saucepan. Cook over medium-low heat, stirring occasionally, until chocolate is melted. Reduce heat to low; continue cooking, stirring occasionally, for 5 to 7 minutes or until thickened. Remove from heat. Stir in vanilla extract. Cool completely.

TO ASSEMBLE:

WRAP *outside* of 9- or 10-inch springform pan with foil. Spread *one third* of chopped cookies on bottom of pan. Top with *half* of ice cream and *half* of chocolate sauce. Combine *remaining* chopped cookies and walnut mixture in medium bowl. Spread *half* of cookie-walnut mixture over chocolate sauce. Top with *remaining* ice cream, chocolate sauce (reserving 2 tablespoons) and cookie-walnut mixture.

PLACE *remaining 2 tablespoons* chocolate sauce in small, *heavy-duty* resealable plastic food storage bag. Cut a hole in corner of bag; squeeze to drizzle chocolate sauce over top of dessert. Freeze for at least 4 hours or overnight.

TO SERVE: Let stand at room temperature for 20 minutes. Remove side of springform pan. Cut into slices.

Makes 16 servings

REFRESHING TREATS

Minty-Licious Ice Cream Freeze

12 chocolate graham crackers, finely ground (about 1½ cups)

½ cup (1 stick) butter or margarine, melted

1⅔ cups (10-ounce package) NESTLÉ® TOLL HOUSE® Dark Chocolate & Mint Morsels, *divided*

1 cup broken-up mini-pretzels (about 40), *divided*

1 container (1.5 quarts) chocolate or vanilla DREYER'S® or EDY'S® SLOW CHURNED™ Light Ice Cream, slightly softened

NESTLÉ® NESQUIK® Chocolate Flavor Syrup (optional)

LINE 13×9-inch baking pan with plastic wrap or foil with edges hanging over sides.

MIX crumbs and butter in small bowl. Press onto bottom of prepared pan. Sprinkle *1 cup* morsels and *½ cup* pretzels over crumb crust. Scoop ice cream over morsels; spread evenly with knife or small spatula.

SPRINKLE with *remaining ⅔ cup* morsels and *½ cup* pretzels; press down lightly. Freeze for at least 2 hours.

TO SERVE: Let stand for 5 minutes. Lift dessert out of pan; remove plastic wrap. Cut into squares. Drizzle each serving with Nesquick.

Makes 15 servings

REFRESHING TREATS

Lemon Bars

CRUST:

- 2 **cups all-purpose flour**
- ½ **cup powdered sugar**
- 1 **cup (2 sticks) butter or margarine, softened**

FILLING:

- 1 **can (14 ounces) NESTLÉ® CARNATION® Sweetened Condensed Milk**
- 4 **large eggs**
- ⅔ **cup lemon juice**
- 1 **tablespoon all-purpose flour**
- 1 **teaspoon baking powder**
- ¼ **teaspoon salt**
- 4 **drops yellow food coloring (optional)**
- 1 **tablespoon grated lemon peel**

  Sifted powdered sugar (optional)

PREHEAT oven to 350°F.

FOR CRUST:

COMBINE flour and sugar in medium bowl. Cut in butter with pastry blender or two knives until mixture is crumbly. Press lightly onto bottom and halfway up sides of ungreased 13×9-inch baking pan.

BAKE for 20 minutes.

FOR FILLING:

BEAT sweetened condensed milk and eggs in large mixer bowl until fluffy. Beat in lemon juice, flour, baking powder, salt and food coloring just until blended. Fold in lemon peel; pour over crust.

BAKE for 20 to 25 minutes or until filling is set and crust is golden brown. Cool in pan on wire rack. Refrigerate for about 2 hours. Cut into bars; sprinkle with powdered sugar.

Makes 4 dozen bars

REFRESHING TREATS

Pumpkin Pie Smoothie

- **1 can (15 ounces) LIBBY'S® 100% Pure Pumpkin,** *chilled*
- **1 can (12 fluid ounces) NESTLÉ® CARNATION® Evaporated Fat Free Milk,** *chilled*
- **1 cup crushed ice**
- **⅔ cup (6 ounces) vanilla light and nonfat yogurt**
- **¼ cup granulated sugar**
- **¼ teaspoon pumpkin pie spice**
- **Light whipped cream**

COMBINE pumpkin, evaporated milk, yogurt, sugar and pumpkin pie spice in blender; cover. Blend until mixture is smooth. If a thinner smoothie is desired, add water, a little at a time, until desired consistency is reached.

TOP with whipped cream; sprinkle with additional pumpkin pie spice.

Makes 5 servings

Note: *For a richer and creamier version of this recipe, substitute NESTLÉ® CARNATION® Evaporated Lowfat 2% Milk or Evaporated Milk for the Evaporated Fat Free Milk.*

Frozen Fudge Pops

- **1 can (12 ounces) NESTLÉ® CARNATION® Evaporated Milk**
- **¾ cup water**
- **1 cup (6 ounces) NESTLÉ® TOLL HOUSE® Milk Chocolate Morsels**
- **10 (3-ounce) paper cups**
- **10 wooden craft sticks***

*Found in cake decorating or hobby shops.

MICROWAVE evaporated milk and water in medium, uncovered, microwave-safe bowl on HIGH (100%) power for 2 minutes or until mixture is very hot but not boiling. Add morsels; whisk until smooth.

CAREFULLY POUR about ⅓ cup chocolate mixture into each cup. Cover each cup with foil. Insert one stick through the center of each foil.

FREEZE for 4 hours or until firm. To remove pops from cups, carefully run warm water over side of cup to loosen. Peel off cup and enjoy. Freeze no longer than 1 month.

Makes 10 servings

Note: *Frozen treat molds can be used. Yield may vary.*

Variation: *For a richer, chocolate flavor, substitute 1 cup (6 ounces) NESTLÉ® TOLL HOUSE® Semi-Sweet Chocolate Morsels for the milk chocolate morsels.*

REFRESHING TREATS

Mini Custard Fruit Tarts

6 *prepared* single-serving graham cracker crumb crusts

1 package (3 ounces) vanilla pudding and pie filling mix (*not instant*)

⅓ cup water

1 can (12 fluid ounces) NESTLÉ® CARNATION® Evaporated Lowfat 2% Milk

1 teaspoon grated lemon peel

Sliced fresh strawberries, kiwi, blueberries, raspberries or orange sections (optional)

Mint leaves (optional)

COMBINE pudding mix and water in small saucepan. Add evaporated milk and lemon peel; stir until smooth. Cook over medium-low heat, stirring constantly, until mixture comes to a boil and thickens.

POUR into crusts; refrigerate for 1 hour or until set. Top with fruit and mint leaves before serving.

Makes 6 servings

Variation: *For a Key Lime twist to this recipe, substitute 2 teaspoons fresh lime juice and 1 teaspoon grated lime peel for the grated lemon peel. Top with lime slice.*

Cookie and Ice Cream Frozen Dessert

1 **package (16.5 ounces) NESTLÉ® TOLL HOUSE® Refrigerated Chocolate Chip Cookie Bar Dough, broken into pieces,** *divided*

4 **cups vanilla DREYER'S® or EDY'S® SLOW CHURNED™ Light Ice Cream, slightly softened**

PREHEAT oven to 350°F. Grease 9-inch springform pan.

PLACE 20 *pieces* (⅚ of bar) of dough in pan. (Refrigerate *remaining* 4 pieces to bake later.) Allow to soften 5 to 10 minutes. Using fingertips, pat dough gently onto bottom and 1 inch up side of prepared pan.

BAKE for 14 to 16 minutes or until light golden brown and center is still slightly soft. Cool completely in pan on wire rack. Bake *remaining* dough into cookies according to package directions.

SPREAD softened ice cream over cookie crust in pan; cover with plastic wrap and freeze for 1 to 2 hours or until firm. Remove side of pan. Cut dessert into wedges; top with crumbled cookies.

Makes 16 servings

Cappuccino Smoothie

1 **can (12 fluid ounce) NESTLÉ® CARNATION® Evaporated Milk,** *chilled*

5 **to 6 teaspoons NESCAFÉ® TASTER'S CHOICE® Decaf House Blend 100% Pure Instant Coffee Granules**

1 **cup vanilla ice cream**

1 **cup ice cubes**

1 **tablespoon granulated sugar**

2 **teaspoons NESTLÉ® TOLL HOUSE® Baking Cocoa**

PLACE evaporated milk and coffee granules in blender; cover. Blend until coffee is dissolved. Add ice cream, ice and sugar; blend until smooth. Pour into glasses. Sprinkle with cocoa.

Makes 4 servings

REFRESHING TREATS

Chocolate Chip Cookie Ice Cream Sandwiches

1 package (16.5 ounces) NESTLÉ® TOLL HOUSE® Refrigerated Chocolate Chip Cookie Bar Dough

2 cups vanilla or chocolate DREYER'S® or EDY'S® SLOW CHURNED™ Light Ice Cream, softened

NESTLÉ® TOLL HOUSE® Semi-Sweet Chocolate Mini Morsels and sprinkles (optional)

PREPARE cookies according to package directions. Cool completely.

PLACE a heaping tablespoon of ice cream on flat side of 1 cookie; top with flat side of second cookie to make a sandwich. Place morsels or sprinkles on plate. Roll sides of sandwiches in morsels and sprinkles. Serve immediately or wrap tightly in plastic wrap and freeze.

Makes 12 sandwiches

Banana Berry Smoothie

1 can (14 ounces) NESTLÉ® CARNATION® Sweetened Condensed Milk

1 can (12 ounces) NESTLÉ® CARNATION® Evaporated Milk

1 ripe banana, sliced

2 cups frozen strawberries,* (about half 16-ounce bag)

If frozen berries are not available, substitute with 2 cups fresh berries and 1 cup of ice cubes.

PLACE sweetened condensed milk, evaporated milk, banana and strawberries in blender; cover. Blend until smooth.

Makes 6 servings

REFRESHING TREATS

Citrus-Iced Mock Margarita Bars

BARS:

- 1 cup *plus* 2 tablespoons all-purpose flour
- 1 teaspoon baking powder
- ¼ teaspoon salt
- ¾ cup granulated sugar
- ⅓ cup butter, softened
- ½ teaspoon vanilla extract
- 2 teaspoons grated lime peel
- 2 teaspoons grated orange peel
- 1 large egg
- 1 cup (6 ounces) NESTLÉ® TOLL HOUSE® Premier White Morsels

CITRUS ICING:

- 1½ cups sifted powdered sugar
- 4 ounces cream cheese, at room temperature
- 1 tablespoon butter, softened
- 1 teaspoon grated lime peel
- 1 teaspoon grated orange peel
- 2 teaspoons lime juice
- 1 teaspoon orange juice
- 1 to 2 teaspoons coarse sea salt (optional)

FOR BARS:

PREHEAT oven to 350°F. Grease 9-inch-square baking pan.

COMBINE flour, baking powder and salt in small bowl. Beat sugar, butter, vanilla extract, lime peel and orange peel in large mixer bowl until creamy. Beat in egg. Gradually beat in flour mixture. Stir in morsels. Press into prepared baking pan.

BAKE for 18 to 20 minutes or until wooden pick inserted in center comes out clean. Cool completely in pan on wire rack. Spread with Citrus Icing. Sprinkle with sea salt. Cut into bars. Store in covered container in refrigerator.

FOR CITRUS ICING:

BEAT powdered sugar, cream cheese, butter, lime peel, orange peel, lime juice and orange juice in small mixer bowl until smooth.

Makes 16 bars

REFRESHING TREATS

Dipped Fruit

1¾ to 2 cups (12-ounce package) NESTLÉ® TOLL HOUSE® Semi-Sweet Chocolate Morsels or Premier White Morsels, or (11.5-ounce package) NESTLÉ® TOLL HOUSE® Milk Chocolate Morsels

2 tablespoons vegetable shortening

36 bite-size pieces fresh fruit (strawberries, orange, kiwi, banana or melon), rinsed and patted dry

LINE baking sheet with wax paper.

MICROWAVE morsels and shortening in medium, uncovered, microwave-safe bowl on MEDIUM-HIGH (70%) power for 1 minute. STIR. Morsels may retain some of their original shape. If necessary, microwave at additional 10- to 15-second intervals, stirring until morsels are melted.

DIP fruit into melted morsels; shake off excess. Place on prepared baking sheet; refrigerate until set.

Makes about 3 dozen pieces

For a fancy drizzle: *MICROWAVE ½ cup NESTLÉ® TOLL HOUSE® Semi-Sweet Chocolate or Premier White Morsels or Baking Bars, broken in pieces, in small, heavy-duty resealable plastic food storage bag on MEDIUM-HIGH (70%) power for 1 minute; knead. Microwave at additional 10- to 15-second intervals, kneading until smooth. Cut tiny corner from bag; squeeze to drizzle over fruit. Refrigerate until set.*

Guava Smoothie

1½ cups (11.5 fluid-ounce can) guava nectar, chilled

⅔ cup (5 fluid-ounce can) NESTLÉ® CARNATION® Evaporated Milk, *chilled*

½ cup ice cubes

2 tablespoons granulated sugar

PLACE nectar, evaporated milk, ice and sugar in blender; cover. Blend until smooth.

Makes 2 servings

Note: *Other nectar flavors such as strawberry banana, mango, pineapple coconut or papaya can be substituted for the guava.*

REFRESHING TREATS

Mini Morsel Ice Cream Pie

1½ **cups graham cracker crumbs**

½ **cup (1 stick) butter, melted**

¼ **cup granulated sugar**

1 **cup (6 ounces) NESTLÉ® TOLL HOUSE® Semi-Sweet Chocolate Mini Morsels**

1 **quart vanilla ice cream, softened**

COMBINE graham cracker crumbs, butter and sugar in medium bowl; stir in morsels. Press 2½ *cups* crumb mixture evenly on bottom and side of 9-inch pie plate. Freeze for 15 minutes or until firm. Spread softened ice cream evenly in pie shell. Top with *remaining* crumb mixture; freeze for 2 hours or until firm.

Makes 8 servings

Concord Grape and Blueberry Freeze with Flax Seed Oil

1 **cup Concord grape juice**

¾ **cup frozen blueberries**

½ **cup ice cubes**

¼ **cup *dry* NESTLÉ® CARNATION® Instant Nonfat Dry Milk**

2 **teaspoons flax seed oil**

PLACE grape juice, blueberries, ice, dry milk and flax seed oil in blender; cover. Blend until smooth. Serve immediately.

Makes 2 servings (about 1 cup each)

Note: *Look for flax seed oil in health food stores or the natural food section of grocery stores.*

Note: *If using fresh blueberries, add 1⁄4 cup extra ice cubes. Substitute cranberry or pomegranate juice for grape juice, if desired.*

Note: *This recipe can easily be doubled.*

REFRESHING TREATS

Frozen Lemonade Pie

1 *prepared* 10-inch (9 ounces) graham cracker crumb crust

1 can (12 fluid ounces) NESTLÉ® CARNATION® Evaporated Milk

1 package (3 ounces) lemon-flavored gelatin

2 tablespoons grated lemon peel

½ cup (3 to 4 lemons) fresh lemon juice

1 container (8 ounces) frozen whipped topping, thawed, *divided*

2 candied lemon half slices, cut into 8 wedges (optional)

MICROWAVE evaporated milk in medium bowl on HIGH (100%) power for 1 minute or until warm. Whisk in gelatin. Refrigerate uncovered for 30 minutes. Add lemon peel and juice; mix well. Gently whisk in *2 cups* whipped topping. Pour into crust.

FREEZE for 4 hours. Dollop *remaining 1 cup* whipped topping around edge of pie. Top each dollop with lemon wedge. Let stand at room temperature for 20 minutes before serving.

Makes 8 servings

Tip: *Sliced fresh lemon can be substituted for the candied lemon slices.*

Tip: *1 can (12 fluid ounces) NESTLÉ® CARNATION® Evaporated Fat Free Milk, 1 package (0.3 ounces) sugar free lemon-flavored gelatin and sugar free whipped topping can be substituted. Prepare as above.*

REFRESHING TREATS

Horchata

- 1 **cup white rice, rinsed, drained**
- 1 **(3-inch) cinnamon stick**
- 4 **cups hot water**
- ¾ **cup granulated sugar**
- 1 **can (12 fluid ounces) NESTLÉ® CARNATION® Evaporated Milk**

  Ice cubes

  Pinch of ground cinnamon

  Lime rind strips (optional)

COMBINE rice, cinnamon stick and water in large bowl; cool. Cover; refrigerate for at least 2 hours, preferably overnight.

REMOVE cinnamon stick. Spoon rice into blender container (reserve soaking water). Cover; blend on High for 3 to 4 minutes until mixture is as smooth as possible. Add the *reserved* soaking water and sugar; blend for an additional 2 minutes. Strain mixture through a cheesecloth or fine sieve into a pitcher, pressing the rice solids until only a dry paste remains; discard paste. Stir evaporated milk into the mixture.

TO SERVE: Pour into tall glasses with ice cubes; sweeten with additional sugar, if desired. Sprinkle with cinnamon. Garnish with lime rind.

Makes 6 servings

REFRESHING TREATS

Triple-Berry Refresher

1 can (12 fluid ounces) NESTLÉ® CARNATION® Evaporated Milk

1 container (6 or 8 ounces) berry-flavored lowfat yogurt

½ cup fresh blueberries

½ cup fresh raspberries

½ cup fresh strawberry halves or blackberries

2 to 3 tablespoons honey

1 tray ice cubes

PLACE evaporated milk, yogurt, blueberries, raspberries, strawberries and honey in blender; cover. Blend until smooth. Strain to remove seeds. Serve over ice.

Makes 4 servings

Note: *Fresh fruit may be substituted with slightly thawed frozen unsweetened or lightly sweetened berries.*

Mango Smoothie

1½ cups chopped mango (fresh, jarred or frozen)

1 cup guava or mango nectar, *chilled*

⅔ cup (5-ounce can) NESTLÉ® CARNATION® Evaporated Milk

   Juice from 2 limes

1 tablespoon packed brown sugar

   Ice cubes (optional)

   Sliced almonds (optional)

COMBINE mango, nectar, evaporated milk, lime juice and sugar in blender; cover. Blend until smooth. Serve over ice and top with almonds, if desired.

Makes 2 servings

Autumn

Trail Bars

Fall means tailgating, or at least getting the gang together to watch the big game at home. These sweet and salty treats offer snack mixes, popcorn, cookies, brownies, and more to help fuel the fun.

2 cups mixed dried fruit (raisins, apricots, cherries, chopped dates, etc.)

½ cup sunflower seeds, shelled

7 cups crisp rice cereal

1 cup quick oats

1½ cups chunky peanut butter

1 cup light corn syrup

½ cup granulated sugar

1 cup *dry* NESTLÉ® CARNATION® Instant Nonfat Dry Milk

1 teaspoon vanilla extract

GREASE 15×10-inch jelly-roll pan.

COMBINE dried fruit and sunflower seeds in food processor; cover. Pulse to chop into small pieces. Transfer to large bowl. Add rice cereal and oats; mix well.

COMBINE peanut butter, corn syrup and sugar in small, microwave-safe bowl. Microwave on HIGH (100%) power until bubbly, about 1 to 2 minutes. Stir in dry milk and vanilla extract. Pour peanut butter mixture over cereal mixture. Stir well to coat. Press mixture into prepared pan. Cut into bars. Let cool completely before removing from pan. Store in airtight container.

Makes 15 bars

GAME DAY GRUB

Sweet & Salty NESTLÉ® TOLL HOUSE® Cookies

2¼ cups all-purpose flour

1 teaspoon baking soda

1 teaspoon salt (optional)

1 cup (2 sticks) butter, softened

¾ cup granulated sugar

¾ cup packed brown sugar

1 teaspoon vanilla extract

2 large eggs

2 cups (12-ounce package) NESTLÉ® TOLL HOUSE® Semi-Sweet Chocolate Morsels

2 cups coarsely broken rippled potato chips

1 cup small pretzel twists, broken into ½-inch pieces

½ cup unsalted peanuts (optional)

PREHEAT oven to 375°F.

COMBINE flour, baking soda and salt in small bowl. Beat butter, granulated sugar, brown sugar and vanilla extract in large mixer bowl until creamy. Add eggs, one at a time, beating well after each addition. Gradually beat in flour mixture. Stir in morsels, potato chips, pretzel pieces and peanuts. Drop by rounded tablespoonful onto ungreased baking sheets.

BAKE for 9 to 11 minutes or until golden brown. Cool on baking sheets for 2 minutes; remove to wire racks to cool completely.

Makes 5 dozen cookies

GAME DAY GRUB

Milk Chocolate Popcorn

12 **cups popped corn**

1 **can (12 ounces) salted peanuts**

1¾ **cups (11.5-ounce package) NESTLÉ® TOLL HOUSE® Milk Chocolate Morsels**

1 **cup light corn syrup**

¼ **cup (½ stick) butter or margarine**

PREHEAT oven to 300°F. Grease large roasting pan. Line serving plate with wax paper.

COMBINE popcorn and nuts in prepared roasting pan. Combine morsels, corn syrup and butter in medium, *heavy-duty* saucepan. Cook over medium heat, stirring constantly, until mixture boils. Pour over popcorn; toss well to coat.

BAKE stirring frequently, for 30 to 40 minutes. Cool slightly in pan; remove to prepared serving plate. Store in airtight container for up to two weeks.

Makes 14 servings

GAME DAY GRUB

Double Chocolate Chunk Cookies

2 cups all-purpose flour

¾ cup NESTLÉ® TOLL HOUSE® Baking Cocoa

1 teaspoon baking soda

½ teaspoon salt

1 cup (2 sticks) butter or margarine, softened

⅔ cup granulated sugar

⅔ cup packed brown sugar

1 teaspoon vanilla extract

2 large eggs

1¾ cups (11.5-ounce package) NESTLÉ® TOLL HOUSE® Semi-Sweet Chocolate Chunks

PREHEAT oven to 350°F.

COMBINE flour, cocoa, baking soda and salt in medium bowl. Beat butter, granulated sugar, brown sugar and vanilla extract in large mixer bowl until creamy. Add eggs, one at a time, beating well after each addition. Gradually beat in flour mixture. Stir in chunks. Drop by rounded tablespoonful onto ungreased baking sheets.

BAKE for 9 to 11 minutes or until cookies are puffed and centers are set but still soft. Cool on baking sheets for 2 minutes; remove to wire racks to cool completely.

Makes about 40 cookies

GAME DAY GRUB

Peanut Butterscotch Pretzel Snacks

1⅔ cups (11-ounce package) NESTLÉ® TOLL HOUSE® Butterscotch Flavored Morsels

⅓ cup creamy peanut butter

60 (3-inch) pretzel twists

2 to 3 tablespoons sesame seeds, toasted

MICROWAVE morsels and peanut butter in medium, uncovered, microwave-safe bowl on MEDIUM-HIGH (70%) power for 1 minute; STIR. Morsels may retain some of their original shape. If necessary, microwave at additional 10- to 15-second intervals, stirring until morsels are melted.

DIP about three-fourths of 1 pretzel into butterscotch mixture; shake off excess. Place on wire rack; sprinkle lightly with sesame seeds. Repeat with remaining pretzels. (If mixture thickens, microwave on MEDIUM-HIGH (70%) power at 10- to 15-second intervals, stirring until smooth.)

REFRIGERATE for 20 minutes or until set. Store in airtight containers or resealable plastic food storage bags.

Makes 5 dozen snacks

GAME DAY GRUB

Dark Chocolate Bark

½ **cup broken mini pretzel twists**

½ **cup coarsely broken rippled potato chips**

¼ **cup coarsely chopped lightly salted peanuts**

1⅔ **cups (10-ounce package) NESTLÉ® TOLL HOUSE® Dark Chocolate Morsels**

LINE baking sheet with wax paper.

COMBINE pretzels, chips and peanuts in small bowl.

MICROWAVE chocolate in small, uncovered, microwave-safe bowl on MEDIUM-HIGH (70%) power for 45 seconds; STIR. If pieces retain some of their original shape, microwave at additional 10- to 15-second intervals, stirring just until melted. Stir in *half* of snack-peanut mixture.

POUR onto prepared baking sheet. Spread mixture to desired thickness. Sprinkle with *remaining* snack-pretzel mixture. Tap sheet several times to spread chocolate and settle pretzels. Refrigerate for 30 minutes or until firm. Break into pieces. Store in airtight container at room temperature. Best when eaten within 24 hours. Makes ¾ pound.

Makes 9 servings

Chocolatey Peanut Pretzel Bars

2½ **cups NESTLÉ® TOLL HOUSE® Refrigerated Chocolate Chip Cookie Tub Dough,** *divided*

1½ **cups (9 ounces) NESTLÉ® TOLL HOUSE® Semi-Sweet Chocolate Morsels,** *divided*

1 **cup small pretzel twists (about 1¼ ounces), broken into ½-inch pieces**

1 **cup honey-roasted peanuts**

PREHEAT oven to 350°F. Grease 13×9-inch baking pan.

PLACE 2 *cups* dough in prepared pan. Using fingertips, pat dough gently to cover bottom.

SPRINKLE 1 *cup* morsels, pretzel pieces and peanuts over dough. Drop 1-inch pieces of *remaining ½ cup* dough over peanuts. Sprinkle with *remaining ½ cup* of morsels and gently press down.

BAKE for 23 to 27 minutes or until browned around edges. Cool completely in pan on wire rack. Cut into bars.

Makes 2 dozen bars

GAME DAY GRUB

Delicious Chocolate Quick Bread

1½ **cups all-purpose flour**

½ **cup NESTLÉ® TOLL HOUSE® Baking Cocoa**

½ **teaspoon salt**

½ **teaspoon baking powder**

½ **teaspoon baking soda**

½ **cup (1 stick) butter, softened**

1 **cup granulated sugar**

2 **large eggs**

1 **cup buttermilk or sour milk***

½ **cup chopped pecans, *divided* (optional)**

¼ **cup NESTLÉ® TOLL HOUSE® Semi-Sweet Chocolate Mini Morsels**

Chocolate Honey Butter (recipe follows)

*If you do not have buttermilk on hand, you can substitute sour milk made with NESTLÉ® CARNATION® Evaporated Milk (Regular, Lowfat or Fat Free). Measure ½ cup NESTLÉ® CARNATION® Evaporated Milk into glass measuring cup. Add ½ cup water and 1 tablespoon vinegar or lemon juice; stir. Let stand for 5 minutes before using.

PREHEAT oven to 350°F. Grease 9×5-inch loaf pan.

COMBINE flour, cocoa, salt, baking powder and baking soda in medium bowl. Beat butter and sugar in large mixer bowl until creamy. Add eggs, one at a time, beating well after each addition. Gradually beat in flour mixture alternately with buttermilk. Fold in ¼ *cup* pecans. Pour into prepared pan.

BAKE for 20 minutes. Top with morsels and *remaining ¼ cup* pecans; continue baking for 30 to 35 minutes or until wooden pick inserted in center comes out clean. Cool in pan on wire rack for 10 minutes; remove to wire rack to cool completely. Serve with Chocolate Honey Butter.

Makes 16 servings

Chocolate Honey Butter

MICROWAVE ½ cup NESTLÉ® TOLL HOUSE® Semi-Sweet Chocolate Mini Morsels in small, uncovered, microwave-safe bowl on HIGH (100%) power for 30 seconds; STIR. Morsels may retain some of their original shape. If necessary, microwave at additional 10- to 15-second intervals, stirring until morsels are melted; let cool. Beat cooled morsels, ½ cup (1 stick) softened butter and 2 tablespoons honey in small mixer bowl until fluffy. Makes about 1 cup.

GAME DAY GRUB

RAISINETS® Cereal Snacking Mix

- **2 cups toasted whole grain oat cereal**
- **½ cup dried cranberries**
- **2 tablespoons granulated sugar**
- **½ teaspoon ground cinnamon**
- **1 tablespoon butter, melted**
- **1 cup (6.5 ounces) NESTLÉ® RAISINETS® Milk Chocolate-Covered Raisins or GOOBERS® Milk Chocolate-Covered Peanuts**

COMBINE cereal and cranberries in large, resealable plastic bag.

COMBINE sugar and cinnamon in small bowl.

POUR cinnamon-sugar mixture and butter over cereal mixture; seal bag. Shake well to combine. Add RAISINETS® or GOOBERS®; shake well.

Makes 6 servings

Butterscotch Party Mix

- **2 cups oven-toasted cereal squares**
- **2 cups small pretzel twists**
- **1 cup dry-roasted peanuts**
- **1 cup (about 20) caramels, unwrapped, coarsely chopped**
- **1 ⅔ cups (11-ounce package) NESTLÉ® TOLL HOUSE® Butterscotch Flavored Morsels**

GREASE 13×9-inch baking pan with nonstick cooking spray.

COMBINE cereal, pretzels, peanuts and caramels in large bowl. Place morsels in medium, uncovered, microwave-safe bowl. Microwave on MEDIUM-HIGH (70%) power for 1 minute. STIR. Morsels may retain some of their original shape. If necessary, microwave at additional 10- to 15-second intervals, stirring until morsels are melted smooth. Pour over cereal mixture; stir to coat evenly.

SPREAD mixture in prepared baking pan; let stand for 20 to 30 minutes or until firm. Break into small pieces.

Makes about 8 servings

GAME DAY GRUB

Jumbo 3-Chip Cookies

4 cups all-purpose flour

1 teaspoon baking powder

1 teaspoon baking soda

1½ cups (3 sticks) butter, softened

1¼ cups granulated sugar

1¼ cups packed brown sugar

2 large eggs

1 tablespoon vanilla extract

1 cup (6 ounces) NESTLÉ® TOLL HOUSE® Milk Chocolate Morsels

1 cup (6 ounces) NESTLÉ® TOLL HOUSE® Semi-Sweet Chocolate Morsels

½ cup NESTLÉ® TOLL HOUSE® Premier White Morsels

1 cup chopped nuts

PREHEAT oven to 375°F.

COMBINE flour, baking powder and baking soda in medium bowl. Beat butter, granulated sugar and brown sugar in large mixer bowl until creamy. Beat in eggs and vanilla extract. Gradually beat in flour mixture. Stir in morsels and nuts. Drop dough by level ¼-cup measure 2 inches apart onto ungreased baking sheets.

BAKE for 12 to 14 minutes or until light golden brown. Cool on baking sheets for 2 minutes; remove to wire racks to cool completely.

Makes about 2 dozen cookies

GAME DAY GRUB

Pumpkin Apple Bread

Nonstick cooking spray

2 cups all-purpose flour

1⅓ cups whole-wheat flour

2 teaspoons baking powder

1 teaspoon ground cinnamon or allspice

½ teaspoon salt

½ teaspoon baking soda

1 can (15 ounces) LIBBY'S® 100% Pure Pumpkin

1 cup refrigerated or frozen egg product

¾ cup sugar blend for baking (such as SPLENDA®)

½ cup Apple NESTLÉ® JUICY JUICE® All Natural 100% Juice

½ cup honey

⅓ cup vegetable oil

1 teaspoon grated orange peel

½ cup peeled, chopped green apple

PREHEAT oven to 350°F. Spray two 8×4-inch loaf pans with nonstick cooking spray.

COMBINE all-purpose flour, whole-wheat flour, baking powder, cinnamon, salt and baking soda in large bowl; stir.

STIR together pumpkin, egg product, sugar blend, Juicy Juice®, honey, oil and orange peel in large bowl. Stir pumpkin mixture into flour mixture just until combined. Stir in apple. Divide mixture between prepared pans.

BAKE for 50 to 55 minutes or until wooden pick inserted in centers comes out clean. Cool in pans on wire racks for 10 minutes. Remove from pans; cool completely on wire racks.

Makes 2 loaves (32 servings)

GAME DAY GRUB

Dark Chocolate Dipped Strawberries & Snacks

1⅔ cups (10-ounce package) NESTLÉ® TOLL HOUSE® Dark Chocolate Morsels

1 tablespoon vegetable shortening

Fresh strawberries (rinsed and patted dry), pretzels, rippled potato chips and/or cookies*

Assorted sprinkles, finely chopped nuts (optional)

*Assorted bite-size fresh fruit rinsed and patted dry, dried fruit, large marshmallows, cut-up pound cake and nuts can also be used for dipping.

LINE baking sheets with wax paper.

MICROWAVE morsels and shortening in medium, uncovered, microwave-safe bowl on MEDIUM-HIGH (70%) power for 45 seconds; STIR. Morsels may retain some of their original shape. If necessary, microwave at additional 10- to 15-second intervals, stirring until morsels are melted.

DIP strawberries (by stem or leaves) or snacks into melted chocolate, tilting bowl to easily dip. Use side of bowl to remove excess. Place on prepared baking sheets. If you are using sprinkles or nuts, sprinkle them on when the chocolate is still wet. Refrigerate for 15 minutes or until set.

Makes 1 cup dip

Blizzard Party Mix

2 cups oven-toasted cereal squares

2 cups small pretzel twists

1 cup dry-roasted peanuts

1 cup (about 20) coarsely chopped caramels

2 cups (12-ounce package) NESTLÉ® TOLL HOUSE® Premier White Morsels

SPRAY 13×9-inch baking pan with nonstick cooking spray.

COMBINE cereal, pretzels, peanuts and caramels in large bowl.

MICROWAVE morsels in medium, uncovered, microwave-safe bowl on MEDIUM-HIGH (70%) power for 1 minute; STIR. Morsels may retain some of their original shape. If necessary, microwave at additional 10- to 15-second intervals, stirring until morsels are melted. Pour over cereal mixture; stir to coat evenly.

SPREAD mixture into prepared baking pan; let stand for 20 to 30 minutes or until firm. Break into bite-size pieces.

Makes 8 servings

GAME DAY GRUB

Crazy Dipped Pretzel Rods

1 **cup (6 ounces) NESTLÉ® TOLL HOUSE® Semi-Sweet Chocolate, Milk Chocolate or Premier White Morsels**

1 **tablespoon vegetable shortening**

16 **pretzel rods**

NESTLÉ® TOLL HOUSE® Semi-Sweet Chocolate Mini Morsels and/or sprinkles (optional)

Additional NESTLÉ® TOLL HOUSE® Morsels for drizzling (optional)

LINE baking sheet with wax paper.

MICROWAVE *1 cup* morsels and vegetable shortening in small, dry, uncovered, microwave-safe bowl on MEDIUM-HIGH (70%) power for 1 minute; STIR. Morsels may retain some of their original shape. If necessary, microwave at additional 10- to 15-second intervals, stirring just until morsels are melted.

DIP pretzel rods about 3 inches into melted morsels, tilting bowl to easily dip. Use side of bowl to remove excess. Sprinkle with morsels or sprinkles. Place on prepared baking sheet. Refrigerate for 20 minutes or until set. Store in airtight container at room temperature.

Makes 16 rods

For a Fancy Drizzle: *MICROWAVE 2 tablespoons of each desired morsel flavor in small, heavy-duty plastic bags on MEDIUM-HIGH (70%) power for 30 seconds; knead. Microwave at additional 10- to 15-second intervals, kneading until smooth. Cut tiny corner from each bag; squeeze to drizzle over already dipped pretzels on baking sheet.*

GOOBERS® Trail Mix

2 **cups NESTLÉ® GOOBERS® Milk Chocolate-Covered Peanuts**

2 **cups small pretzel twists**

2 **cups miniature marshmallows**

1 **cup raisins**

1 **cup coarsely chopped dried apricots**

1 **cup coarsely chopped dried apples**

COMBINE Goobers, pretzels, marshmallows, raisins, apricots and apples in large bowl.

Makes 10 servings

GAME DAY GRUB

Mexican Hot Chocolate Shots with Spicy Foam

2 cans (12 fluid ounces *each*) NESTLÉ® CARNATION® Evaporated Milk, *divided*

1 cup water

1½ cups (9 ounces)* NESTLÉ® TOLL HOUSE® Semi-Sweet Chocolate Morsels

1¼ teaspoons vanilla extract, *divided*

½ plus ⅛ teaspoon ground cinnamon, *divided*

⅛ teaspoon ground cayenne pepper, *divided* (optional)

*May substitute NESTLÉ® TOLL HOUSE® Milk Chocolate Morsels for the Semi-Sweet Morsels.

POUR *½ cup* evaporated milk into medium mixer bowl; place beaters into mixture. Freeze for about 30 minutes or until ice crystals form around edge of bowl.

HEAT *remaining* evaporated milk, water, morsels, *1 teaspoon* vanilla extract, *½ teaspoon* cinnamon and a pinch of cayenne pepper in medium saucepan over low heat, stirring frequently, until melted. Do not boil. Set aside.

REMOVE chilled evaporated milk from freezer. Beat on high speed for 1 minute or until very frothy. Add *remaining ¼ teaspoon* vanilla extract, *remaining ⅛ teaspoon* cinnamon and a pinch of cayenne pepper. Continue beating for 3 to 4 minutes or until mixture forms soft peaks.

POUR hot chocolate into eight 4-ounce demitasse cups and immediately dollop with foam topping.

Makes 8 servings

GAME DAY GRUB

Chocolate Turtle Brownies

2 cups (12-ounce package) NESTLÉ® TOLL HOUSE® Semi-Sweet Chocolate Morsels, *divided*

½ cup (1 stick) butter or margarine, cut into pieces

3 large eggs

1¼ cups all-purpose flour

1 cup granulated sugar

¼ teaspoon baking soda

1 teaspoon vanilla extract

½ cup chopped walnuts

12 caramels

1 tablespoon milk

PREHEAT oven to 350° F. Grease 13×9-inch baking pan.

MELT *1 cup* morsels and butter in large, *heavy-duty* saucepan over low heat, stirring constantly until smooth. Remove from heat; stir in eggs. Add flour, sugar, baking soda and vanilla extract; stir well.

SPREAD batter into prepared baking pan; sprinkle with *remaining 1 cup* morsels and walnuts.

BAKE for 20 to 25 minutes or until wooden pick inserted in center comes out slightly sticky.

MICROWAVE caramels and milk in small, microwave-safe bowl on HIGH (100%) power for 1 minute; STIR. Microwave at additional 10- to 15-second intervals, stirring until melted. Drizzle over warm brownies. Cool in pan on wire rack.

Make 2 dozen brownies

GAME DAY GRUB

NESTLÉ® TOLL HOUSE® Spicy Party Mix

1½ **quarts water**

1 **pound pecan halves**

½ **cup granulated sugar**

2 **tablespoons plus 1½ teaspoons canola oil**

1 **vanilla bean (optional)**

1 **teaspoon fine sea salt**

½ **teaspoon chili powder**

½ **teaspoon curry powder**

½ **teaspoon ground coriander**

½ **teaspoon ground cumin**

½ **teaspoon garlic salt**

¼ **teaspoon ground allspice**

¼ **teaspoon ground cinnamon**

¼ **teaspoon ground nutmeg**

¼ **teaspoon cayenne pepper (optional)**

2 **cups pretzel nuggets**

1¾ **cups (11.5-ounce package) NESTLÉ® TOLL HOUSE® Semi-Sweet Chocolate Chunks**

1 **package (6 ounces) sweetened dried cranberries**

BRING water to boil in large saucepan. Pour nuts into boiling water. Boil for 1 minute; strain. Pour nuts into large bowl. Add sugar and oil; stir to coat. Let stand for 10 minutes.

SPLIT vanilla bean in half lengthwise and with edge of knife, scrape inside of bean into a large bowl. Add spices to bowl; combine well and set aside.

PREHEAT oven to 325°F.

BAKE nuts, stirring often, for 30 to 35 minutes or until nuts are light brown and crisp. While still warm, carefully pour nuts into spice mixture and toss. Spread spiced nuts in a single layer on clean, large baking sheet with sides. Cool completely.

POUR cooled nuts into large bowl. Add pretzel nuggets, chunks and cranberries; mix well. Store in airtight container at room temperature for up to 2 weeks. Makes 10 cups.

Makes 40 servings (⅓ cup each)

GAME DAY GRUB

Football Cookies

1 **package (16.5 ounces) NESTLÉ® TOLL HOUSE® Refrigerated Chocolate Chip Cookie Bar Dough, softened at room temperature for 30 minutes***

⅓ **cup NESTLÉ® TOLL HOUSE® Baking Cocoa, *plus* additional for rolling**

1 **(3-inch) football cutter**

Decorator icings (various colors)

Red or black thin licorice rope

Substitute 2 cups NESTLÉ® TOLL HOUSE® Refrigerated Chocolate Chip Tub Dough can be substituted for the bar dough.

PREHEAT oven to 325°F. Grease two baking sheets.

COMBINE softened cookie dough and cocoa in large mixer bowl. This can be done with a mixer or with clean hands.

ROLL dough to ¼-inch thickness between sheets of wax paper, using additional cocoa to prevent sticking. Cut out footballs with cookie cutter. Place 1-inch apart on prepared baking sheets. Repeat with trimmings.

BAKE for 12 to 13 minutes or until edges are set. (If using dark baking sheets, check at 12 minutes). Cool for 2 minutes; remove to wire racks to cool completely.

DECORATE cookies with icings as desired. Cut licorice into small pieces to form laces. Let stand for 15 minutes to set icing. Store cookies in between wax paper layers in covered container.

Makes 18 to 20 cookies

GAME DAY GRUB

Nutty Nougat Caramel Bites

COOKIE BASE:

- 2¼ cups all-purpose flour
- 1 teaspoon baking soda
- 1 teaspoon salt
- 1 cup (2 sticks) butter, softened
- ¾ cup packed brown sugar
- ¼ cup granulated sugar
- 1 package (3.4 ounces) butterscotch-flavored instant pudding mix
- 2 large eggs, lightly beaten
- 1 teaspoon vanilla extract
- 1⅓ cups (about 8 ounces) NESTLÉ® TOLL HOUSE® Butterscotch Flavored Morsels

NOUGAT FILLING:

- ¼ cup (½ stick) butter
- 1 cup granulated sugar
- ¼ cup NESTLÉ® CARNATION® Evaporated Milk
- 1 jar (7 ounces) marshmallow creme
- ¼ cup creamy peanut butter
- 1 teaspoon vanilla extract
- 1½ cups (about 8 ounces) coarsely chopped salted peanuts

CARAMEL LAYER:

- 1 package (14 ounces) caramels, unwrapped
- ¼ cup heavy whipping cream

ICING:

- 1 cup (6 ounces) NESTLÉ® TOLL HOUSE® Milk Chocolate Morsels
- ⅓ cup NESTLÉ® TOLL HOUSE® Butterscotch Flavored Morsels
- ¼ cup creamy peanut butter

FOR COOKIE BASE:

PREHEAT oven to 350°F. Line 17×11×1-inch baking pan with parchment paper.

COMBINE flour, baking soda and salt in small bowl. Beat butter, brown sugar and granulated sugar in large mixer bowl until creamy. Add pudding mix, eggs and vanilla extract; mix well. Gradually beat in flour mixture. Stir in 1⅓ cups butterscotch morsels. Spread and pat dough evenly into prepared baking pan.

BAKE for 10 to 11 minutes or until light golden brown. Carefully hold pan 2 to 3 inches above a heat-resistant surface and allow pan to drop. (This creates a chewier cookie base.) Cool completely in pan on wire rack.

FOR NOUGAT FILLING:

MELT butter in medium, *heavy-duty* saucepan over medium heat. Add granulated sugar and evaporated milk; stir. Bring to a boil, stirring constantly. Boil, stirring constantly, for 5 minutes. Remove from heat.

STIR in marshmallow creme, peanut butter and vanilla extract. Add peanuts; stir well. Spread nougat mixture over cookie base. Refrigerate for 15 minutes or until set.

FOR CARAMEL LAYER:

COMBINE caramels and cream in medium, *heavy-duty* saucepan. Cook over low heat, stirring constantly, until caramels are melted and mixture is smooth. Spread caramel mixture over nougat layer. Refrigerate for 15 minutes or until set.

FOR ICING:

MELT milk chocolate morsels, ⅓ cup butterscotch morsels and peanut butter in medium, microwave-safe bowl on MEDIUM-HIGH (70%) power for 1 minute; STIR. Microwave at additional 10- to 20-second intervals, stirring until smooth. Spread icing over caramel layer. Refrigerate for at least 1 hour.

TO SERVE: Let stand at room temperature for 5 to 10 minutes. Cut into 1-inch pieces. Store in airtight container in refrigerator.

Makes 90 servings (2 pieces per serving)

GAME DAY GRUB

Fudgy Chocolate Brownies

1⅓ cups all-purpose flour

¼ teaspoon baking soda

¼ teaspoon salt

1⅔ cups granulated sugar

½ cup (1 stick) butter or margarine, melted

4 packets (1 ounce *each*) NESTLÉ® TOLL HOUSE® CHOCO BAKE® Pre-Melted Unsweetened Chocolate Flavor

2 large eggs

2 tablespoons water

1½ teaspoons vanilla extract

½ cup chopped nuts (optional)

PREHEAT oven to 350°F. Grease 13×9-inch baking pan.

COMBINE flour, baking soda and salt in small bowl. Stir in sugar, butter, Choco Bake, eggs, water and vanilla extract vigorously in large bowl. Stir in flour mixture. Stir in nuts. Spread into prepared baking pan.

BAKE for 18 to 22 minutes or until wooden pick inserted in center comes out slightly sticky. Cool completely in pan on wire rack. Cut into bars.

Makes 2 dozen brownies

Rocky Road Squares

1 package (19.5 to 21 ounces) fudge brownie mix

Vegetable oil, per package directions

Egg(s), per package directions

NESTLÉ® CARNATION® Evaporated Milk

1 cup (6 ounces) NESTLÉ® TOLL HOUSE® Semi-Sweet Chocolate Morsels

2 cups miniature marshmallows

1 cup coarsely chopped walnuts

PREHEAT oven according to brownie mix package directions. Grease 13×9-inch baking pan.

PREPARE brownie mix according to package directions, using vegetable oil and egg(s) and substituting evaporated milk for water. Spread into prepared baking pan.

BAKE according to package directions. Do not overbake. Remove from oven. Immediately sprinkle with morsels. Let stand 5 minutes or until morsels are shiny. Spread evenly. Top with marshmallows and walnuts.

BAKE for 3 to 5 minutes or just until marshmallows begin to melt. Cool in pan on wire rack for 20 to 30 minutes. Cut into squares. Serve warm.

Makes 2 dozen brownies

GAME DAY GRUB

Creamy Crunchy Haystacks

2 cups (12-ounce package) NESTLÉ® TOLL HOUSE® Premier White Morsels

1 tablespoon vegetable shortening

1 cup pretzel sticks, broken into 1-inch pieces

1 cup almond slivers, toasted

½ cup unsweetened or sweetened flaked coconut, toasted

MICROWAVE morsels and shortening in large, uncovered, microwave-safe bowl on MEDIUM-HIGH (70%) for 1 minute; STIR. Morsels may retain some of their original shape. If necessary, microwave at additional 10- to 15-second intervals, stirring until morsels are melted. Stir in pretzel sticks, almonds and coconut; toss until all ingredients are coated. Drop by level tablespoon onto prepared trays. Refrigerate for 30 minutes. Store in tightly covered container.

Makes 40 candies

Double Boiler Method: *COMBINE pretzel sticks, almonds and coconut in large bowl. Place morsels and shortening in top of double boiler over hot (not boiling) water. Do not cover. When most of the morsels are shiny, stir just until melted. (Prevent water from coming in contact with morsels.) Remove from heat. Pour melted morsels over pretzel mixture; toss until all ingredients are coated. Proceed as above.*

Peanut Butter Crunchy Haystacks: *SUBSTITUTE ¾ cup creamy or crunchy peanut butter for the vegetable shortening. Proceed as above.*

Tip: *If you do not have on hand or a preference for pretzel sticks, almonds and/or coconut, try using granola, popcorn, toasted rice cereal, pecans, macadamia nuts, peanuts, pistachios and/or crumbled shredded wheat cereal instead.*

Autumn

Polka Dot Pumpkin Cupcakes

Revup the kids for their after-school activities with these tasty snacks—or better yet, get the kids involved in the cooking! Whether it's baking crisp cookies and moist brownies or dipping ingredients in chocolate, everyone's sure to have a great time!

TOPPING:

½ **cup (4 ounces) cream cheese, softened**

1 **large egg**

2 **tablespoons granulated sugar**

⅔ **cup NESTLÉ® TOLL HOUSE® Semi-Sweet Chocolate Mini Morsels**

CUPCAKES:

1 **package (16 ounces) pound cake mix**

1 **cup LIBBY'S® 100% Pure Pumpkin**

⅓ **cup water**

2 **large eggs**

2 **teaspoons pumpkin pie spice**

1 **teaspoon baking soda**

PREHEAT oven to 325°F. Grease or paper-line 18 muffin cups.

FOR TOPPING:

BEAT cream cheese, egg and granulated sugar in small mixer bowl until smooth. Stir in morsels.

FOR CUPCAKES:

COMBINE cake mix, pumpkin, water, eggs, pumpkin pie spice and baking soda in large mixer bowl; beat on medium speed for 3 minutes. Pour batter into prepared muffin cups, filling three fourths full. Spoon about 1 tablespoon topping over batter.

BAKE for 25 to 30 minutes or until wooden pick inserted in center comes out clean. Cool in pans on wire racks for 10 minutes; remove to wire racks to cool completely.

Makes 1½ dozen cupcakes

AFTER SCHOOL SNACKS

Rocky Road Bars

2 cups (12-ounce package) **NESTLÉ® TOLL HOUSE®** **Semi-Sweet Chocolate Morsels,** *divided*

1½ cups all-purpose flour

1½ teaspoons baking powder

1 cup granulated sugar

6 tablespoons (¾ stick) butter or margarine, softened

1½ teaspoons vanilla extract

2 large eggs

2 cups miniature marshmallows

1½ cups coarsely chopped walnuts

PREHEAT oven to 375°F. Grease 13×9-inch baking pan.

MICROWAVE *1 cup* morsels in medium, uncovered, microwave-safe bowl on HIGH (100%) power for 1 minute. STIR. Morsels may retain some of their original shape. If necessary, microwave at additional 10- to 15-second intervals, stirring until morsels are melted. Cool to room temperature. Combine flour and baking powder in small bowl.

BEAT sugar, butter and vanilla extract in large mixer bowl until crumbly. Beat in eggs. Add melted chocolate; beat until smooth. Gradually beat in flour mixture. Spread batter into prepared baking pan.

BAKE for 16 to 20 minutes or until wooden pick inserted in center comes out slightly sticky.

REMOVE from oven; sprinkle immediately with marshmallows, nuts and *remaining 1 cup* morsels. Return to oven for 2 minutes or just until marshmallows begin to melt. Cool in pan on wire rack for 20 to 30 minutes. Cut into bars with wet knife. Serve warm.

Makes 2½ dozen bars

AFTER SCHOOL SNACKS

Chocolate Oatmeal Chippers

1¼ cups all-purpose flour

½ cup NESTLÉ® TOLL HOUSE® Baking Cocoa

1 teaspoon baking soda

¼ teaspoon salt

1 cup (2 sticks) butter or margarine, softened

1 cup packed brown sugar

½ cup granulated sugar

1 teaspoon vanilla extract

2 large eggs

1¾ cups (11.5-ounce package) NESTLÉ® TOLL HOUSE® Milk Chocolate Morsels

1¾ cups quick or old-fashioned oats

1 cup chopped nuts (optional)

PREHEAT oven to 375°F.

COMBINE flour, cocoa, baking soda and salt in medium bowl. Beat butter, brown sugar, granulated sugar and vanilla extract in large mixer bowl until creamy. Beat in eggs. Gradually beat in flour mixture. Stir in morsels, oats and nuts. Drop dough by rounded tablespoonful onto ungreased baking sheets.

BAKE for 9 to 12 minutes or until edges are set but centers are still soft. Cool on baking sheets for 2 minutes; remove to wire racks to cool completely.

Makes about 4 dozen cookies

Bar Cookie Variation: *PREHEAT oven to 350°F. Grease 15×10-inch jelly-roll pan. Prepare dough as above. Spread into prepared pan. Bake for 25 to 30 minutes. Cool in pan on wire rack. Makes about 4 dozen bars.*

AFTER SCHOOL SNACKS

Monster Pops

1⅔ cups all-purpose flour

1 teaspoon baking soda

½ teaspoon salt

1 cup (2 sticks) butter or margarine, softened

¾ cup granulated sugar

¾ cup packed brown sugar

2 teaspoons vanilla extract

2 large eggs

2 cups (12-ounce package) NESTLÉ® TOLL HOUSE® Semi-Sweet Chocolate Morsels

2 cups quick or old-fashioned oats

1 cup raisins

24 wooden craft sticks

1 container (16 ounces) prepared vanilla frosting, colored as desired, or colored icing in tubes

PREHEAT oven to 325°F.

COMBINE flour, baking soda and salt in small bowl. Beat butter, granulated sugar, brown sugar and vanilla extract in large mixer bowl until creamy. Beat in eggs. Gradually beat in flour mixture. Stir in morsels, oats and raisins. Drop dough by level ¼-cup measure 3 inches apart onto ungreased baking sheets. Shape into round mounds. Insert wooden stick into side of each mound.

BAKE for 14 to 18 minutes or until golden brown. Cool on baking sheets on wire racks for 2 minutes; remove to wire racks to cool completely.

DECORATE pops as desired.

Makes about 2 dozen cookies

For Speedy Monster Pops: *SUBSTITUTE 2 packages (16.5 ounces each), NESTLÉ® TOLL HOUSE® Refrigerated Chocolate Chip Cookie Dough for the first nine ingredients, adding 1 cup quick or old-fashioned oats and ½ cup raisins to the dough. Bake as stated above for 16 to 20 minutes or until golden brown. Makes 1½ dozen cookies.*

AFTER SCHOOL SNACKS

Triple Treat Chocolate Cupcakes

- 1 **package (18.25 ounces) devil's food cake mix**
- 1 **package (3.9 ounces) chocolate instant pudding and pie filling mix**
- 1 **container (8 ounces) sour cream**
- 4 **large eggs**
- ½ **cup vegetable oil**
- ½ **cup warm water**
- 1⅔ **cups (10-ounce package) NESTLÉ® TOLL HOUSE® SWIRLED™ Semi-Sweet Chocolate & Premier White Morsels,** *divided*
- 1 **container (16 ounces) prepared white frosting**

PREHEAT oven to 350°F. Paper-line 30 muffin cups.

COMBINE cake mix, pudding mix, sour cream, eggs, vegetable oil and water in large mixer bowl; beat on low speed until just blended. Beat on medium speed for 2 minutes. Stir in *1 cup* morsels. Fill each cup two-thirds full.

BAKE for 25 to 28 minutes or until wooden pick inserted in center comes out clean. Cool in pans for 10 minutes; remove to wire racks to cool completely. Frost; decorate with *remaining ⅔ cup* morsels.

Makes 2½ dozen cupcakes

AFTER SCHOOL SNACKS

NESTLÉ® Graham Dippers

Wax paper

**3 to 4 tablespoons candy sprinkles, NESTLÉ®
TOLL HOUSE® Semi-Sweet Chocolate
Mini Morsels or chopped nuts**

**⅓ cup NESTLÉ® TOLL HOUSE® Premier White
Morsels or Semi-Sweet Chocolate Mini
Morsels**

16 honey or cinnamon graham sticks

LINE tray with wax paper. Place candy sprinkles on plate or in shallow bowl.

MELT morsels according to package directions in small bowl. Dip one graham stick halfway into melted morsels, then into candy sprinkles. Transfer to prepared tray. Repeat with remaining graham sticks.

REFRIGERATE for 10 minutes or until set. Store in airtight container at room temperature for up to 1 week.

Makes 8 servings (2 sticks each)

Kids' Favorite Chocolate Chip Muffins

1½ cups all-purpose flour

1½ cups whole wheat flour

2 teaspoons baking soda

2 teaspoons baking powder

**2 teaspoons ground cinnamon or pumpkin
pie spice**

½ teaspoon salt

4 large eggs, slightly beaten

2 cups granulated sugar

**1 can (15 ounces) LIBBY'S® 100% Pure
Pumpkin**

1 cup vegetable oil

**2 cups (12-ounce package) NESTLÉ®
TOLL HOUSE® Semi-Sweet Chocolate
Morsels**

PREHEAT oven to 350°F. Grease 36 (2½-inch) muffin cups or line with paper bake cups.

COMBINE all-purpose flour, whole wheat flour, baking soda, baking powder, cinnamon and salt in medium bowl. Combine eggs and sugar in large bowl. Add pumpkin and oil; mix well. Stir in flour mixture until moistened. Stir in morsels. Spoon batter into prepared muffin cups.

BAKE for 20 to 25 minutes or until top springs back when lightly touched. Cool in pans on wire racks for 5 minutes; remove from pans.

Makes 3 dozen muffins

AFTER SCHOOL SNACKS

Mini Dessert Burgers

1 **box (12 ounces) vanilla wafer cookies,* divided**

½ **cup powdered sugar**

¼ **teaspoon salt**

¾ **cup NESTLÉ® TOLL HOUSE® Semi-Sweet Chocolate Morsels**

⅓ **cup milk**

½ **cup sweetened flaked coconut**

½ **teaspoon water**

3 **drops green food coloring**

Red and yellow decorating gels (for ketchup and mustard)

1 **teaspoon melted butter (optional)**

1 **tablespoon sesame seeds (optional)**

*A 12-ounce box of vanilla wafers contains about 88 wafers.

RESERVE 48 wafers for bun tops and bottoms.

PLACE remaining wafers in large resealable bag. Crush into small pieces using a rolling pin. Combine wafer crumbs (about 1½ cups) with powdered sugar and salt in medium bowl.

MICROWAVE morsels and milk in medium, uncovered, microwave-safe bowl on HIGH (100%) power for 45 seconds; STIR. If necessary, microwave at additional 10- to 15-second intervals, stirring just until smooth.

POUR chocolate mixture into wafer mixture; stir until combined. Cool for 10 minutes. Line baking sheet with wax paper. Roll mixture into 24, 1-inch (about 1 tablespoonful each) balls. Place each ball on prepared sheet; flatten slightly to form burger patties.

COMBINE coconut, water and green food coloring in small, resealable plastic bag. Seal bag and shake to coat evenly with color.

TO ASSEMBLE:

PLACE 24 wafers, rounded side down on prepared baking sheet. Top each wafer with 1 burger patty. Top each burger patty with 1 teaspoon colored coconut. Squeeze decorating gels on top of coconut. Top with remaining wafers. Brush tops of wafers with melted butter and sprinkle with sesame seeds, if desired.

Makes 24 servings

Tip: *Recipe can easily be doubled or tripled. Great birthday or slumber party activity.*

Cheeseburgers!: *Cut apricot fruit rollups into small ½-inch squares to create cheese for the mini burgers.*

AFTER SCHOOL SNACKS

Chocolate-Cherry Thumbprints

2 cups (12-ounce package) NESTLÉ® TOLL HOUSE® Semi-Sweet Chocolate Morsels, *divided*

1¾ cups quick or old fashioned oats

1½ cups all-purpose flour

¼ cup NESTLÉ® TOLL HOUSE® Baking Cocoa

1 teaspoon baking powder

¼ teaspoon salt (optional)

¾ cup granulated sugar

⅔ cup butter or margarine, softened

2 large eggs

1 teaspoon vanilla extract

2 cups (two 10-ounce jars) maraschino cherries, drained and patted dry

MICROWAVE *1 cup* morsels in small, uncovered, microwave-safe bowl on HIGH (100%) power for 1 minute. STIR. Morsels may retain some of their original shape. If necessary, microwave at additional 10- to 15-second intervals, stirring until morsels are melted. Combine oats, flour, cocoa, baking powder and salt in medium bowl.

BEAT sugar, butter, eggs and vanilla extract in large mixer bowl until smooth. Beat in melted chocolate. Stir in oat mixture. Cover; refrigerate dough for 1 hour.

PREHEAT oven to 350°F.

SHAPE dough into 1-inch balls. Place 2 inches apart on ungreased baking sheet. Press thumb into tops to make deep depression. Place maraschino cherry into each depression.

BAKE for 10 to 12 minutes or until set. Cool on baking sheets for 2 minutes; remove to wire racks to cool completely. Melt *remaining 1 cup* morsels; drizzle over cookies.

Makes about 4 dozen cookies

AFTER SCHOOL SNACKS

Surprise Prize Cupcakes

1 **package (18.25 ounces) plain chocolate cake mix**

⅓ **cup water**

3 **large eggs**

⅓ **cup vegetable oil**

1 **package (16.5 ounces) NESTLÉ® TOLL HOUSE® Refrigerated Chocolate Chip Cookie Bar Dough**

1 **container (16 ounces) prepared chocolate frosting**

NESTLÉ® TOLL HOUSE® Semi-Sweet Chocolate Mini Morsels

PREHEAT oven to 350°F. Paper-line 24 muffin cups.

BEAT cake mix, water, eggs and oil in large mixer bowl on low speed for 30 seconds. Beat on medium speed for 2 minutes or until smooth. Spoon about ¼ cup batter into each cup, filling about two-thirds full.

CUT cookie dough into 24 pieces; roll each into a ball. Place one ball of dough in each muffin cup, pressing it into the bottom.

BAKE for 19 to 22 minutes or until top springs back when gently touched. Let stand for 15 minutes. Remove to wire rack to cool completely. Spread with frosting and sprinkle with morsels.

Makes 2 dozen cupcakes

AFTER SCHOOL SNACKS

Chunky Chocolate Chip Peanut Butter Cookies

1¼ **cups all-purpose flour**

½ **teaspoon baking soda**

½ **teaspoon salt**

½ **teaspoon ground cinnamon**

¾ **cup (1½ sticks) butter or margarine, softened**

½ **cup granulated sugar**

½ **cup packed brown sugar**

½ **cup creamy peanut butter**

1 **large egg**

1 **teaspoon vanilla extract**

2 **cups (12-ounce package) NESTLÉ® TOLL HOUSE® Semi-Sweet Chocolate Morsels**

½ **cup coarsely chopped peanuts**

PREHEAT oven to 375°F.

COMBINE flour, baking soda, salt and cinnamon in small bowl. Beat butter, granulated sugar, brown sugar and peanut butter in large mixer bowl until creamy. Beat in egg and vanilla extract. Gradually beat in flour mixture. Stir in morsels and peanuts.

DROP dough by rounded tablespoonful onto ungreased baking sheets. Press down slightly to flatten into 2-inch circles.

BAKE for 7 to 10 minutes or until edges are set but centers are still soft. Cool on baking sheets for 4 minutes; remove to wire racks to cool completely.

Makes about 3 dozen cookies

AFTER SCHOOL SNACKS

Mini Pumpkin Muffin Mix

3 **cups all-purpose flour**

1 **cup granulated sugar**

4 **teaspoons baking powder**

1½ **teaspoons salt**

1 **teaspoon ground cinnamon**

1 **teaspoon ground nutmeg**

1 **cup raisins, sweetened dried cranberries or chopped nuts (optional)**

1 **can (15 ounces) LIBBY'S® 100% Pure Pumpkin**

COMBINE all ingredients, except pumpkin, in large bowl. Pour into 1-quart resealable plastic food storage bag; seal. Wrap muffin mix and can of pumpkin in fabric; tie with ribbon or twine.

Makes about 5 dozen mini muffins

Recipe to Attach: *POUR muffin mix into large bowl. Cut in ½ cup vegetable shortening with pastry blender until mixture is fine. Add 1 cup LIBBY'S 100% Pure Pumpkin, 1 cup milk and 2 large eggs; mix until just moistened. Spoon into greased or paper-lined mini-muffin pans, filling two thirds full. Bake in preheated 400°F oven for 15 minutes; remove to wire racks. Sprinkle with powdered sugar. Makes about 5 dozen mini muffins.*

Peanut Butter and Jelly Bars

1¼ cups all-purpose flour

½ cup graham cracker crumbs

½ teaspoon baking soda

½ teaspoon salt

½ cup (1 stick) butter, softened

½ cup granulated sugar

½ cup packed brown sugar

½ cup creamy peanut butter

1 large egg

1 teaspoon vanilla extract

1¾ cups (11.5-ounce package) NESTLÉ® TOLL HOUSE® Milk Chocolate Morsels

¾ cup coarsely chopped peanuts

½ cup jelly or jam

PREHEAT oven to 350°F.

COMBINE flour, graham cracker crumbs, baking soda and salt in small bowl.

BEAT butter, granulated sugar, brown sugar and peanut butter in large mixer bowl until creamy. Beat in egg and vanilla extract. Gradually beat in flour mixture. Stir in morsels and nuts. Press ¾ dough into ungreased 13×9-inch baking pan.

BAKE for 15 minutes; remove from oven. Dollop jelly by heaping teaspoonful over partially baked dough. Let stand for 1 minute; spread to cover. Dollop remaining dough by heaping teaspoonful over jelly.

BAKE for an additional 20 to 25 minutes or until edges are set. Cool in pan on wire rack. Cut into bars.

Makes 4 dozen bars

Chunky Milk Chocolate Chip Cookies

- 2 **cups all-purpose flour**
- 1 **teaspoon baking soda**
- ¼ **teaspoon salt**
- 1¼ **cups packed brown sugar**
- 1 **cup (2 sticks) butter or margarine, softened**
- 1 **teaspoon vanilla extract**
- 1 **large egg**
- 1¾ **cups (11.5-ounce package) NESTLÉ® TOLL HOUSE® Milk Chocolate Morsels**
- 1 **cup chopped nuts**
- 1 **cup raisins**

PREHEAT oven to 375°F.

COMBINE flour, baking soda and salt in small bowl. Beat sugar, butter and vanilla extract in large mixer bowl until creamy. Beat in egg. Gradually beat in flour mixture. Stir in morsels, nuts and raisins. Drop by heaping tablespoonful onto ungreased baking sheets; flatten slightly.

BAKE for 9 to 11 minutes or until edges are lightly browned. Cool on baking sheets for 2 minutes; remove to wire racks to cool completely.

Makes about 2½ dozen cookies

AFTER SCHOOL SNACKS

Candy Bars

1⅔ cups (11-ounce package) NESTLÉ®
     TOLL HOUSE® Butterscotch Flavored
     Morsels

4 cups toasted rice cereal

2 packages (11.5 ounces *each*) NESTLÉ®
     TOLL HOUSE® Milk Chocolate Morsels,
     divided

GREASE 13×9-inch baking pan.

MICROWAVE butterscotch morsels in large,
microwave-safe bowl on MEDIUM-HIGH (70%)
power for 1 minute; STIR. Microwave at additional
10- to 20-second intervals, stirring until morsels
are melted. Stir in cereal and *1 cup* milk chocolate
morsels. Press evenly into prepared baking pan.

MICROWAVE *remaining* milk chocolate morsels in
small, microwave-safe bowl on MEDIUM-HIGH (70%)
power for 1 minute; STIR. Microwave at additional
10- to 20-second intervals, stirring until morsels
are melted. Spread evenly over mixture in pan.
Refrigerate until firm. Cut into bars.

Makes 2 dozen bars

Candy Shop Pizza

1 package (16.5 ounces) NESTLÉ®
     TOLL HOUSE® Refrigerated Chocolate
     Chip Cookie Bar Dough

½ cup (3 ounces) NESTLÉ® TOLL HOUSE®
     Semi-Sweet Chocolate Morsels

¼ cup creamy or chunky peanut butter

1 cup coarsely chopped assorted
     NESTLÉ® candy such as BUTTERFINGER®,
     NESTLÉ® CRUNCH®, BABY RUTH®,
     GOOBERS®, NESTLÉ® RAISINETS® and/or
     BUNCHA CRUNCH®

PREHEAT oven to 325°F. Grease pizza pan or baking
sheet.

PLACE whole bar of dough on prepared pan. Allow
to soften for 5 to 10 minutes. Using fingertips, pat
dough gently to form 8-inch circle.

BAKE for 18 to 20 minutes or until golden brown.
Immediately sprinkle morsels over hot crust; drop
peanut butter by spoonfuls onto morsels. Let stand
for 5 minutes or until morsels become shiny. Gently
spread chocolate and peanut butter evenly over
cookie crust.

SPRINKLE candy in single layer over pizza. Cut into
wedges; serve warm or at room temperature.

Makes about 12 servings

AFTER SCHOOL SNACKS

Easy Double Chocolate Chip Brownies

2 cups (12-ounce package) NESTLÉ® TOLL HOUSE® Semi-Sweet Chocolate Morsels, *divided*

½ cup (1 stick) butter or margarine, cut into pieces

3 large eggs

1¼ cups all-purpose flour

1 cup granulated sugar

1 teaspoon vanilla extract

¼ teaspoon baking soda

½ cup chopped nuts

PREHEAT oven to 350°F. Grease 13×9-inch baking pan.

MELT *1 cup* morsels and butter in large, *heavy-duty* saucepan over low heat; stir until smooth. Remove from heat. Stir in eggs. Stir in flour, sugar, vanilla extract and baking soda. Stir in *remaining* morsels and nuts. Spread into prepared baking pan.

BAKE for 18 to 22 minutes or until wooden pick inserted in center comes out slightly sticky. Cool completely in pan on wire rack.

Makes 2 dozen brownies

AFTER SCHOOL SNACKS

Magical Cookie Wands

- **1 package (16.5 ounces) NESTLÉ® TOLL HOUSE® Refrigerated Chocolate Chip Cookie Bar Dough**
- **2 tablespoons all-purpose flour plus additional for rolling**
- **12 pretzel rods**
- **1 (3-inch) star cookie cutter**
- **½ cup NESTLÉ® TOLL HOUSE® Morsels (Premier White, Semi-Sweet Chocolate, Milk Chocolate)**
- **Decorator sugars or sprinkles (optional)**
- **Thin ribbons (optional)**

You may substitute 1¾ cups NESTLÉ® TOLL HOUSE® Refrigerated Chocolate Chip Cookie Tub Dough for the bar dough.

PREHEAT oven to 350°F.

BREAK dough apart into medium bowl. Combine dough and flour until mixed. Roll cookie dough to ¼-inch thickness between two sheets of floured wax paper. Remove top piece of paper. Cut cookie dough into stars with cutter. Transfer stars to baking sheet placing about 4 inches apart (2 to 3 baking sheets will be needed, pending size of sheet-stars will spread). Place pretzel rod under star (make sure to have rod at least to middle of star or close to top). Press down lightly. Refrigerate for 15 minutes.

BAKE for 13 to 14 minutes or until lightly browned. Remove from oven and immediately pat sides of each star with edge of knife to help retain shape. Cool on baking sheets for 5 minutes; remove to wire racks to cool completely.

TO DECORATE:

MICROWAVE morsels on MEDIUM-HIGH (70%) power for 30 seconds in small, *heavy-duty* plastic bag; knead. Microwave at additional 10- to 15-second intervals, kneading until smooth. Cut a small corner from bag. Squeeze bag to drizzle melted morsels over cookie stars in design desired. Immediately sprinkle with sugar or sprinkles. Let stand for 15 minutes to set drizzles.

Makes 12 wands

Tip: *Refrigerating cookie wands before baking helps to prevent cookies from spreading and retain their shape during baking.*

AFTER SCHOOL SNACKS

Chocolatey Chocolate Chip Cookie Cups

- 1 package (16.5 ounces) NESTLÉ® TOLL HOUSE® Refrigerated Chocolate Chip Cookie Bar Dough
- 1 cup (6 ounces) NESTLÉ® TOLL HOUSE® Peanut Butter & Milk Chocolate Morsels

PREHEAT oven to 350°F. Grease or paper-line 24 mini muffin cups.

PLACE squares of dough into prepared muffin cups; press down lightly in center to make a well.

BAKE for 9 to 11 minutes or until edges are set. Cool in pans on wire racks for 5 minutes; remove to wire racks to cool completely.

MICROWAVE morsels in small, *heavy-duty* plastic food storage bag on MEDIUM-HIGH (70%) power for 30 seconds; knead until smooth. Microwave at additional 10- to 15-second intervals, kneading until smooth. Cut tiny corner from bag; squeeze chocolate into each cup.

Makes 2 dozen cookie cups

For Extra Chocolatey Chocolate Chip Cookie Cups: *SUBSTITUTE 1 cup (6 ounces) NESTLÉ® TOLL HOUSE® Semi-Sweet Chocolate Morsels for Peanut Butter & Milk Chocolate Morsels.*

Apple Butterscotch Tart

- Pastry for single-crust pie
- 5 cups (about 5 medium) peeled and thinly sliced tart green apples
- 1 cup (6 ounces) NESTLÉ® TOLL HOUSE® Butterscotch Flavored Morsels
- ¾ cup all-purpose flour
- ½ cup packed brown sugar
- ½ teaspoon ground cinnamon
- ¼ cup (½ stick) butter or margarine, chilled
- Ice cream or sweetened whipped cream (optional)

PREHEAT oven to 375°F.

LINE 9-inch tart pan with removable bottom with pastry; trim away excess pastry. Arrange apples in pastry shell; sprinkle morsels over apples. Combine flour, sugar and cinnamon in medium bowl. Cut in butter with pastry blender or two knives until mixture resembles coarse crumbs. Sprinkle mixture over filling.

BAKE for 40 to 45 minutes or until apples are tender when pierced with sharp knife. Remove side of tart pan. Serve warm with ice cream.

Makes 8 servings

NESTLÉ® TOLL HOUSE® Cookie Puzzle

1 tub (36 ounces) NESTLÉ® TOLL HOUSE® Refrigerated Chocolate Chip Cookie Tub Dough

Frosting, colored decorator icing, assorted NESTLÉ® candies and/or sprinkles, NESTLÉ® TOLL HOUSE® Morsels, any flavor

Two packages (16.5 ounces each) NESTLÉ® TOLL HOUSE® Refrigerated Chocolate Chip Cookie Bar Dough can be substituted for the Tub Dough.

PREHEAT oven to 325°F. Foil-line 15×10-inch jelly-roll pan, allowing 1-inch of foil to hang over sides of pan. Grease foil.

PLACE whole tub of dough in prepared pan. Allow to soften for 5 to 10 minutes. Using fingertips, gently press dough to evenly fill pan.

BAKE for 25 to 30 minutes or until golden brown and edges are set. Cool completely in pan on wire rack. Carefully lift from pan using foil handles to cutting board. Carefully remove foil; return to cutting board.

CUT cookie bar into 24 (2- to 4-inch) random shaped pieces with pizza cutter or sharp knife. Leave pieces on cutting board, return pieces to baking sheet or place pieces on platter.

DECORATE puzzle as desired. Allow icing to set. Carefully separate using knife into individual puzzle pieces.

Makes 24 servings

Tip: *Puzzle may be decorated for a variety of holidays or occasions.*

Ultimate Chocolate Chocolate Chip Cookies

4 cups (two 12-ounce packages) NESTLÉ® TOLL HOUSE® Semi-Sweet Chocolate Morsels, *divided*

2⅔ cups all-purpose flour

1 teaspoon baking soda

1 teaspoon salt

1 cup (2 sticks) butter or margarine, softened

1 cup packed brown sugar

½ cup granulated sugar

1 teaspoon vanilla extract

3 large eggs

PREHEAT oven to 375°F.

MELT *2 cups* morsels in small, *heavy-duty* saucepan over low heat; stir until smooth. Remove from heat.

COMBINE flour, baking soda and salt in medium bowl. Beat butter, brown sugar, granulated sugar and vanilla extract in large mixer bowl. Add eggs, one at a time, beating well after each addition. Beat in melted chocolate. Gradually beat in flour mixture. Stir in *remaining 2 cups* morsels. Drop by rounded tablespoonful onto ungreased baking sheets.

BAKE for 8 to 9 minutes or until cookies are puffed. Cool on baking sheets for 2 minutes; remove to wire racks to cool completely.

Makes 4 dozen cookies

AFTER SCHOOL SNACKS

NESTLÉ® TOLL HOUSE® Cookie S'mores

48 graham cracker squares, *divided*

 1 package (16.5 ounces) NESTLÉ® TOLL HOUSE® Refrigerated Chocolate Chip Cookie Bar Dough

12 large marshmallows, cut in half

PREHEAT oven to 350°F. Line baking sheet with foil. Arrange 24 graham cracker squares on prepared baking sheet; set aside.

BAKE cookie dough on another baking sheet according to package instructions. Cool for 2 minutes on baking sheet. Remove cookies from baking sheet and place one warm cookie on each graham cracker square on foil. Top each cookie with one marshmallow half.

BAKE for 1 to 2 minutes or until marshmallows are soft. Immediately top s'mores with *remaining* graham cracker squares.

Makes 2 dozen s'mores

Cookie on a Stick

 1 package (16.5 ounces) NESTLÉ® TOLL HOUSE® Refrigerated Chocolate Chip Cookie Dough

 8 wooden craft sticks

    Decorator icing, various colors (optional)

    Candies (optional)

    Melted chocolate (optional)

    Thin ribbons (optional)

PREHEAT oven to 375°F.

SHAPE cookie dough into eight 2-inch balls. Place four balls at a time onto an ungreased baking sheet. Insert wooden sticks into each ball to resemble a lollipop; flatten dough slightly.

BAKE for 12 to 14 minutes or until edges are crisp. Cool on baking sheet for 1 minute; remove to wire racks to cool completely.

DECORATE as desired. Tie ribbons around sticks and give as a cookie bouquet.

Makes 8 cookies

Note: *Dough from one batch Original NESTLÉ® TOLL HOUSE® Chocolate Chip Cookies (NESTLÉ® TOLL HOUSE® Semi-Sweet Chocolate Morsels 6-ounce package recipe) may be used.*

Autumn

Frosted Double Chocolate Cookies

Who needs a reason to celebrate? These delectable cookies, fluffy cakes, chewy brownies, classic pies, creamy puddings, and much more are perfect ways to show you care at any time.

- 2 **cups (12-ounce package) NESTLÉ® TOLL HOUSE® Semi-Sweet Chocolate Morsels, *divided***
- 1¼ **cups all-purpose flour**
- ¾ **teaspoon baking soda**
- ½ **teaspoon salt**
- ½ **cup (1 stick) butter or margarine, softened**
- ½ **cup packed brown sugar**
- ¼ **cup granulated sugar**
- 1 **teaspoon vanilla extract**
- 1 **large egg**
- ½ **cup chopped nuts (optional)**

 Chocolate Frosting (recipe follows)

PREHEAT oven to 375°F.

MICROWAVE *¾ cup* morsels in small, uncovered, microwave-safe bowl on HIGH (100%) power for 1 minute. STIR. Morsels may retain some of their original shape. If necessary, microwave at additional 10- to 15-second intervals, stirring until morsels are melted. Cool to room temperature. Combine flour, baking soda and salt in small bowl.

BEAT butter, brown sugar, granulated sugar and vanilla extract in large mixer bowl until creamy. Beat in melted chocolate and egg. Gradually beat in flour mixture. Stir in *¾ cup* morsels and nuts. Drop by rounded tablespoonful onto ungreased baking sheets.

BAKE for 8 to 9 minutes or until edges are set but centers are still slightly soft. Cool on baking sheets for 3 minutes; remove to wire racks to cool completely. Thinly frost centers of cookies with Chocolate Frosting.

Makes about 2½ dozen cookies

Chocolate Frosting

MICROWAVE *remaining ½ cup* morsels and 2 tablespoons butter or margarine in medium, uncovered, microwave-safe bowl on HIGH (100%) power for 30 seconds; STIR. Microwave at additional 10- to 15-second intervals, stirring until smooth. Add 1¼ cups sifted powdered sugar and 2 tablespoons milk; stir until smooth.

EVERYDAY DESSERTS

Chocolate Chip Cheesecake

CRUST:

1½ cups (about 15) crushed chocolate sandwich cookies

2 tablespoons butter or margarine, melted

2 cups (12-ounce package) NESTLÉ® TOLL HOUSE® Semi-Sweet Chocolate Mini Morsels, *divided*

FILLING:

2 packages (8 ounces *each*) cream cheese, softened

½ cup granulated sugar

1 tablespoon vanilla extract

2 large eggs

2 tablespoons all-purpose flour

¾ cup NESTLÉ® CARNATION® Evaporated Milk

½ cup sour cream

FOR CRUST:

PREHEAT oven to 300°F.

COMBINE cookie crumbs and butter in medium bowl until moistened; press onto bottom of ungreased 9-inch springform pan. Sprinkle with *1 cup* morsels.

FOR FILLING:

BEAT cream cheese, sugar and vanilla extract in large mixer bowl until smooth. Beat in eggs and flour. Gradually beat in evaporated milk and sour cream. Pour over crust. Sprinkle with *remaining ½ cup* morsels.

BAKE for 25 minutes. Cover loosely with aluminum foil. Bake for additional 30 to 40 minutes or until edge is set but center still moves slightly. Place in refrigerator immediately; refrigerate for 2 hours or until firm. Remove side of springform pan.

Makes 12 to 14 servings

Note: *Cheesecake may be baked in 13×9-inch pan. Prepare as above. Bake in preheated 300°F oven for 20 minutes. Cover loosely with aluminum foil. Bake for additional 20 to 30 minutes.*

EVERYDAY DESSERTS

Rich Chocolate Cake with Creamy Peanut Butter Milk Chocolate Frosting

CAKE:

- 2 cups all-purpose flour
- 1¾ cups granulated sugar
- ⅔ cup NESTLÉ® TOLL HOUSE® Baking Cocoa
- 1½ teaspoons baking powder
- 1½ teaspoons baking soda
- ½ teaspoon salt
- 1 cup milk
- 1 cup water
- ½ cup vegetable oil
- 2 large eggs
- 2 teaspoons vanilla extract
- 1⅔ cups (11-ounce package) NESTLÉ® TOLL HOUSE® Peanut Butter & Milk Chocolate Morsels, *divided*

CREAMY PEANUT BUTTER MILK CHOCOLATE FROSTING:

- 1 package (8 ounces) cream cheese, softened
- 1 teaspoon vanilla extract
- ⅛ teaspoon salt
- 3 cups powdered sugar

FOR CAKE:

PREHEAT oven to 350°F. Grease and flour two 9-inch-round cake pans.

COMBINE flour, granulated sugar, cocoa, baking powder, baking soda and salt in large mixer bowl. Add milk, water, vegetable oil, eggs and vanilla extract; blend until moistened. Beat for 2 minutes (batter will be thin). Pour into prepared pans. Sprinkle ⅓ cup morsels over each cake layer.

BAKE for 25 to 30 minutes or until wooden pick inserted in center comes out clean. Cool in pans on wire racks for 10 minutes; remove to wire racks to cool completely. Frost with Creamy Peanut Butter Milk Chocolate Frosting.

FOR CREAMY PEANUT BUTTER MILK CHOCOLATE FROSTING:

MICROWAVE *remaining 1⅓ cup* morsels in small, uncovered, microwave-safe bowl on MEDIUM-HIGH (70%) power for 1 minute. STIR. Morsels may retain some of their original shape. If necessary, microwave at additional 10- to 15-second intervals, stirring until morsels are melted. Beat cream cheese, melted morsels, vanilla extract and salt in small mixer bowl until light and fluffy. Gradually beat in powdered sugar.

Makes 12 servings

EVERYDAY DESSERTS

Turtle Cheesecake

CRUST:

1¾ cups chocolate graham cracker crumbs

⅓ cup butter or margarine, melted

FILLING:

3 packages (8 ounces *each*) cream cheese, softened

1 can (14 ounces) NESTLÉ® CARNATION® Sweetened Condensed Milk

½ cup granulated sugar

3 large eggs

3 tablespoons lime juice

1 tablespoon vanilla extract

1½ cups (9 ounces) NESTLÉ® TOLL HOUSE® Semi-Sweet Chocolate Morsels

2 tablespoons NESTLÉ® NESQUIK® Chocolate Flavor Syrup

2 tablespoons caramel syrup or ice cream topping

½ cup coarsely chopped pecans

¼ cup NESTLÉ® TOLL HOUSE® Semi-Sweet Chocolate Mini Morsels

PREHEAT oven to 300°F. Grease 9-inch springform pan.

FOR CRUST:

COMBINE crumbs and butter in medium bowl. Press onto bottom and 1 inch up side of prepared pan.

FOR FILLING:

BEAT cream cheese and sweetened condensed milk in large mixer bowl until smooth. Add sugar, eggs, lime juice and vanilla extract; beat until combined.

MICROWAVE 1½ cups morsels in medium, uncovered, microwave-safe bowl on HIGH (100%) power for 1 minute. STIR. Morsels may retain some of their original shape. If necessary, microwave at additional 10- to 15-second intervals, stirring until morsels are melted. Stir 2 *cups* of cheesecake batter into melted morsels; mix well. Alternately spoon batters into crust, beginning and ending with yellow batter.

BAKE for 70 to 75 minutes or until edge is set and center moves slightly. Cool in pan on wire rack for 10 minutes; run knife around edge of cheesecake. Cool completely. Drizzle Nesquik and caramel syrup over cheesecake. Sprinkle with pecans and mini morsels. Refrigerate for several hours or overnight. Remove side of pan.

Makes 12 to 16 servings

EVERYDAY DESSERTS

Chocolate Mint Brownie Cookies

1½ cups (9 ounces) NESTLÉ® TOLL HOUSE® Semi-Sweet Chocolate Morsels, *divided*

1¾ cups all-purpose flour

½ teaspoon baking soda

¼ teaspoon salt

½ cup (1 stick) butter or margarine, softened

½ cup granulated sugar

¼ cup packed brown sugar

½ teaspoon peppermint extract

½ teaspoon vanilla extract

2 large eggs

¾ cup chopped nuts

PREHEAT oven to 350°F.

MELT ¾ cup morsels in small, *heavy-duty* saucepan over *lowest possible* heat. When morsels begin to melt, remove from heat; stir. Return to heat for a few seconds at a time, stirring until smooth. Cool to room temperature.

COMBINE flour, baking soda and salt in small bowl. Beat butter, granulated sugar, brown sugar, peppermint extract and vanilla extract in large mixer bowl until creamy. Add eggs, one at a time, beating well after each addition. Beat in melted chocolate. Gradually beat in flour mixture. Stir in *remaining ¾ cup* morsels and nuts. Drop dough by rounded tablespoonful onto ungreased baking sheets.

BAKE for 8 to 12 minutes or until sides are set but centers are still soft. Let stand for 2 minutes; remove to wire racks to cool completely.

Makes 3 dozen cookies

EVERYDAY DESSERTS

Mini LIBBY'S® Famous Pumpkin Pies

- 4 **(1-cup volume *each*) 4-inch diameter mini-pie shells**
- ¾ **cup granulated sugar**
- 1 **teaspoon ground cinnamon**
- ½ **teaspoon salt**
- ½ **teaspoon ground ginger**
- ¼ **teaspoon ground cloves**
- 2 **large eggs**
- 1 **can (15 ounces) LIBBY'S® 100% Pure Pumpkin**
- 1 **can (12 fluid ounces) NESTLÉ® CARNATION® Evaporated Milk**

PREHEAT oven to 425°F.

MIX sugar, cinnamon, salt, ginger and cloves in small bowl. Beat eggs lightly in large bowl. Stir in pumpkin and sugar-spice mixture. Gradually stir in evaporated milk.

POUR into shells.

BAKE for 15 minutes. Reduce oven temperature to 350°F. Bake for 30 to 35 minutes or until knife inserted near center comes out clean. Cool on wire rack for 2 hours. Serve immediately or refrigerate. (Do not freeze as this may cause filling to separate from the crust.)

Makes 4 mini pies

Note: *May use refrigerated or homemade single pie crust to make 4 mini-pie shells. Lay rim of mini-pie pan on rolled out dough. Cut circle ½ inch larger than mini-pie to allow for dough to form fluted edge.*

Lower Fat & Calorie Pies: *Substitute NESTLÉ® CARNATION® Lowfat Evaporated or Fat Free Evaporated Milk.*

EVERYDAY DESSERTS

Triple-Chocolate Cupcakes

1 package (18.25 ounces) chocolate cake mix

1 package (3.9 ounces) chocolate instant pudding and pie filling mix

1 container (8 ounces) sour cream

4 large eggs

½ cup vegetable oil

½ cup warm water

2 cups (12-ounce package) NESTLÉ® TOLL HOUSE® Semi-Sweet Chocolate Morsels

1 container (16 ounces) prepared frosting

Assorted candy sprinkles

PREHEAT oven to 350°F. Grease or paper-line 30 muffin cups.

COMBINE cake mix, pudding mix, sour cream, eggs, vegetable oil and water in large mixer bowl; beat on low speed just until blended. Beat on high speed for 2 minutes. Stir in morsels. Pour into prepared muffin cups, filling ⅔ full.

BAKE for 25 to 28 minutes or until wooden pick inserted in centers comes out clean. Cool in pans for 10 minutes; remove to wire racks to cool completely. Frost; decorate with candy sprinkles.

Makes 2½ dozen cupcakes

EVERYDAY DESSERTS
NESTLÉ® TOLL HOUSE® Grand Chocolate Brownie Wedges with Chocolate Sauce

3 bars (12 ounces) NESTLÉ® TOLL HOUSE® Dark Chocolate Baking Bar, *divided*

1 cup granulated sugar

⅓ cup butter, cut into pieces

2 tablespoons water

2 large eggs

1 teaspoon vanilla extract

¾ cup all-purpose flour

¼ teaspoon salt

½ cup chopped walnuts or pecans (optional)

⅓ cup heavy whipping cream

Whipped cream (optional)

PREHEAT oven to 325°F. Line 8-inch-square baking pan with foil; grease.

HEAT *10 ounces (2½ bars)* chocolate (broken into small pieces), sugar, butter and water in small, *heavy-duty* saucepan over low heat, stirring constantly, until chocolate and butter are melted. Pour into medium bowl. Stir in eggs, one at a time, until mixed in. Stir in vanilla extract. Add flour and salt; stir well. Stir in nuts, if desired. Pour into prepared baking pan.

BAKE for 35 to 40 minutes or until wooden pick inserted in center comes out slightly sticky (may be up to 45 minutes). Cool in pan on wire rack. Lift brownie from pan with foil to cutting board. Carefully remove foil. Cut brownie square in half. Cut each half into thirds for a total of 6 pieces. Cut each piece in half diagonally to form triangles for a total of 12.

PLACE cream in small, uncovered, microwave-safe dish. Microwave on HIGH (100%) power for 25 to 30 seconds. Add *remaining 2 ounces (½ bar)* chocolate, broken into small pieces; stir until smooth. (Sauce will thicken as it cools.) Place wedge on serving plate; top or drizzle with a teaspoon of sauce. Top with whipped cream, if desired.

Makes 12 servings

EVERYDAY DESSERTS

Oatmeal Scotchies

1¼ **cups all-purpose flour**

1 **teaspoon baking soda**

½ **teaspoon salt**

½ **teaspoon ground cinnamon**

1 **cup (2 sticks) butter or margarine, softened**

¾ **cup granulated sugar**

¾ **cup packed brown sugar**

2 **large eggs**

1 **teaspoon vanilla extract *or* grated peel of 1 orange**

3 **cups quick or old-fashioned oats**

1⅔ **cups (11-ounce package) NESTLÉ® TOLL HOUSE® Butterscotch Flavored Morsels**

PREHEAT oven to 375°F.

COMBINE flour, baking soda, salt and cinnamon in small bowl. Beat butter, granulated sugar, brown sugar, eggs and vanilla extract in large mixer bowl. Gradually beat in flour mixture. Stir in oats and morsels. Drop by rounded tablespoonful onto ungreased baking sheets.

BAKE for 7 to 8 minutes for chewy cookies or 9 to 10 minutes for crispy cookies. Cool on baking sheets for 2 minutes; remove to wire racks to cool completely.

Makes about 4 dozen cookies

Pan Cookie Variation: *Grease 15×10-inch jelly-roll pan. Prepare dough as above. Spread into prepared pan. Bake for 18 to 22 minutes or until light brown. Cool completely in pan on wire rack. Makes 4 dozen bars.*

EVERYDAY DESSERTS

Creamy Chocolate Pudding

6 tablespoons granulated sugar

¼ cup NESTLÉ® TOLL HOUSE® Baking Cocoa

¼ cup cornstarch

⅛ teaspoon salt

1 can (12 fluid ounces) NESTLÉ® CARNATION® Evaporated Fat Free Milk

½ cup water

1 tablespoon butter or margarine

½ teaspoon vanilla extract

COMBINE sugar, cocoa, cornstarch and salt in medium saucepan. Add evaporated milk and water; whisk to blend.

COOK over medium heat, stirring constantly, for about 7 minutes or until pudding thickens. Do not boil. Remove from heat; stir in butter and vanilla extract.

Makes about 4 (½-cup) servings

NESTLÉ® TOLL HOUSE® Easy Chocolate Cheesecake

1 package (16.5 ounces) NESTLÉ® TOLL HOUSE® Refrigerated Chocolate Chip Cookie Dough

2 packages (8 ounces *each*) cream cheese, softened

1 cup granulated sugar

4 packets (1 ounce *each*) NESTLÉ® TOLL HOUSE® CHOCO BAKE® Pre-Melted Unsweetened Chocolate Flavor

2 containers (8 ounces *each*) frozen whipped topping, thawed

½ cup NESTLÉ® TOLL HOUSE® Semi-Sweet Chocolate Morsels, *melted*

PREHEAT oven to 350°F. Grease 9-inch springform pan.

PLACE whole bar of dough in prepared pan. Allow to soften for 5 to 10 minutes. Using fingertips, pat dough gently to cover bottom.

BAKE for 18 to 19 minutes or until light golden brown. Cool completely in pan on wire rack.

COMBINE cream cheese, sugar and Choco Bake in large mixer bowl until well blended. Add whipped topping; stir until just blended. Spoon over cookie crust; smooth top. Drizzle with melted chocolate. Refrigerate for 3 to 4 hours or overnight. Remove side of pan.

Makes 16 servings

EVERYDAY DESSERTS

Peanut Butter & Chocolate Cookie Cups

¾ cup (1½ sticks) butter or margarine, softened

⅓ cup granulated sugar

1½ cups all-purpose flour

1⅔ cups (11-ounce package) NESTLÉ® TOLL HOUSE® Peanut Butter & Milk Chocolate Morsels, *divided*

2 large eggs

1 can (14 ounces) NESTLÉ® CARNATION® Sweetened Condensed Milk

1 teaspoon vanilla extract

PREHEAT oven to 350°F. Heavily grease 36 mini-muffin cups.

BEAT butter and sugar in small mixer bowl until creamy. Add flour; beat until mixture is evenly moist and crumbly. Roll rounded teaspoonful dough into ball; press onto bottom and halfway up side of muffin cup. Repeat with remaining dough. Place 5 *morsels* in each cup.

BEAT eggs in medium bowl with wire whisk. Stir in sweetened condensed milk and vanilla extract. Spoon into muffin cups, filling almost to the top of each cup.

BAKE for 15 to 18 minutes or until centers are puffed and edges are just beginning to brown. Remove from oven to wire rack(s). Gently run knife around edges of cookies. Let centers flatten. While still warm, top cookies with *half of remaining morsels* (they will soften and retain their shape). Repeat with *remaining morsels*. Cool completely in pan on wire rack. With tip of knife, release cookies from cups.

Makes 3 dozen cookie cups

EVERYDAY DESSERTS

Chocolate Hazelnut Terrine with Raspberry Sauce

DARK CHOCOLATE LAYER:

- **2 cups (12-ounce package) NESTLÉ® TOLL HOUSE® Semi-Sweet Chocolate Morsels**
- **⅓ cup butter, cut into pieces**
- **¼ cup hazelnut liqueur**
- **1½ cups heavy whipping cream**

MILK CHOCOLATE LAYER:

- **1¾ cups (11.5-ounce package) NESTLÉ® TOLL HOUSE® Milk Chocolate Morsels**
- **⅓ cup butter, cut into pieces**

RASPBERRY SAUCE:

- **1 package (10 ounces) frozen raspberries in syrup, thawed, puréed and strained**
- **½ cup water**
- **1 tablespoon cornstarch**
- **1 teaspoon granulated sugar**

LINE 9×5-inch loaf pan with plastic wrap.

FOR DARK CHOCOLATE LAYER:

MICROWAVE semi-sweet morsels and ⅓ cup butter in medium, uncovered, microwave-safe bowl on HIGH (100%) power for 1 minute. STIR. Morsels may retain some of their original shape. If necessary, microwave at additional 10- to 15-second intervals, stirring just until morsels are melted. Stir in liqueur; cool to room temperature.

WHIP cream in small mixer bowl until stiff peaks form. Fold 2 *cups* whipped cream into chocolate mixture. Spoon into prepared loaf pan. Refrigerate *remaining* whipped cream.

FOR MILK CHOCOLATE LAYER:

MICROWAVE milk chocolate morsels and ⅓ cup butter in medium, uncovered, microwave-safe bowl on MEDIUM-HIGH (70%) power for 1 minute. STIR. Morsels may retain some of their original shape. If necessary, microwave at additional 10- to 15-second intervals, stirring just until morsels are melted. Cool to room temperature. Stir *remaining* whipped cream into chocolate mixture. Spread over dark chocolate layer. Cover; refrigerate for at least 2 hours or until firm.

FOR RASPBERRY SAUCE:

COOK raspberry purée, water, cornstarch and sugar over medium heat, stirring constantly, until mixture comes to a boil; boil for 1 minute. Cover; refrigerate.

TO SERVE: Invert terrine onto serving platter; remove plastic wrap. Cut into ½-inch-thick slices; serve in pool of Raspberry Sauce.

Makes 16 servings

EVERYDAY DESSERTS

Molasses Spice Cookies

1¾ cups all-purpose flour

1 teaspoon baking soda

1 teaspoon ground ginger

1 teaspoon ground cinnamon

¼ teaspoon ground cloves

¼ teaspoon salt

1 cup granulated sugar

¾ cup (1½ sticks) butter or margarine, softened

1 large egg

¼ cup unsulphured molasses

2 cups (12-ounce package) NESTLÉ® TOLL HOUSE® Premier White Morsels

1 cup finely chopped walnuts

COMBINE flour, baking soda, ginger, cinnamon, cloves and salt in small bowl. Beat sugar and butter in large mixer bowl until creamy. Beat in egg and molasses. Gradually beat in flour mixture. Stir in morsels. Refrigerate for 20 minutes or until slightly firm.

PREHEAT oven to 375°F.

ROLL dough into 1-inch balls; roll in walnuts. Place on ungreased baking sheets.

BAKE for 9 to 11 minutes or until golden brown. Cool on baking sheets for 2 minutes; remove to wire racks to cool completely.

Makes about 2½ dozen cookies

EVERYDAY DESSERTS

Milk Chocolate Oatmeal Cookies

1¼ cups all-purpose flour

½ teaspoon baking powder

½ teaspoon baking soda

½ teaspoon ground cinnamon

¼ teaspoon salt

¾ cup (1½ sticks) butter or margarine, softened

¾ cup packed brown sugar

⅓ cup granulated sugar

1½ teaspoons vanilla extract

1 large egg

2 tablespoons milk

1¾ cups (11.5-ounce package) NESTLÉ® TOLL HOUSE® Milk Chocolate Morsels

1 cup quick or old-fashioned oats

½ cup raisins (optional)

PREHEAT oven to 375°F.

COMBINE flour, baking powder, baking soda, cinnamon and salt in small bowl. Beat butter, brown sugar, granulated sugar and vanilla extract in large mixer bowl until creamy. Beat in egg. Gradually beat in flour mixture and milk. Stir in morsels, oats and raisins. Drop by rounded tablespoonful onto ungreased baking sheets.

BAKE for 10 to 14 minutes or until edges are crisp but centers are still soft. Cool on baking sheets for 2 minutes; remove to wire racks to cool completely.

Makes about 3 dozen cookies

EVERYDAY DESSERTS

Chocolate Crumb Bars

1 cup (2 sticks) butter or margarine, softened

1¾ cups all-purpose flour

½ cup granulated sugar

¼ teaspoon salt

2 cups (12-ounce package) NESTLÉ® TOLL HOUSE® Semi-Sweet Chocolate Morsels, *divided*

1 can (14 ounces) NESTLÉ® CARNATION® Sweetened Condensed Milk

1 teaspoon vanilla extract

1 cup chopped walnuts (optional)

PREHEAT oven to 350°F. Grease 13×9-inch baking pan.

BEAT butter in large mixer bowl until creamy. Beat in flour, sugar and salt until crumbly. With floured fingers, press 2 *cups* crumb mixture onto bottom of prepared baking pan; reserve *remaining* mixture.

BAKE for 10 to 12 minutes or until edges are golden brown.

COMBINE *1 cup* morsels and sweetened condensed milk in small, *heavy-duty* saucepan. Warm over low heat, stirring until smooth. Stir in vanilla extract. Spread over hot crust.

STIR nuts and *remaining 1 cup* morsels into *reserved* crumb mixture; sprinkle over chocolate filling. Bake for 25 to 30 minutes or until center is set. Cool in pan on wire rack.

Makes 2½ dozen bars

EVERYDAY DESSERTS

Razz-Ma-Tazz Bars

½ cup (1 stick) butter or margarine

2 cups (12-ounce package) **NESTLÉ® TOLL HOUSE® Premier White Morsels,** *divided*

2 large eggs

½ cup granulated sugar

1 cup all-purpose flour

½ teaspoon salt

½ teaspoon almond extract

½ cup seedless raspberry jam

¼ cup toasted sliced almonds

PREHEAT oven to 325°F. Grease and sugar 9-inch-square baking pan.

MELT butter in medium, microwave-safe bowl on HIGH (100%) power for 1 minute; stir. Add *1 cup* morsels; let stand. Do not stir.

BEAT eggs in large mixer bowl until foamy. Add sugar; beat until light lemon colored, about 5 minutes. Stir in morsel-butter mixture. Add flour, salt and almond extract; mix at low speed until combined. Spread ⅔ of batter into prepared pan.

BAKE for 15 to 17 minutes or until light golden brown around edges. Remove from oven to wire rack.

HEAT jam in small, microwave-safe bowl on HIGH (100%) power for 30 seconds; stir. Spread jam over warm crust. Stir *remaining 1 cup* morsels into *remaining* batter. Drop spoonfuls of batter over jam. Sprinkle with almonds.

BAKE for 25 to 30 minutes or until edges are browned. Cool completely in pan on wire rack. Cut into bars.

Makes 16 bars

Tip: *To sugar a baking pan, simply sprinkle it with a tablespoon of sugar after greasing.*

EVERYDAY DESSERTS

Super-Easy Rocky Road Fudge

2 cups (12-ounce package) NESTLÉ® TOLL HOUSE® Semi-Sweet Chocolate Morsels

1 can (14 ounces) NESTLÉ® CARNATION® Sweetened Condensed Milk

1 teaspoon vanilla extract

3 cups miniature marshmallows

1½ cups coarsely chopped walnuts

LINE 13×9-inch baking pan with foil; grease lightly.

MICROWAVE morsels and sweetened condensed milk in large, uncovered, microwave-safe bowl on HIGH (100%) power for 1 minute; STIR. Morsels may retain some of their original shape. If necessary, microwave at additional 10- to 15-second intervals, stirring until morsels are melted. Stir in vanilla extract. Fold in marshmallows and nuts.

PRESS mixture into prepared baking pan. Refrigerate until ready to serve. Lift from pan; remove foil. Cut into pieces.

Makes 48 pieces

EVERYDAY DESSERTS

Chewy Chocolate Brownies

1 **cup all-purpose flour**

¼ **teaspoon baking soda**

¼ **teaspoon salt**

¾ **cup granulated sugar**

½ **cup (1 stick) butter or margarine**

2 **tablespoons water**

2 **bars (8 ounces) NESTLÉ®
    TOLL HOUSE® Semi-Sweet
    Chocolate Baking Bar, broken
    into pieces**

2 **large eggs**

2 **teaspoons vanilla extract**

½ **cup chopped nuts (optional)**

PREHEAT oven to 350°F. Grease 13×9-inch baking pan.

COMBINE flour, baking soda and salt in small bowl. Microwave sugar, butter and water in large, microwave-safe bowl on HIGH (100%) power for 3 minutes until mixture boils, stirring once. Add baking bars; stir until melted. Add eggs, one at a time, stirring well after each addition. Stir in vanilla extract. Add flour, baking soda and salt; stir well. Stir in nuts. Pour into prepared baking pan.

BAKE for 16 to 20 minutes until wooden pick inserted in center comes out slightly sticky. Cool completely in pan on wire rack. Cut into bars.

Makes 2 dozen brownies

Saucepan Method: *HEAT sugar, butter and water in medium saucepan just to a boil, stirring constantly. Remove from heat. Add baking bars; stir until melted. Proceed as above.*

EVERYDAY DESSERTS

Old-Fashioned Lemon Bread

1½ **cups all-purpose flour**

1 **cup granulated sugar**

1 **teaspoon baking powder**

½ **teaspoon salt**

2 **large eggs**

⅔ **cup (5 fluid-ounce can) NESTLÉ® CARNATION® Evaporated Milk**

⅓ **cup olive or vegetable oil**

1½ **teaspoons grated lemon peel (about 1 lemon-reserve lemon for later use)**

Lemon Syrup (recipe follows)

PREHEAT oven to 350°F. Grease and flour 8×4-inch baking pan.

COMBINE flour, sugar, baking powder and salt in large bowl. Beat eggs, evaporated milk, oil and lemon peel together in medium bowl. Pour egg mixture into flour mixture. Stir until just combined. Pour into prepared pan.

BAKE for 55 to 60 minutes or until wooden skewer inserted in center comes out clean. Using the skewer, poke numerous holes in the hot bread, piercing all the way to the bottom. Slowly drizzle the hot Lemon Syrup over the bread (syrup will soak into the bread). Cool on wire rack for 15 minutes; run knife around edge of bread. Remove bread to wire rack to cool completely.

Makes 1 loaf (10 servings)

Lemon Syrup

COMBINE ⅓ cup granulated sugar and ¼ cup lemon juice (1 lemon) in small, heavy-duty saucepan. Cook over medium-low heat, stirring constantly, for about 5 minutes or until sugar is dissolved and a light syrup is formed.

EVERYDAY DESSERTS

Jumbo Dark Chocolate Cookies

1⅔ cups (10-ounce package) NESTLÉ® TOLL HOUSE® Dark Chocolate Morsels, divided

1 cup all-purpose flour

¼ cup NESTLÉ® TOLL HOUSE® Baking Cocoa

1 teaspoon baking soda

½ teaspoon salt

½ cup (1 stick) butter, softened

½ cup packed light brown sugar

¼ cup granulated sugar

1 large egg

1 teaspoon vanilla extract

PREHEAT oven to 325°F. Line baking sheets with parchment paper or lightly grease.

MELT ⅔ *cup* morsels in microwave-safe bowl on MEDIUM-HIGH (70%) power for 30 seconds. STIR. Morsels may retain some of their original shape. If necessary, microwave at additional 10- to 15-second intervals, stirring just until morsels are melted. Set aside.

SIFT flour, cocoa, baking soda and salt into medium bowl. Beat butter, brown sugar and granulated sugar in large mixer bowl until creamy. Add melted chocolate and mix well. Add egg and vanilla extract, mixing until well blended, about 1 minute. Add flour mixture, mixing just until blended. Stir in *remaining 1 cup* morsels. Drop dough by level ¼-cup measure 3 inches apart onto prepared baking sheets.

BAKE for 16 to 18 minutes or until wooden pick inserted in center comes out with moist crumbs and the tops have a cracked appearance. Cool on baking sheets for 5 minutes. Remove to wire rack to cool completely.

Make 1 dozen cookies

EVERYDAY DESSERTS

Peanut Butter Fudge

1½ **cups granulated sugar**

⅔ **cup (5 fluid-ounce can) NESTLÉ® CARNATION® Evaporated Milk**

2 **tablespoons butter or margarine**

¼ **teaspoon salt**

2 **cups miniature marshmallows**

1½ **cups (9 ounces) NESTLÉ® TOLL HOUSE® Semi-Sweet Chocolate Morsels**

1 **cup chunky or regular peanut butter**

1 **teaspoon vanilla extract**

½ **cup chopped peanuts (optional)**

COMBINE sugar, evaporated milk, butter and salt in a medium, *heavy-duty* saucepan. Bring to a *full rolling boil* over medium heat, stirring constantly. Boil, stirring constantly, for 4 to 5 minutes. Remove from heat.

STIR in marshmallows, morsels, peanut butter and vanilla extract. Stir vigorously for 1 minute or until marshmallows are melted. Pour into foil-lined 8-inch-square baking pan; cool for 1 minute. Top with peanuts, pressing in slightly. Refrigerate for 2 hours or until firm. Lift from pan; remove foil. Cut into 48 pieces.

Makes 24 servings (2 pieces each)

EVERYDAY DESSERTS

Chocolate Cherry Merlot Brownies

1¼ **cups (6-ounce package) dried sweet cherries, chopped***

½ **cup Merlot wine (optional)**

2 **bars (8 ounces) NESTLÉ® TOLL HOUSE® Dark Chocolate Baking Bar, broken into small pieces**

1⅓ **cups all-purpose flour**

½ **teaspoon salt**

1 **cup granulated sugar**

⅓ **cup butter, softened**

2 **large eggs**

1 **teaspoon vanilla extract**

*Sweetened dried cranberries can be substituted for the dried cherries.

PREHEAT oven to 350°F. Grease 9-inch square baking pan.

MICROWAVE dried cherries and wine in small, uncovered, microwave-safe bowl on HIGH (100%) power for 1 minute. Set aside for 15 minutes, stirring occasionally. Drain cherries; discard wine.

MICROWAVE small chocolate pieces in small, uncovered, microwave-safe bowl on MEDIUM-HIGH (70%) power for 1 minute; STIR. If pieces retain some of their original shape, microwave at additional 10- to 15-second intervals, stirring just until melted. Cool to room temperature.

COMBINE flour and salt in small bowl. Beat sugar and butter in medium mixer bowl until well mixed. Add eggs and beat until light and fluffy. Beat in melted chocolate and vanilla extract. Stir in flour mixture until blended. Stir in drained cherries. Spread into prepared pan.

BAKE for 33 to 37 minutes or until wooden pick inserted in center comes out slightly sticky. Cool completely in pan on wire rack. Cut into bars.

Makes 16 brownies

EVERYDAY DESSERTS

S'more Brownies

Nonstick cooking spray

9 **broken in half (18 pieces) whole graham crackers,** *divided*

1 **package (18.3 ounces) traditional 13×9-inch chewy fudge brownie mix**

¼ **cup water**

⅔ **cup vegetable oil**

2 **large eggs**

2 **cups (12-ounce package) NESTLÉ® TOLL HOUSE® Semi-Sweet Chocolate Morsels,** *divided*

2 **cups miniature marshmallows**

PREHEAT oven to 350°F.

LINE 13×9-inch metal baking pan with foil leaving an overhang on two sides. Spray foil with nonstick cooking spray.

PLACE 15 graham cracker halves into bottom of pan, overlapping slightly. Break remaining graham cracker halves into ½-inch pieces; set aside.

COMBINE brownie mix, water, oil and eggs in medium bowl until blended. Stir in *1 cup* morsels. Spread over graham crackers in pan.

BAKE for 25 to 30 minutes or until wooden pick inserted into center comes out still slightly sticky; remove from oven.

PREHEAT broiler.

SPRINKLE *remaining* graham cracker pieces and marshmallows over warm brownies. Broil for 30 to 45 seconds or until marshmallows are light brown. Watch carefully as browning occurs very fast! A handheld kitchen butane torch can be used as well. Remove from oven to wire rack. Sprinkle immediately with *remaining 1 cup* morsels.

COOL for at least 1 hour at room temperature. Lift out by foil edges to cutting board. Carefully remove foil. Cut into bars with wet knife. Store in tightly covered container.

Makes 30 servings

EVERYDAY DESSERTS

Flourless Chocolate Brownies

2 cups (12-ounce package) NESTLÉ® TOLL HOUSE® Semi-Sweet Chocolate Morsels, *divided*

¾ cup (1½ sticks) butter, cut into pieces

2 tablespoons water

¼ cup NESTLÉ® TOLL HOUSE® Baking Cocoa

4 large eggs

⅓ cup granulated sugar

1 teaspoon vanilla extract

1 cup pecans, finely ground (optional)

¼ cup heavy whipping cream

PREHEAT oven to 300°F. Line 9-inch-square baking pan with foil. Grease bottom and sides.

HEAT *1½ cups* morsels, butter and water in medium, *heavy-duty* saucepan over low heat, stirring constantly, until morsels and butter are melted and mixture is smooth. Stir in cocoa until smooth. Remove from heat.

BEAT eggs and sugar in medium mixer bowl until thick, about 4 minutes. Stir in vanilla extract. Fold ⅓ of egg mixture into chocolate mixture. Fold in remaining egg mixture, one half at a time, until thoroughly incorporated. Fold in pecans. Pour into prepared pan.

BAKE for 35 to 40 minutes or until risen in center and edges start to get firm and shiny (center may still move and appear underbaked). Cool completely in pan on wire rack (center may sink slightly). Cover; refrigerate for 4 hours or overnight.

PLACE cream in small, uncovered, microwave-safe dish. Microwave on HIGH (100%) power for 25 to 30 seconds. Add *remaining ½ cup* morsels. Let stand for 2 to 3 minutes; stir until chocolate is melted.

SPREAD ganache over chilled brownie. Refrigerate for 30 minutes. Using two opposite sides of foil, carefully lift the entire brownie out of the pan and place on cutting board. Carefully peel away foil from brownie. Cut into bars. Store in tightly covered container in refrigerator.

Makes 16 brownies

EVERYDAY DESSERTS

Sweet & Salty Chewy Pecan Bars

1 **package (16.5 ounces) NESTLÉ® TOLL HOUSE® Refrigerated Chocolate Chip Cookie Bar Dough,** *divided*

1 **tablespoon butter, melted**

¾ **cup chopped pecans**

1 **tablespoon granulated sugar**

¼ **teaspoon salt**

⅓ **cup NESTLÉ® TOLL HOUSE® Semi-Sweet Chocolate Morsels**

2 **tablespoons caramel sauce**

PREHEAT oven to 350°F. Grease 8-inch-square baking pan.

PRESS ¾ *package (18 squares)* cookie dough into prepared baking pan and refrigerate remaining cookie dough.

BAKE for 10 minutes; remove from oven.

COMBINE butter, sugar and salt in small bowl until coated. Sprinkle over dough. Top with teaspoonfuls of *remaining* cookie dough; pressing down gently. Sprinkle with morsels.

BAKE for an additional 22 to 24 minutes or until edges are browned and set. Cool 30 minutes in pan on wire rack.

DRIZZLE caramel sauce over bar. Cool completely in pan on wire rack. Cut into bars.

Makes 16 servings

Tip: *For chewier caramel top, microwave 6 unwrapped caramel candies with 1 teaspoon milk for 20 to 30 seconds or until melted; stir until smooth. Drizzle sauce over bar.*

Tip: *Toasted pecans may also be used, if desired.*

Spicy Chocolate Cake

CAKE:

- 1 cup (6 ounces) NESTLÉ® TOLL HOUSE® Semi-Sweet Chocolate Morsels
- 1¼ cups granulated sugar
- ¾ cup (1½ sticks) butter or margarine, softened
- 1 teaspoon vanilla extract
- 3 large eggs
- 2 cups all-purpose flour
- 1 tablespoon ground cinnamon
- 1 teaspoon baking soda
- ½ teaspoon salt
- 1 cup milk
- 1 to 2 tablespoons diced jalapeños (optional)

FROSTING:

- 3 to 3¼ cups sifted powdered sugar
- ⅓ cup milk
- ¼ cup (½ stick) butter or margarine, softened
- 2 packets (1 ounce *each*) NESTLÉ® TOLL HOUSE® CHOCO BAKE® Unsweetened Chocolate Flavor
- 2 teaspoons vanilla extract
- ¼ teaspoon salt

FOR CAKE:

PREHEAT oven to 350°F. Grease two 9-inch-round cake pans or one 13×9-inch baking pan.

MICROWAVE morsels in medium, uncovered, microwave-safe bowl on HIGH (100%) power for 1 minute. STIR. Morsels may retain some of their original shape. If necessary, microwave at additional 10- to 15-second intervals, stirring until morsels are melted. Let cool to room temperature.

BEAT granulated sugar, butter and vanilla extract in large mixer bowl until creamy. Add eggs; beat for 1 minute. Beat in melted chocolate. Combine flour, cinnamon, baking soda and salt in medium bowl; beat into chocolate mixture alternately with milk. Stir in jalapeños. Pour into prepared pan(s).

BAKE for 30 to 35 minutes or until wooden pick inserted in center comes out clean. Cool in pan(s) for 20 minutes; invert onto wire rack(s) to cool completely.

FOR FROSTING:

BEAT powdered sugar, milk, butter, Choco Bake, vanilla extract and salt in small mixer bowl until mixture is smooth and creamy. Frost cake.

Makes 10 to 12 servings

EVERYDAY DESSERTS

Original NESTLÉ® TOLL HOUSE® Chocolate Chip Cookies

2¼ cups all-purpose flour

1 teaspoon baking soda

1 teaspoon salt

1 cup (2 sticks) butter, softened

¾ cup granulated sugar

¾ cup packed brown sugar

1 teaspoon vanilla extract

2 large eggs

2 cups (12-ounce package) NESTLÉ® TOLL HOUSE® Semi-Sweet Chocolate Morsels

1 cup chopped nuts

PREHEAT oven to 375°F.

COMBINE flour, baking soda and salt in small bowl. Beat butter, granulated sugar, brown sugar and vanilla extract in large mixer bowl until creamy. Add eggs, one at a time, beating well after each addition. Gradually beat in flour mixture. Stir in morsels and nuts. Drop by rounded tablespoonful onto ungreased baking sheets.

BAKE for 9 to 11 minutes or until golden brown. Cool on baking sheets for 2 minutes; remove to wire racks to cool completely.

Makes about 5 dozen cookies

Pan Cookie Variation: *GREASE 15×10-inch jelly-roll pan. Prepare dough as above. Spread in prepared pan. Bake for 20 to 25 minutes or until golden brown. Cool in pan on wire rack. Makes 4 dozen bars.*

Autumn

Baked Ziti with Pumpkin & Sausage

Discover a delicious variety of dinnertime solutions for hectic weeknight meals. You'll be able to feed the family on the busiest of nights.

Nonstick cooking spray

4 **cups (12 ounces) dry regular or whole-wheat ziti**

1 **can (15 ounces) LIBBY'S® 100% Pure Pumpkin**

2 **tablespoons all-purpose flour**

1 **teaspoon garlic powder**

½ **teaspoon salt**

¼ **teaspoon ground nutmeg**

Pinch cayenne pepper

1 **can (12 fluid ounces) NESTLÉ® CARNATION® Evaporated Fat Free Milk**

4 **links (12 ounces) fully-cooked Italian-seasoned chicken sausage, cut into ¼-inch slices**

1 **package (6 ounces) or about 4 cups pre-washed baby spinach**

1 **cup (4 ounces) shredded part-skim or 2% milk reduced-fat mozzarella cheese**

1 **cup (1.5 ounces) shredded Parmesan cheese**

PREHEAT oven to 425° F. Spray 4-quart baking dish with nonstick cooking spray.

PREPARE pasta according to package directions. *Reserve ½ cup pasta cooking water and set aside for later use.* Drain pasta; return to cooking pot.

MEANWHILE, COMBINE pumpkin, flour, garlic powder, salt, nutmeg and cayenne pepper in medium skillet over medium heat. Slowly add evaporated milk, stirring until smooth. Cook, stirring occasionally, for 2 to 3 minutes or until mixture begins to thicken slightly. Pour over pasta in pot. Add sausage and *reserved* pasta cooking water; stir well.

SPREAD *half* of the pasta mixture into prepared baking dish. Top with spinach. Cover with *remaining* pasta mixture. Lightly spray piece of foil with nonstick cooking spray. Cover ziti with foil, greased-side-down.

BAKE for 20 minutes or until heated through. Combine mozzarella and Parmesan cheeses in small bowl. Remove foil; sprinkle with cheese mixture. Bake, uncovered, for an additional 5 minutes or until cheese is melted.

Makes 12 servings

Mexican Meatloaf Muffins

- **3 pounds lean ground beef**
- **1 can (12 fluid ounces) NESTLÉ® CARNATION® Evaporated Milk**
- **2 large eggs**
- **½ cup ketchup**
- **2 cups quick oats**
- **2 packets (1.25 ounces *each*) taco seasoning mix**
- **1 teaspoon ground black pepper**
- **1 tablespoon dried parsley (optional)**
- **Shredded lettuce, shredded cheddar, chopped tomatoes, taco sauce (optional)**

PREHEAT oven to 350°F.

COMBINE ground beef, evaporated milk, eggs, ketchup, quick oats, taco seasoning, black pepper and parsley in large bowl until just mixed. Divide meat mixture into 20 ungreased muffin cups; mound tops slightly.

BAKE for 25 to 30 minutes or until no longer pink in center. Cool for 5 minutes before removing from muffin cups.

SERVE *half* the meatloaf muffins over lettuce, cheese and tomatoes, if desired.

Makes 20 muffins

Tip: *Freeze half the meatloaf muffins for another meal. Wrap each in freezer wrap; freeze. To reheat, microwave unwrap meatloaf muffin on HIGH (100%) power for 2 minutes. If thawed, microwave for 1 minute.*

Tip: *Meatloaf mixture can be divided into two ungreased 8×4-inch loaf pans instead of muffin cups. Bake 55 to 60 minutes or until no longer pink in center.*

Chicken & Rice Casserole

- **2 cups cooked rice**
- **2 cups (8 ounces) shredded Monterey Jack cheese**
- **1½ cups cooked, chopped chicken breast meat**
- **1 can (12 fluid ounces) NESTLÉ® CARNATION® Evaporated Milk**
- **½ cup finely chopped red onion**
- **2 large eggs, lightly beaten**
- **¼ cup finely chopped cilantro**
- **2 tablespoons butter or margarine, melted**
- **1 tablespoon diced jalapeños**

PREHEAT oven to 350°F. Lightly grease 2-quart casserole dish.

COMBINE rice, cheese, chicken, evaporated milk, onion, eggs, cilantro, butter and jalapeños in prepared casserole dish; stir well.

BAKE for 45 to 50 minutes or until knife inserted in center comes out clean. Season with salt.

Makes 6 servings

To Make Ahead and Freeze: *PREPARE as above; do not bake. Cover; freeze for up to 2 months. Thaw overnight in refrigerator. Uncover. Preheat oven to 350ºF. Bake for 60 to 70 minutes or until knife inserted in center comes out clean. Season with salt.*

EASY WEEKNIGHT MEALS

Crispy Oat Crusted Fish Fillets with CARNATION® Tartar Sauce

TARTAR SAUCE:

- 1 **package (8 ounces) ⅓ less fat cream cheese (Neufchâtel), at room temperature**
- 1 **can (12 fluid ounces) NESTLÉ® CARNATION® Evaporated Lowfat 2% Milk, divided**
- ½ **cup sweet pickle relish**
- 2 **tablespoons white vinegar**
- ¼ **teaspoon salt**
- ¼ **teaspoon ground black pepper**

CRUSTED FISH:

- 2 **large egg whites, beaten**
- 1½ **cups quick-cooking oats**
- 1½ **teaspoons garlic powder**
- 1 **teaspoon paprika**
- 1½ **pounds fresh or frozen (thawed) white fish fillets (such as tilapia)**
- 2 **to 3 tablespoons olive oil**

   Lemon wedges (optional)

FOR TARTAR SAUCE:

BEAT cream cheese and ⅔ cup evaporated milk in small mixer bowl until creamy. (Save remaining evaporated milk for the fish). Stir in relish, vinegar, salt and pepper. Store refrigerated in covered container for up to 4 days. Makes about 2½ cups.

FOR CRUSTED FISH:

COMBINE remaining evaporated milk and egg whites in shallow dish. Combine oats, garlic powder and paprika in medium bowl. Dip fish fillets into evaporated milk mixture, coating both sides and then into oat mixture. Press oats gently onto both sides of fish to form crust. Place coated fillets on baking sheet. Discard evaporated milk and oat mixtures after dipping.

HEAT oil in large, nonstick skillet over medium-high heat. Add fillets; cook for 4 to 5 minutes on each side or until fish flakes easily when tested with a fork. (Thicker fillets may take longer to cook.) Season with salt and pepper to taste. Serve with Carnation Tartar Sauce and lemon wedges.

Makes 6 servings

Variation: *For Tartar Sauce with a kick, add hot pepper sauce to taste.*

Tip: *If your quick-cooking oats are large in size, they can be processed to a smaller size in a blender or food processor.*

EASY WEEKNIGHT MEALS

Turkey Veggie Tetrazzini

- **8** ounces dry whole wheat spaghetti
- **1** package (16 ounces) frozen Italian-style vegetable blend (broccoli, red peppers, mushrooms and onions)
- **1** tablespoon olive oil
- **¼** cup all-purpose flour
- **½** teaspoon garlic powder
- **¼** teaspoon salt
- **¼** teaspoon ground black pepper
- **1** can (14.5 fluid ounces) reduced sodium chicken broth
- **1** can (12 fluid ounces) NESTLÉ® CARNATION® Evaporated Lowfat 2% Milk
- **¾** cup (2.25 ounces) shredded Parmesan cheese, *divided*
- **2** cups cooked, chopped turkey breast meat

PREHEAT oven to 350°F. Lightly grease 13×9-inch baking dish.

PREPARE pasta according to package directions, adding frozen vegetables to boiling pasta water for last minute of cooking time; drain. Return pasta and vegetables to cooking pot.

MEANWHILE, HEAT oil in medium saucepan over medium heat. Stir in flour, garlic powder, salt and pepper; cook, stirring constantly, for 1 minute. Remove from heat; gradually stir in broth. Return to heat; bring to boil over medium heat, stirring constantly. Stir in evaporated milk and ½ cup cheese; cook over low heat until cheese melts. Remove from heat. Stir in turkey.

POUR cheese sauce over pasta and vegetables; mix lightly. Pour into prepared baking dish. Sprinkle with *remaining ¼ cup* cheese.

BAKE for 20 to 25 minutes or until lightly browned. Serve immediately.

Makes 12 servings

Creamy Smashed Red Potatoes with Cheese

3 pounds red new potatoes, unpeeled, cut into quarters

1 cup or more NESTLÉ® CARNATION® Evaporated Lowfat 2% Milk

2 tablespoons butter, cut into pieces

¾ cup grated Parmesan cheese blend

   Salt and ground black pepper to taste

PLACE potatoes in large saucepan. Cover with water; bring to a boil. Cook over medium-high heat for 15 to 20 minutes or until potatoes are tender; drain.

RETURN potatoes to saucepan. Beat with hand-held mixer for a few seconds to break up. Add evaporated milk and butter; beat until milk and butter are mixed in (some lumps will still be present). Add additional evaporated milk if a smoother consistency is desired. Stir in cheese. Season with salt and pepper to taste.

Makes 15 (½-cup) servings

Crispy Baked Dijon Chicken

   Nonstick cooking spray

¼ cup NESTLÉ® CARNATION® Evaporated Fat Free Milk

3 to 4 tablespoons Dijon mustard

¼ cup plain, dry bread crumbs

¼ cup (0.75 ounce) BUITONI® Refrigerated Freshly Shredded Parmesan Cheese

4 (about 1¼ pounds *total*) boneless, skinless chicken breast halves

PREHEAT oven to 475°F. Spray 13×9-inch baking dish with nonstick cooking spray.

COMBINE evaporated milk and mustard in shallow bowl. Combine bread crumbs and cheese in separate shallow bowl. Dip chicken into milk mixture, coating both sides, then into bread crumb mixture. Place in prepared dish.

BAKE for 15 to 20 minutes or until chicken is golden brown and no longer pink in center.

Makes 4 servings

Stovetop Beef & Penne Casserole

- **2 cups (8 ounces) dry penne pasta (or small pasta of your choice)**
- **2 pounds lean ground beef**
- **1 medium onion, chopped**
- **2 cans (12 fluid ounces *each*) NESTLÉ® CARNATION® Evaporated Milk**
- **1 can (15 ounces) LIBBY'S® 100% Pure Pumpkin**
- **1 can (15 ounces) tomato sauce**
- **1 tablespoon packed brown sugar**
- **1 tablespoon paprika**
- **1 tablespoon Worcestershire sauce**
- **2 teaspoons salt**
- **½ teaspoon garlic powder**
- **½ teaspoon ground black pepper**
- **2 cups frozen peas, thawed**

COOK pasta in large saucepan for 1 to 2 minutes less than package directions (pasta should be slightly firm in texture); drain.

COOK beef and onion in large saucepan over medium-high heat until beef is no longer pink; drain. Reduce heat to medium. Stir in evaporated milk, pumpkin, tomato sauce, sugar, paprika, Worcestershire sauce, salt, garlic powder and black pepper. Cook, stirring occasionally, until mixture begins to simmer. Add pasta and peas; stir until heated.

Makes 12 servings (two 6-serving meals)

Tip: *Freeze half the casserole for another meal. Thaw in refrigerator and reheat in microwave or on stovetop.*

Tip: *Using pumpkin and evaporated milk not only adds depth of flavor, but also sneaks in extra nutrition to the casserole.*

"Thank You Very Much" Pumpkin Peanut Butter Sandwich

- **½ cup LIBBY'S® 100% Pure Pumpkin**
- **½ cup creamy or crunchy peanut butter**
- **4 slices whole wheat or white bread**
- **1 medium banana, cut into ¼-inch slices**

COMBINE pumpkin and peanut butter in small bowl until well blended. Makes 1 cup.

SPREAD *1 tablespoon* pumpkin peanut butter spread on *each* slice. Top *2 slices* with banana slices. Top *each* with second slice of bread to make sandwiches.

REFRIGERATE leftover pumpkin-peanut butter spread in tightly covered container for up to 5 days.

Makes 2 sandwiches

Tip: *Sandwiches can also be made with pita bread, English muffins or tortillas. The pumpkin-peanut butter spread is also good on crackers or with celery sticks.*

EASY WEEKNIGHT MEALS

Take-Two Turkey Tetrazzini

8 ounce dry spaghetti

1 package (16 ounces) frozen vegetable blend (peas, carrots, corn, beans)

1 tablespoon olive oil

¼ cup all-purpose flour

½ teaspoon garlic powder

½ teaspoon salt

½ teaspoon ground black pepper

1 can (14.5 fluid ounces) chicken broth

1 can (12 fluid ounces) NESTLÉ® CARNATION® Evaporated Milk

¾ cup (2¼ ounces) shredded Parmesan cheese, *divided*

2 cups (about 10 ounces) cooked turkey, cut into ½-inch pieces

PREHEAT oven to 350°F. Lightly grease 13×9-inch baking dish.

PREPARE pasta according to package directions, adding frozen vegetables to boiling pasta water for last minute of cooking time; drain. Return pasta and vegetables to cooking pot.

MEANWHILE, HEAT oil in medium saucepan over medium heat. Stir in flour, garlic powder, salt and pepper; cook, stirring constantly, for 1 minute. Remove from heat; gradually stir in broth. Return to heat; bring to boil over medium heat, stirring constantly. Stir in evaporated milk and ½ *cup* cheese; cook over low heat until cheese melts. Remove from heat. Stir in turkey.

POUR cheese sauce over pasta and vegetables; mix lightly. Pour into prepared baking dish. Sprinkle with *remaining ¼ cup* cheese.

BAKE for 20 to 25 minutes or until lightly browned. Serve immediately.

Makes 12 servings

EASY WEEKNIGHT MEALS

Italian Pumpkin Strata

1 tablespoon vegetable oil

1 pound sweet Italian sausage, casings removed

1 small onion, chopped

½ cup chopped green bell pepper

½ cup chopped red bell pepper

2 cloves garlic, finely chopped

12 cups (about 1 pound loaf) 1½-inch cubes Italian or French bread

2 cups (8 ounces) shredded mozzarella cheese

2 cans (12 fluid ounces *each*) NESTLÉ® CARNATION® Evaporated Milk

1 can (15 ounces) LIBBY'S® 100% Pure Pumpkin

4 large eggs

1 teaspoon salt

½ teaspoon ground black pepper

½ teaspoon dried oregano, crushed

½ teaspoon dried basil, crushed

½ teaspoon dried marjoram, crushed

PREHEAT oven to 350°F. Grease 13×9-inch baking pan.

HEAT oil in large skillet over medium-high heat. Add sausage, onion, bell peppers and garlic. Cook, stirring to break up sausage, for 7 to 10 minutes or until sausage is no longer pink; drain.

COMBINE bread cubes, cheese and sausage mixture in a large bowl. Beat evaporated milk, pumpkin, eggs, salt, pepper, oregano, basil and marjoram in medium bowl. Pour over bread mixture, stirring gently to moisten bread. Pour into prepared baking pan.

BAKE for 30 to 35 minutes or until set. Serve warm.

Makes 12 servings

EASY WEEKNIGHT MEALS

Crowd Pleasin' Cheesy Sausage Ziti

1 **box (16 ounces) dry ziti, cooked and drained**

2 **tablespoons olive oil**

1 **large yellow onion, chopped**

2 **tablespoons all-purpose flour**

3 **cans (12 fluid ounces *each*) NESTLÉ® CARNATION® Evaporated Milk**

1½ **teaspoons garlic powder**

1 **teaspoon salt**

1 **teaspoon ground black pepper**

4 **cups (two 8-ounce packages) shredded cheddar cheese, *divided***

4 **links (12 ounces) fully-cooked chicken sausage, cut lengthwise into quarters and into ¼-inch slices**

½ **cup crumbled cheese snack crackers**

PREHEAT oven to 375°F. Grease 13×9-inch baking dish.

HEAT oil in large saucepan over medium heat. Add onions; cook until softened. Whisk in flour; cook, stirring constantly, until mixture turns light brown, about 3 minutes. Gradually whisk in evaporated milk, garlic powder, salt and pepper; cook, stirring constantly, until sauce is thickened, about 5 minutes. Add 3½ *cups* cheese; stir until melted. Add pasta and sausage; stir until thoroughly coated. Pour mixture into prepared baking dish. Sprinkle with crackers and *remaining ½ cup* cheese.

BAKE for 20 to 25 minutes or until bubbling around edges and golden brown.

Makes 18 servings

Creamy Chicken and Rice Bake

1   can (12 fluid ounces) NESTLÉ® CARNATION® Evaporated Milk

1   package (3 ounces) cream cheese, softened

1   can (10¾ ounces) cream of chicken soup

½   cup water

½   teaspoon garlic powder

⅛   teaspoon ground black pepper

1   bag (16 ounces) frozen broccoli, cauliflower and carrot mix, thawed

2   cups cubed, precooked chicken

1½   cups uncooked instant white rice

½   cup (2 ounces) shredded cheddar cheese

PREHEAT oven to 350°F. Grease 13×9-inch baking dish.

COMBINE evaporated milk and cream cheese in baking dish with wire whisk until smooth. Add soup, water, garlic powder and black pepper; mix well. Add vegetables, chicken and rice. Cover tightly with foil.

BAKE for 35 minutes. Uncover; top with cheese. Bake for an additional 10 to 15 minutes or until cheese is melted and mixture is bubbly. Let stand 5 minutes before serving.

Makes 8 to 10 servings

EASY WEEKNIGHT MEALS

Simple Risotto with Peas & Parmesan

1 **tablespoon olive oil**

1 **small onion, finely chopped**

2 **cloves garlic, finely chopped**

1 **cup uncooked arborio rice**

2 **cups chicken broth or stock**

1 **cup NESTLÉ® CARNATION® Evaporated Lowfat 2% Milk**

½ **cup frozen peas, thawed**

¼ **to ½ teaspoon lemon zest (optional)**

Salt and ground black pepper to taste

¼ **cup (about 1 ounce) finely shredded Parmesan cheese**

HEAT oil in medium, nonstick saucepan over medium-high heat. Add onion; cook, stirring occasionally, for about 3 minutes or until onion is tender. Stir in garlic and cook until aroma is released (do not brown). Stir in rice; cook, stirring frequently, for 1 minute.

STIR in broth and evaporated milk. Reduce heat to medium. Cook, stirring frequently, for 20 to 25 minutes or until rice is tender but firm to the bite (mixture will be creamy and more stirring will be needed as it becomes thicker). Remove from heat; stir in peas and lemon zest. Season with salt and pepper to taste. Serve immediately with Parmesan cheese.

Makes 9 servings

EASY WEEKNIGHT MEALS

CARNATION® Cornbread

1¼ cups yellow corn meal

¾ cup all-purpose flour

½ cup dry NESTLÉ® CARNATION® Instant Nonfat Dry Milk

¼ cup granulated sugar

1½ teaspoons baking powder

1 teaspoon salt

1 can (8.5 ounces) creamed corn

½ cup vegetable oil

⅓ cup water

1 large egg

PREHEAT oven to 375°F. Grease 8-inch-square baking pan.

COMBINE corn meal, flour, dry milk, sugar, baking powder and salt in large bowl. Add creamed corn, vegetable oil, water and egg; stir just until moistened. Pour into prepared baking pan.

BAKE for 25 to 30 minutes or until wooden pick inserted in center comes out clean. Cool in pan on wire rack for 10 minutes. Serve warm.

Makes 12 servings

EASY WEEKNIGHT MEALS

Spicy Jack Mac & Cheese with Broccoli

- 2 **cups (8 ounces) dry elbow macaroni**
- 2 **cups chopped frozen or fresh broccoli**
- 2 **cups (8 ounces) shredded sharp cheddar cheese**
- 2 **cups (8 ounces) shredded Pepper Jack cheese***
- 1 **can (12 fluid ounces) NESTLÉ® CARNATION® Evaporated Milk**
- ½ **cup grated Parmesan cheese, *divided***
- ½ **teaspoon ground black pepper**
- 2 **tablespoons bread crumbs**

For a less spicy version, substitute 2 cups (8 ounces) shredded Monterey Jack cheese and a few dashes of hot pepper sauce (optional) for Pepper Jack cheese.

PREHEAT oven to 350°F. Lightly butter 2½-quart casserole dish.

COOK macaroni in large saucepan according to package directions, adding broccoli to boiling pasta water for last 3 minutes of cooking time; drain.

COMBINE cooked pasta, broccoli, cheddar cheese, Pepper Jack cheese, evaporated milk, ¼ cup Parmesan cheese and black pepper in large bowl. Pour into prepared casserole dish. Combine remaining Parmesan cheese and bread crumbs; sprinkle over macaroni mixture. Cover tightly with aluminum foil.

BAKE covered for 20 minutes. Remove foil; bake for additional 10 minutes or until lightly browned.

Makes 8 servings

EASY WEEKNIGHT MEALS

Traditional Macaroni & Cheese

1⅔ cups (about 7 ounces) dry small elbow macaroni, cooked and drained

2 tablespoons cornstarch

1 teaspoon salt

½ teaspoon dry mustard

¼ teaspoon ground black pepper

1 can (12 fluid ounces) NESTLÉ® CARNATION® Evaporated Milk

1 cup water

2 tablespoons butter or margarine

2 cups (8 ounces) shredded sharp cheddar cheese, divided

PREHEAT oven to 375°F. Grease 2-quart casserole dish.

COMBINE cornstarch, salt, mustard and pepper in medium saucepan. Stir in evaporated milk, water and butter. Cook over medium-heat, stirring constantly, until mixture comes to a boil. Boil for 1 minute. Remove from heat. Stir in 1½ cups cheese until melted. Add macaroni; mix well. Pour into prepared casserole dish. Top with *remaining ½ cup* cheese.

BAKE for 20 to 25 minutes or until cheese is melted and light brown.

Makes 6 servings

Note: *To transform Macaroni & Cheese from a simple dish to a savory one-dish meal, add 1 cup chopped ham or hot dogs after milk mixture comes to a boil.*

EASY WEEKNIGHT MEALS

Suppertime Sausage Bake

1 pound hot bulk pork sausage, cooked, drained and crumbled

2 cans (12 fluid ounces *each*) NESTLÉ® CARNATION® Evaporated Milk

8 large eggs, beaten

2 cups (8-ounce package) shredded cheddar cheese

½ cup chopped red pepper

2 green onions (green parts only), sliced

½ teaspoon onion powder

¼ teaspoon garlic powder

8 cups ½-inch cubed Italian or French bread (about 9 slices)*

Substitute multi-grain bread for Italian or French bread.

PREHEAT oven to 350°F. Grease 13×9-inch baking dish.

COMBINE milk, eggs, sausage, cheese, red pepper, green onions, onion powder and garlic powder in large bowl. Add bread cubes, stirring gently to moisten bread. Pour mixture into baking dish.

BAKE for 45 minutes or until set. Serve warm.

Makes 10 to 12 servings

Tip: *Substitute pre-cooked, sliced sausage links for bulk pork sausage to save time.*

"Wheely" Easy Mac & Cheesy

2 cups (8 ounces) dry wagon wheel or rotelle pasta

1 cup frozen shelled edamame (shelled soybeans)

1 can (12 fluid ounces) NESTLÉ® CARNATION® Evaporated Milk

2 cups (8-ounce package) shredded Monterey Jack and cheddar cheese blend or other cheese blend

½ teaspoon garlic powder

½ teaspoon ground black pepper

½ cup cherry or grape tomatoes, cut in half

Look for edamame in the frozen food or organic section of your local store.

COOK pasta according to package directions, adding edamame to boiling pasta water for last 2 minutes of cooking time; drain.

MEANWHILE, COMBINE evaporated milk, cheese, garlic powder and black pepper in medium saucepan. Cook over medium low heat, stirring occasionally, until cheese is melted. Remove from heat.

ADD pasta and edamame to cheese sauce; stir until combined. Add tomatoes; stir gently until combined.

Makes 4 servings

Tip: *Frozen peas can be used in place of edamame.*

EASY WEEKNIGHT MEALS

One-Dish Fiesta Casserole

1 **can (12 fluid ounces) NESTLÉ® CARNATION® Evaporated Milk**

1 **can (10¾ ounces) condensed cheddar cheese soup**

½ **cup mild, medium or hot salsa**

¼ **teaspoon ground black pepper**

1 **bag (14 to 16 ounces) frozen Southwest-style vegetable blend: broccoli, corn, black beans and red peppers, thawed**

2 **cups cooked turkey or chicken (about 10 ounces), cut into ½-inch pieces**

1½ **cups uncooked instant white rice**

1 **cup (4 ounces) shredded Mexican-blend cheese**

¼ **cup sour cream**

1 **tablespoon water**

1 **avocado, peeled and sliced (optional)**

PREHEAT oven to 350°F. Grease 13×9-inch baking dish.

COMBINE evaporated milk and condensed soup in baking dish with wire whisk until smooth. Add salsa and black pepper; mix well. Add vegetables, turkey and rice; mix well. Cover dish tightly with foil.

BAKE for 35 minutes. Uncover; top with cheese. Bake for an additional 10 to 15 minutes or until cheese is melted and mixture is bubbly. Let stand for 5 minutes before serving.

COMBINE sour cream with water in small bowl. Drizzle over casserole. Top with avocado slices just prior to serving.

Makes 10 servings

Tip: *To keep avocado slices from browning, squeeze fresh lime juice over slices.*

EASY WEEKNIGHT MEALS

Creamy Rice & Mushroom Bake

2 tablespoons margarine

3 cups (about 8 ounces) mushrooms, sliced

1 small onion, chopped

2 garlic cloves, finely chopped

1 teaspoon Worcestershire sauce

2 packages (3 ounces *each*) ⅓ less fat cream cheese (Neufchâtel), softened

2 large eggs

1 can (12 fluid ounces) NESTLÉ® CARNATION® Evaporated Lowfat 2% Milk

3 teaspoons dried parsley flakes or 3 tablespoons chopped fresh parsley

1½ teaspoons salt

½ teaspoon ground black pepper

3 cups cooked rice

PREHEAT oven to 350°F. Grease 11×7-inch baking dish.

MELT margarine in large skillet over medium heat. Add mushrooms, onion, garlic and Worcestershire sauce; cook, stirring occasionally, for 3 to 4 minutes or until mushrooms are soft. Beat cream cheese and eggs in large mixer bowl until creamy. Mix in evaporated milk, parsley, salt, and pepper. Stir in rice and mushroom mixture. Pour into prepared casserole dish.

BAKE for 35 to 40 minutes or until set and light brown around edges.

Makes 6 servings

Winter

Pumpkin Cheesecake

Holiday entertaining made easy! Choose from an assortment of delectable entrées, flavorful side dishes, and mouthwatering desserts for all your dinner party needs.

CRUST:

1½ cups graham cracker crumbs

⅓ cup butter or margarine, melted

¼ cup granulated sugar

FILLING:

3 packages (8 ounces *each*) cream cheese, softened

1 cup granulated sugar

¼ cup packed light brown sugar

2 large eggs

1 can (15 ounces) LIBBY'S® 100% Pure Pumpkin

⅔ cup (5 fluid-ounce can) NESTLÉ® CARNATION® Evaporated Milk

2 tablespoons cornstarch

1¼ teaspoons ground cinnamon

½ teaspoon ground nutmeg

TOPPING:

1 container (16 ounces) sour cream, at room temperature

⅓ cup granulated sugar

1 teaspoon vanilla extract

PREHEAT oven to 350°F.

FOR CRUST:

COMBINE graham cracker crumbs, butter and granulated sugar in medium bowl. Press onto bottom and 1 inch up side of 9-inch springform pan. Bake for 6 to 8 minutes (do not allow to brown). Cool on wire rack for 10 minutes.

FOR FILLING:

BEAT cream cheese, granulated sugar and brown sugar in large mixer bowl until fluffy. Beat in eggs, pumpkin and evaporated milk. Add cornstarch, cinnamon and nutmeg; beat well. Pour into crust.

BAKE for 55 to 60 minutes or until edge is set but center still moves slightly.

FOR TOPPING:

COMBINE sour cream, granulated sugar and vanilla extract in small bowl; mix well. Spread over surface of warm cheesecake. Bake for 5 minutes. Cool on wire rack. Refrigerate for several hours or overnight. Remove side of springform pan.

Makes 16 servings

CLASSIC HOLIDAY FAVORITES

Butterscotch Pecan Perfection Pie

1   *unbaked* 9-inch (4-cup volume) deep-dish pie shell*

1⅔   cups (11-ounce package) NESTLÉ® TOLL HOUSE® Butterscotch Flavored Morsels, *divided*

¾   cup light corn syrup

3   large eggs, at room temperature

1   tablespoon all-purpose flour

¼   teaspoon salt

1½   cups pecan halves, coarsely chopped

1½   cups whipped cream (optional)

If using frozen pie shell, use deep-dish style. Do not thaw. Bake on baking sheet.

PREHEAT oven to 350°F.

MELT 1⅓ *cups* morsels in medium, uncovered microwave-safe bowl on MEDIUM-HIGH (70%) power for 1 minute; STIR. Morsels may retain some of their original shape. If necessary, microwave at additional 10- to 15-second intervals, stirring just until morsels are melted.

ADD corn syrup, eggs, flour and salt to melted morsels. Beat on medium until smooth. Stir in pecans. Pour pecan mixture into pie shell.

BAKE for 40 to 45 minutes or until knife inserted into center comes out with little bits of filling attached. If browning too quickly, cover with foil. Cool on wire rack for 2 hours. Refrigerate 1 hour or until serving time.

TO GARNISH AND SERVE:

LINE baking sheet with wax paper.

PLACE *remaining* morsels in *heavy-duty* plastic bag. Microwave on MEDIUM-HIGH (70%) power for 30 to 45 seconds; knead. Microwave at 10- to 15-second intervals, kneading until smooth. Cut tiny corner from bag. Drizzle 10 circular designs about 2 inches high and wide onto prepared baking sheet. Refrigerate for 5 to 10 minutes or until firm.

PLACE 10 dollops of whipped cream around edge of pie. Remove drizzle designs from refrigerator. With tip of knife, gently remove designs from wax paper and insert, standing up, into dollops. Serve immediately.

Makes 10 servings

Variation: *You may use ⅓ cup NESTLÉ® TOLL HOUSE® Semi-Sweet Chocolate Morsels melted and made into drizzle designs instead of the Butterscotch Flavored Morsels.*

Tip: *Two shallow (2-cup volume) pie shells can be substituted for the one deep-dish pie shell. Follow directions above and bake for 30 to 35 minutes.*

CLASSIC HOLIDAY FAVORITES

Butterscotch Pumpkin Cake

1⅔ cups (11-ounce package) NESTLÉ® TOLL HOUSE® Butterscotch Flavored Morsels, *divided*

2 cups all-purpose flour

1¾ cups granulated sugar

1 tablespoon baking powder

1½ teaspoons ground cinnamon

1 teaspoon salt

½ teaspoon ground nutmeg

1 cup LIBBY'S® 100% Pure Pumpkin

½ cup vegetable oil

3 large eggs

1 teaspoon vanilla extract

Powdered sugar (optional)

Butterscotch Sauce (recipe follows)

PREHEAT oven to 350°F. Grease 12-cup Bundt pan.

MICROWAVE *1 cup* morsels in small, uncovered, microwave-safe bowl on MEDIUM-HIGH (70%) power for 1 minute. STIR. Morsels may retain some of their original shape. If necessary, microwave at additional 10- to 15-second intervals, stirring just until morsels are melted. Cool to room temperature.

COMBINE flour, granulated sugar, baking powder, cinnamon, salt and nutmeg in medium bowl. Stir together melted morsels, pumpkin, vegetable oil, eggs and vanilla extract in large bowl with wire whisk. Stir in flour mixture. Spoon batter into prepared Bundt pan.

BAKE for 40 to 50 minutes or until wooden pick inserted in cake comes out clean. Cool in pan on wire rack for 30 minutes; remove to wire rack to cool completely. Sprinkle with powdered sugar. Serve with Butterscotch Sauce.

Makes 24 servings

Butterscotch Sauce: *HEAT ⅓ cup NESTLÉ® CARNATION® Evaporated Milk in medium, heavy-duty saucepan over medium heat just to a boil; remove from heat. Add remaining ⅔ cup morsels; stir until smooth. Return to heat. Stirring constantly, bring mixture just to a boil. Cool to room temperature. Stir before serving.*

CLASSIC HOLIDAY FAVORITES

Southwest Corn Soufflé

3 tablespoons butter

¼ cup all-purpose flour

⅔ cup (5 fluid-ounce can) NESTLÉ® CARNATION® Evaporated Milk

⅓ cup water

1 can (11 ounces) Mexican-style corn, drained

1 can (4 ounces) chopped green chilies

1 large egg, separated

¾ cup (3 ounces) shredded cheddar cheese, *divided*

PREHEAT oven to 325°F. Grease 1½-quart baking dish. Chill small mixer bowl.

MELT butter in large saucepan. Remove from heat. Stir in flour. Gradually stir in evaporated milk and water. Cook over medium heat, stirring constantly, until mixture comes just to a boil. Stir in corn, chilies, egg yolks and ½ *cup* cheese. Beat egg whites in chilled mixer bowl until stiff peaks form. Fold into corn mixture. Pour into prepared baking dish.

BAKE for 50 to 55 minutes or until knife inserted near center comes out clean. Top with *remaining ¼ cup* cheese. Bake for additional 2 to 3 minutes or until cheese is melted.

Makes 6 servings

CLASSIC HOLIDAY FAVORITES

Mocha Dream Cake

CAKE:

1½ cups hot water

1 tablespoon NESCAFÉ® TASTER'S CHOICE® House Blend 100% Pure Instant Coffee

1 cup original NESTLÉ® COFFEE-MATE® Powdered Coffee Creamer

2⅓ cups all-purpose flour, *divided*

1½ teaspoons baking soda

1⅓ cups (8 ounces) NESTLÉ® TOLL HOUSE® Premier White Morsels

⅓ cup vegetable oil

1⅔ cups granulated sugar

4 large eggs

⅔ cup (5 fluid-ounce can) NESTLÉ® CARNATION® Evaporated Milk

2 tablespoons white vinegar

1 teaspoon vanilla extract

⅔ cup NESTLÉ® TOLL HOUSE® Baking Cocoa

FROSTING:

⅔ cup NESTLÉ® TOLL HOUSE® Premier White Morsels

⅓ cup butter or margarine

1 tablespoon NESCAFÉ® TASTER'S CHOICE® House Blend 100% Pure Instant Coffee Granules

1½ teaspoons water

2 packages (3 ounces *each*) cream cheese, softened

4 to 4½ cups powdered sugar

PREHEAT oven to 350°F. Grease and flour two 9-inch-round cake pans.

FOR CAKE:

COMBINE water and coffee granules in medium bowl. Stir in Coffee-mate with wire whisk. Combine 1⅔ cups flour and baking soda in another medium bowl.

MICROWAVE 1⅓ cups morsels and vegetable oil in large, uncovered, microwave-safe bowl on MEDIUM-HIGH (70%) power for 1 minute. STIR. Morsels may retain some of their original shape. If necessary, microwave at additional 10- to 15-second intervals, stirring just until morsels are melted. Add coffee mixture, granulated sugar, eggs, evaporated milk, vinegar and vanilla extract to melted morsels; mix with wire whisk. Gradually beat in flour mixture until combined. (Batter will be thin.) Pour 3¼ *cups* batter into medium bowl; stir in *remaining* flour. Pour into prepared pans.

BLEND cocoa into *remaining* batter with wire whisk until blended. Slowly pour even amounts of cocoa batter into center of each pan. (Cocoa batter will spread evenly outward from center.)

BAKE for 40 to 45 minutes or until wooden pick inserted in center comes out clean. Cool in pans on wire racks for 10 minutes; remove to wire racks to cool completely. Frost cake with frosting between layers and on top and side of cake.

FOR FROSTING:

MICROWAVE ⅔ cup morsels and butter in large, uncovered, microwave-safe bowl on MEDIUM-HIGH (70%) power for 1 minute. STIR. Morsels may retain some of their original shape. If necessary, microwave at additional 10- to 15-second intervals, stirring just until melted. Combine coffee granules and water in small bowl. Beat cream cheese and coffee mixture into melted morsels. Gradually beat in powdered sugar until mixture reaches spreading consistency. Makes about 2½ cups.

Makes 10 to 12 servings

CLASSIC HOLIDAY FAVORITES

Pumpkin Apple Gingerbread Cake

3½ cups all-purpose flour

1 tablespoon baking powder

2½ teaspoons ground ginger

½ teaspoon baking soda

½ teaspoon pumpkin pie spice

½ teaspoon salt

1 cup (2 sticks) butter or margarine, softened

1 cup granulated sugar

½ cup packed brown sugar

4 large eggs

1 can (15 ounces) LIBBY'S® 100% Pure Pumpkin

1 cup (1 large) baking apple (such as Granny Smith) peeled, shredded

½ cup molasses

Powdered sugar

Hard Sauce (recipe follows)

PREHEAT oven to 350°F. Grease and flour 12-cup Bundt pan.

COMBINE flour, baking powder, ginger, baking soda, pumpkin pie spice and salt in medium bowl. Beat butter, granulated sugar and brown sugar in large mixer bowl until creamy. Beat in eggs, two at a time, beating well after each addition. Beat in pumpkin, apple and molasses. Gradually beat in flour mixture.

SPOON batter into prepared Bundt pan. Bake for 55 to 60 minutes or until wooden pick inserted in bread comes out clean. Cool in pan on wire rack for 15 minutes; invert onto serving platter. Dust with powdered sugar before serving. Serve warm with Hard Sauce.

Makes 12 servings

Hard Sauce

BEAT ½ cup (1 stick) softened butter and 1 teaspoon vanilla extract in small mixer bowl until smooth. Gradually beat in 2 cups sifted powdered sugar until fluffy.

Three-Vegetable Bake

- 3 **cups (about 3 medium) coarsely chopped red or other waxy potatoes**
- 1 **cup (1 medium) peeled and coarsely chopped parsnip**
- 3 **cups fresh broccoli and/or cauliflower florets**
- 3 **tablespoons butter or margarine, *divided***
- 2 **tablespoons all-purpose flour**
- 1 **can (12 fluid ounces) NESTLÉ® CARNATION® Evaporated Fat Free Milk**
- 1 **MAGGI® Vegetarian Vegetable Flavor Bouillon Cube**
- ⅛ **teaspoon ground white pepper**
- ¼ **cup seasoned dry bread crumbs**

PREHEAT oven to 350°F.

MICROWAVE potatoes and parsnip in covered, medium, microwave-safe casserole dish on HIGH (100%) power for 9 minutes; drain. Return to dish; top with broccoli.

MELT 2 *tablespoons* butter in small saucepan over medium heat. Stir in flour; cook, stirring constantly, for 30 seconds. Gradually stir in evaporated milk, bouillon and pepper; cook, stirring occasionally, for 3 to 4 minutes or until bouillon is dissolved and sauce is slightly thickened. Pour sauce over vegetables.

MICROWAVE *remaining 1 tablespoon* butter in small, microwave-safe bowl on HIGH (100%) power for 10 to 20 seconds or until melted. Stir in bread crumbs until combined. Sprinkle over vegetables; cover.

BAKE for 30 minutes. Uncover; bake for an additional 10 minutes or until top is golden brown.

Makes 6 servings

Marbled Chocolate Sour Cream Cake

1 cup (6 ounces) NESTLÉ® TOLL HOUSE® Semi-Sweet Chocolate Morsels

1 package (18.5 ounces) yellow cake mix

4 large eggs

¾ cup sour cream

½ cup vegetable oil

¼ cup water

¼ cup granulated sugar

   Powdered sugar (optional)

PREHEAT oven to 375°F. Grease 10-cup Bundt or round tube pan.

MICROWAVE morsels in medium, uncovered, microwave-safe bowl on HIGH (100%) power for 1 minute. STIR. Morsels may retain some of their original shape. If necessary, microwave at additional 10- to 15-second intervals, stirring just until morsels are melted.

COMBINE cake mix, eggs, sour cream, vegetable oil, water and granulated sugar in large mixer bowl. Beat on low speed until moistened. Beat on high speed for 2 minutes.

STIR *2 cups* batter into melted chocolate. Alternately spoon batters into prepared pan, beginning and ending with yellow batter.

BAKE for 35 to 40 minutes or until wooden pick inserted in cake comes out clean. Cool in pan for 20 minutes; invert onto wire rack to cool completely. Dust with powdered sugar before serving.

Makes 20 servings

Sweet & White Scalloped Potatoes with Parmesan & Thyme

1 can (12 fluid ounces) NESTLÉ® CARNATION® Evaporated Milk

2 MAGGI® Reduced Sodium Chicken Flavor Bouillon Cubes

1 teaspoon onion powder

½ teaspoon dried thyme leaves

4 cups (1½ pounds) potatoes, peeled, cut into ¼-inch slices

2 cups (½ pound) sweet potatoes or yams, peeled, cut into ¼-inch slices

½ cup grated Parmesan cheese

HEAT evaporated milk, bouillon cubes, onion powder and thyme in large skillet over medium high heat, stirring occasionally until mixture comes to a boil and bouillon is dissolved. Add potatoes.

COOK, stirring occasionally, until mixture comes to boil. Cover; reduce heat to low. Cook, rearranging potatoes gently and occasionally, for 35 to 40 minutes or until potatoes are tender. Sprinkle with cheese; serve immediately.

Makes 8 servings

Tip: *For quick and consistently thin potato slices, use the slicing blade of a food processor.*

CLASSIC HOLIDAY FAVORITES

LIBBY'S® Famous Pumpkin Pie

¾ **cup granulated sugar**

1 **teaspoon ground cinnamon**

½ **teaspoon salt**

½ **teaspoon ground ginger**

¼ **teaspoon ground cloves**

2 **large eggs**

1 **can (15 ounces) LIBBY'S® 100% Pure Pumpkin**

1 **can (12 fluid ounces) NESTLÉ® CARNATION® Evaporated Milk**

1 *unbaked* **9-inch (4-cup volume) deep-dish pie shell**

Whipped cream

MIX sugar, cinnamon, salt, ginger and cloves in small bowl. Beat eggs in large bowl. Stir in pumpkin and sugar-spice mixture. Gradually stir in evaporated milk.

POUR into pie shell.

BAKE in preheated 425°F oven for 15 minutes. Reduce oven temperature to 350°F; bake for 40 to 50 minutes or until knife inserted near center comes out clean. Cool on wire rack for 2 hours. Serve immediately or refrigerate. Top with whipped cream before serving.

Makes 8 servings

Note: *Do not freeze this pie because this will result in the crust separating from the filling.*

Tip: *You can substitute 1¾ teaspoons pumpkin pie spice for the cinnamon, ginger and cloves; however, the flavor will be slightly different.*

For 2 shallow pies:
Substitute two 9-inch (2-cup volume) pie shells. Bake in preheated 425°F oven for 15 minutes. Reduce temperature to 350°F; bake for 20 to 30 minutes or until pies test done.

Crumble-Top Pumpkin Muffins

4 **cups all-purpose baking mix**

1 **cup raisins (optional)**

⅔ **cup quick or old-fashioned oats**

⅔ **cup granulated sugar**

1 **teaspoon ground cinnamon**

1 **can (30 ounces) LIBBY'S® Easy Pumpkin Pie Mix**

2 **large eggs**

   Streusel Topping (recipe follows)

PREHEAT oven to 400°F. Paper-line or grease 24 muffin cups.

COMBINE baking mix, raisins, oats, sugar and cinnamon in large bowl. Combine pumpkin pie mix and eggs in medium bowl; mix well. Stir into oat mixture just until moistened. Spoon batter into prepared muffin cups, filling three-fourths full. Sprinkle with Streusel Topping.

BAKE for 14 to 16 minutes or until wooden pick inserted in center comes out clean. Remove from pans to wire rack; cool slightly. Serve warm.

Makes 2 dozen muffins

Streusel Topping

COMBINE 3 tablespoons all-purpose flour, 3 tablespoons granulated sugar and ¾ teaspoon ground cinnamon in small bowl. Cut in 2 tablespoons butter with pastry blender or two knives until mixture is crumbly.

Sweet Potato Soufflé

- 2 **cans (29 ounces *each*) sweet potatoes, packed in light syrup, drained**
- ¾ **cup NESTLÉ® CARNATION® Evaporated Milk**
- ½ **cup packed brown sugar**
- 2 **large eggs**
- 2 **tablespoons butter or margarine, melted**
- ¾ **teaspoon pumpkin pie spice**
- ½ **teaspoon salt**
- ⅓ **cup finely chopped nuts**

PREHEAT oven to 350°F. Lightly grease 3-quart casserole.

PLACE sweet potatoes, evaporated milk, sugar, eggs, butter, pumpkin pie spice and salt in food processor or blender; cover. Process until smooth. Pour into prepared casserole; sprinkle with nuts.

BAKE for 40 to 45 minutes or until golden brown.

Makes 10 servings, ½ cup each

Scrumptious Chocolate Mint Layer Bars

- 2 **cups (about 15) finely ground creme-filled chocolate sandwich cookies**
- ¼ **cup (½ stick) butter or margarine**
- 1½ **cups chopped nuts**
- 1 **cup flaked coconut**
- 1 **can (14 ounces) NESTLÉ® CARNATION® Sweetened Condensed Milk**
- 1⅔ **cups (10-ounce package) NESTLÉ® TOLL HOUSE® Dark Chocolate & Mint Morsels**

PREHEAT oven to 350°F.

MELT butter in 13×9-inch baking pan in oven; remove from oven. Sprinkle cookie crumbs over butter. Stir well; press mixture onto bottom of pan. Sprinkle with nuts and coconut. Pour sweetened condensed milk evenly over top. Sprinkle with morsels; press down slightly.

BAKE for 20 to 25 minutes or until coconut is light golden brown. Cool completely in pan on wire rack. Cut into bars.

Makes 2 dozen bars

CLASSIC HOLIDAY FAVORITES

Pumpkin Sausage Lasagna

- 1   container (15 ounces) light ricotta cheese
- 2   tablespoons BUITONI® Refrigerated Freshly Shredded Parmesan Cheese
- 1   teaspoon Italian seasoning
- 12 ounces sweet or hot light turkey sausage, casings removed
- ¾   cup LIBBY'S® 100% Pure Pumpkin
- ½   cup dry white wine
- ½   cup chicken broth
- 1   container (15 ounces) BUITONI® Refrigerated Roasted Garlic Marinara Sauce
- 8   no-boil lasagna noodles
- 1½ cups (6 ounces) shredded mozzarella cheese, *divided*
- ⅓   cup hot water

PREHEAT oven to 350°F.

COMBINE ricotta cheese, Parmesan cheese and seasoning in medium bowl; mix well.

HEAT large, nonstick skillet over medium-high heat. Add sausage; cook, stirring to break into pieces, until browned. Transfer sausage to paper towel-lined plate to drain.

ADD pumpkin, wine and broth to skillet; cook over medium heat, stirring frequently, until bubbly. Stir in sauce and sausage; heat through.

SPREAD *1 cup* mixture over bottom of 11×7-inch or 13×9-inch baking dish. Top with *4* lasagna noodles. Spread *1 cup* ricotta mixture over noodles. Sprinkle with *1 cup* mozzarella cheese. Spread *1 cup* sauce mixture over mozzarella cheese; top with *remaining 4* lasagna noodles, *remaining* sauce mixture. Sprinkle with *remaining ½ cup* mozzarella cheese. Pour water around edges of lasagna. Cover with foil.

BAKE for 40 to 45 minutes or until bubbly. Let stand for 10 minutes before serving.

Makes 6 to 8 servings

Variation: *Can substitute BUITONI® Refrigerated Marinara Sauce. If this is preferred, add 2 cloves finely chopped garlic when cooking sausage.*

Date Bars

- 1   package (8 ounces) chopped dates
- ¾   cup NESTLÉ® CARNATION® Evaporated Milk
- 2   tablespoons granulated sugar
- 1   teaspoon vanilla extract
- ½   cup (1 stick) butter or margarine, softened
- ½   cup packed light brown sugar
- 1   cup all-purpose flour
- ¾   cup quick oats
- ½   teaspoon baking soda
- ½   teaspoon salt
- ½   teaspoon ground cinnamon

PREHEAT oven to 400°F. Grease 8-inch-square baking pan.

COMBINE dates, evaporated milk, granulated sugar and vanilla extract in medium saucepan. Cook over medium-low heat, stirring occasionally, for 8 to 10 minutes or until thickened. Remove from heat.

BEAT butter and brown sugar in large mixer bowl until creamy. Beat in flour, oats, baking soda, salt and cinnamon. With floured fingers, press *half* of crust mixture onto bottom of prepared baking pan. Spread date filling over crust. Top with *remaining* crust.

BAKE for 20 to 25 minutes or until golden. Cut into bars. Serve warm.

Makes 16 bars

CLASSIC HOLIDAY FAVORITES

Scrumptious Cheddar Bacon Scalloped Potatoes

- **6 slices turkey bacon, cooked and chopped, divided**
- **2 to 2½ pounds (about 6 medium) potatoes, unpeeled and thinly sliced**
- **3 tablespoons butter or margarine**
- **3 tablespoons all-purpose flour**
- **½ teaspoon salt**
- **¼ teaspoon ground black pepper**
- **1 can (12 fluid ounces) NESTLÉ® CARNATION® Evaporated Lowfat 2% Milk**
- **1 cup water**
- **2 cups (8 ounces) shredded 2% cheddar cheese, divided**
- **2 green onions, sliced**

PLACE potatoes in large saucepan. Cover with water; bring to a boil. Cook over medium-high heat for 8 to 10 minutes or until just fork tender; drain.

MEANWHILE, HEAT butter in medium saucepan over medium heat. Stir in flour, salt and pepper. Gradually stir in evaporated milk, water and ⅓ cup bacon. Cook for about 8 to 10 minutes, stirring constantly, until mixture comes to a boil. Remove from heat. Stir in 1½ *cups* cheese and green onion.

LAYER *half* of potatoes in ungreased 3-quart microwave-safe dish. Pour half of sauce over potatoes. Top with *remaining* potatoes and sauce. Top with *remaining* cheese and bacon. Microwave uncovered on HIGH (100%) power for 2 to 3 minutes or until cheese is melted.

Makes about 16 servings, ½ cup each

CLASSIC HOLIDAY FAVORITES

Pork Tenderloin with Dijon Mustard Sauce

- 1 **pound pork tenderloin**
- 1 **teaspoon vegetable oil**
- ½ **cup NESTLÉ® CARNATION® Evaporated Fat Free Milk**
- 2 **tablespoons Dijon mustard**
- 2 **to 3 green onions, sliced**

CUT pork into 1-inch-thick slices. Place pork between two pieces of plastic wrap. Flatten to ¼-inch thickness using meat mallet or rolling pin. Season with salt and ground black pepper, if desired.

HEAT oil in large, nonstick skillet over medium-high heat. Add *half* of the pork; cook on each side for 2 minutes or until browned and cooked through. Remove from skillet; set aside and keep warm. Repeat with *remaining* pork.

REDUCE heat to low. Add evaporated milk; stir to loosen brown bits from bottom of skillet. Stir in mustard and green onions. Return pork to skillet. Cook for 1 to 2 minutes or until sauce is slightly thickened, turning pork to coat with sauce.

Makes 4 servings

Milk Chocolate Florentine Cookies

- ⅔ **cup butter**
- 2 **cups quick oats**
- 1 **cup granulated sugar**
- ⅔ **cup all-purpose flour**
- ¼ **cup light or dark corn syrup**
- ¼ **cup milk**
- 1 **teaspoon vanilla extract**
- ¼ **teaspoon salt**
- 1¾ **cups (11.5-ounce package) NESTLÉ® TOLL HOUSE® Milk Chocolate Morsels**

PREHEAT oven to 375°F. Line baking sheets with foil.

MELT butter in medium saucepan; remove from heat. Stir in oats, sugar, flour, corn syrup, milk, vanilla extract and salt; mix well. Drop by level teaspoonful, about 3 inches apart, onto prepared baking sheets. Spread thinly with rubber spatula.

BAKE for 6 to 8 minutes or until golden brown. Cool completely on baking sheets on wire racks. Peel foil from cookies.

MICROWAVE morsels in medium, uncovered, microwave-safe bowl on MEDIUM-HIGH (70%) power for 1 minute; STIR. Morsels may retain some of their original shape. If necessary, microwave at additional 10- to 15-second intervals, stirring just until morsels are melted. Spread thin layer of melted chocolate onto flat side of *half* the cookies. Top with *remaining* cookies.

Makes about 3½ dozen sandwich cookies

Pan Cookie Variation: *Grease 15×10-inch jelly-roll pan. Prepare dough as above. Spread in prepared pan. Bake for 20 to 25 minutes or until golden brown. Cool in pan on wire rack. Makes 4 dozen bars.*

CLASSIC HOLIDAY FAVORITES

LIBBY'S® Pumpkin Roll

CAKE:

- ¼ **cup powdered sugar**
- ¾ **cup all-purpose flour**
- ½ **teaspoon baking powder**
- ½ **teaspoon baking soda**
- ½ **teaspoon ground cinnamon**
- ½ **teaspoon ground cloves**
- ¼ **teaspoon salt**
- 3 **large eggs**
- 1 **cup granulated sugar**
- ⅔ **cup LIBBY'S® 100% Pure Pumpkin**
- 1 **cup chopped walnuts (optional)**

FILLING:

- 1 **package (8 ounces) cream cheese, at room temperature**
- 1 **cup powdered sugar, sifted**
- 6 **tablespoons butter or margarine, softened**
- 1 **teaspoon vanilla extract**

   Powdered sugar (optional for decoration)

FOR CAKE:

PREHEAT oven to 375°F. Grease 15×10-inch jelly-roll pan; line with wax paper. Grease and flour paper. Sprinkle a thin, cotton kitchen towel with powdered sugar.

COMBINE flour, baking powder, baking soda, cinnamon, cloves and salt in small bowl. Beat eggs and granulated sugar in large mixer bowl until thick. Beat in pumpkin. Stir in flour mixture. Spread evenly into prepared pan. Sprinkle with nuts.

BAKE for 13 to 15 minutes or until top of cake springs back when touched. (If using a dark-colored pan, begin checking doneness at 11 minutes.) Immediately loosen and turn cake onto prepared towel. Carefully peel off paper. Roll up cake and towel together, starting with narrow end. Cool on wire rack.

FOR FILLING:

BEAT cream cheese, *1 cup* powdered sugar, butter and vanilla extract in small mixer bowl until smooth. Carefully unroll cake. Spread cream cheese mixture over cake. Reroll cake. Wrap in plastic wrap and refrigerate at least one hour. Sprinkle with powdered sugar before serving, if desired.

Makes 10 servings

CLASSIC HOLIDAY FAVORITES

Chicken Tetrazzini

8 ounces dry spaghetti, cooked, drained and kept warm

¼ cup dry bread crumbs

3 tablespoons butter or margarine, *divided*

¾ cup BUITONI® Shredded Parmesan Cheese, *divided*

½ cup chopped onion

¼ cup all-purpose flour

¼ teaspoon salt

⅛ teaspoon ground white pepper

1 can (14.5 ounces) chicken broth

1 can (12 ounces) NESTLÉ® CARNATION® Evaporated Milk

2 cups chopped cooked chicken or turkey breast meat

2 cans (4 ounces each) sliced mushrooms, drained

1 cup frozen peas, thawed

2 tablespoons dry sherry

PREHEAT oven to 350°F. Lightly grease 13×9-inch baking dish.

COMBINE bread crumbs and *2 tablespoons* butter in small bowl. Stir in ¼ *cup* cheese.

MELT *remaining 1 tablespoon* butter in medium saucepan over medium heat. Add onion; cook, stirring occasionally, for 1 to 2 minutes or until tender. Stir in flour, salt and pepper; cook, stirring constantly, for 1 minute. Remove from heat; gradually stir in broth. Return to heat; bring to boil over medium heat, stirring constantly. Stir in evaporated milk and *remaining* cheese; cook over low heat until cheese melts. Remove from heat. Stir in chicken, mushrooms, peas and sherry.

COMBINE pasta and chicken mixture in large bowl. Pour into prepared baking dish. Sprinkle with bread crumb topping.

BAKE for 20 to 25 minutes or until topping is lightly browned. Serve immediately.

Makes 8 servings

CLASSIC HOLIDAY FAVORITES

Chocolate Truffle Cake with Strawberry Sauce

TRUFFLE CAKE:

1¾ cups (11.5-ounce package) NESTLÉ® TOLL HOUSE® Milk Chocolate Morsels, *divided*

½ cup (1 stick) butter

3 large eggs

⅔ cup granulated sugar

1 teaspoon vanilla extract

¼ teaspoon salt

⅔ cup all-purpose flour

GLAZE:

¼ cup NESTLÉ® TOLL HOUSE® Butterscotch Flavored Morsels

¼ cup creamy peanut butter

STRAWBERRY SAUCE:

2 cups fresh or frozen strawberries, thawed

2 tablespoons granulated sugar

Garnish suggestions: whipped topping, fresh strawberries, fresh mint leaves

FOR TRUFFLE CAKE:

PREHEAT oven to 350°F. Grease and flour 9-inch springform pan. Melt *1 cup* milk chocolate morsels and butter in small, uncovered, microwave-safe bowl on MEDIUM-HIGH (70%) power for 1 minute. STIR. Morsels may retain some of their original shape. If necessary, microwave at additional 10- to 15-second intervals, stirring just until morsels are melted. Cool for 10 minutes.

BEAT eggs, ⅔ cup sugar, vanilla extract and salt in large mixer bowl. Blend in chocolate mixture. Stir in flour; mix well. Pour into prepared pan.

BAKE for 30 to 35 minutes or until wooden pick inserted in center comes out clean. Cool completely in pan on wire rack. Remove side of pan.

FOR GLAZE:

MELT *remaining* milk chocolate morsels, butterscotch morsels and peanut butter in small, uncovered, microwave-safe bowl on MEDIUM-HIGH (70%) power for 1 minute. STIR. Morsels may retain some of their original shape. If necessary, microwave at additional 10- to 15-second intervals, stirring just until morsels are melted. Cool slightly. Spread glaze over top and side of cooled cake. Refrigerate for 30 minutes or until glaze is set.

FOR STRAWBERRY SAUCE:

PLACE strawberries and 2 tablespoons sugar in blender; cover. Blend until smooth. Refrigerate until serving time. To serve, cut into wedges. Garnish with Strawberry Sauce, whipped topping, strawberries and mint leaves.

Makes 12 servings

CLASSIC HOLIDAY FAVORITES

Premier Cheesecake Cranberry Bars

2   **cups all-purpose flour**

1½   **cups quick or old-fashioned oats**

¼   **cup packed light brown sugar**

1   **cup (2 sticks) butter or margarine, softened**

2   **cups (12-ounce package) NESTLÉ® TOLL HOUSE® Premier White Morsels**

1   **package (8 ounces) cream cheese, softened**

1   **can (14 ounces) NESTLÉ® CARNATION® Sweetened Condensed Milk**

¼   **cup lemon juice**

1   **teaspoon vanilla extract**

1   **can (14 ounces) whole-berry cranberry sauce**

2   **tablespoons cornstarch**

PREHEAT oven to 350°F. Grease 13×9-inch baking pan.

COMBINE flour, oats and brown sugar in large bowl. Add butter; mix until crumbly. Stir in morsels. Reserve 2½ *cups* morsel mixture for topping. With floured fingers, press *remaining* mixture into prepared pan.

BEAT cream cheese in large mixer bowl until creamy. Add sweetened condensed milk, lemon juice and vanilla extract; mix until smooth. Pour over crust. Combine cranberry sauce and cornstarch in medium bowl. Spoon over cream cheese mixture. Sprinkle *reserved* morsel mixture over cranberry mixture.

BAKE for 35 to 40 minutes or until center is set. Cool completely in pan on wire rack. Cover; refrigerate until serving time (up to 1 day). Cut into bars.

Makes 2½ dozen bars

CLASSIC HOLIDAY FAVORITES

Sweet Potato Pies

2   *unbaked* 9-inch (2-cup volume) pie shells

2   large or 3 medium (about 1½ to 2 pounds total) sweet potatoes

½   cup (1 stick) butter or margarine, softened

1   cup granulated sugar

⅔   cup (5 fluid-ounce can) NESTLÉ® CARNATION® Evaporated Milk

2   large eggs, beaten

2   tablespoons packed brown sugar

1   teaspoon lemon juice

1   teaspoon vanilla extract

1   teaspoon ground cinnamon

¼   teaspoon ground nutmeg

⅛   teaspoon salt

     Whipped cream

COOK sweet potatoes in boiling water for 45 to 50 minutes or until tender. Drain, cool slightly and peel.

PREHEAT oven to 425°F.

MASH warm sweet potatoes and butter in large bowl. Stir in granulated sugar, brown sugar, evaporated milk and eggs. Stir in lemon juice, vanilla extract, cinnamon, nutmeg and salt. Pour into prepared pie shells.

BAKE for 15 minutes. Reduce heat to 350°F; bake for 30 to 40 minutes or until knife inserted near center comes out clean. Cool on wire rack for 2 hours. Top with whipped cream. Serve immediately or refrigerate.

Makes 16 servings

Cheesy Spoon Bread

¾   cup *dry* NESTLÉ® CARNATION® Instant Nonfat Dry Milk

½   cup yellow corn meal

2   cups water

1¼   cups (5 ounces) shredded cheddar cheese, *divided*

3   large eggs, separated

2   tablespoons margarine or butter

¼   teaspoon baking powder

PREHEAT oven to 375°F. Grease 1½-quart casserole dish.

COMBINE dry milk and corn meal in large saucepan. Stir in water. Cook over medium heat, stirring constantly, until mixture comes to a boil and thickens. Remove from heat. Stir in ¾ *cup* cheese, egg yolks, margarine and baking powder.

BEAT egg whites in small mixer bowl until stiff peaks form. Fold into corn meal mixture lightly but thoroughly. Pour into prepared dish. Sprinkle with *remaining* cheese.

BAKE for 30 to 35 minutes or until top is golden and filling is set. Serve warm.

Makes 6 servings

Easy Pumpkin-Pasta Bake

Nonstick cooking spray

1 box (14.5 ounces) whole wheat penne or other short-cut pasta, prepared according to package directions

1 pound (about 4 links) sweet or spicy lean Italian turkey sausage, casings removed

1 tablespoon finely chopped garlic

1 jar (24 to 26 ounces) marinara sauce

½ cup water or dry red or white wine

1 can (15 ounces) LIBBY'S® 100% Pure Pumpkin

4 tablespoons (0.75 ounce) shredded Parmesan cheese, *divided*

1 cup (4 ounces) shredded low-moisture part-skim mozzarella cheese

PREHEAT oven to 375°F. Spray 3-quart casserole dish or 13×9-inch baking dish with nonstick cooking spray.

COOK sausage in large skillet over medium-high heat until cooked through. Stir in garlic; cook for 1 minute. Stir in marinara sauce (reserve jar). Add water or wine to jar; cover and shake. Pour into skillet along with pumpkin and 2 *tablespoons* Parmesan cheese. Stir well. Stir in prepared pasta. Spoon into prepared dish. Sprinkle with *remaining 2 tablespoons* Parmesan cheese and mozzarella cheese; cover.

BAKE for 15 minutes. Carefully remove cover; bake for an additional 5 minutes or until cheese is melted and bubbly.

Makes 10 servings

CLASSIC HOLIDAY FAVORITES

Double Chocolate Warm Pudding Cake

Nonstick cooking spray

1 **cup all-purpose flour**

1¼ **cups granulated sugar,** *divided*

3 **tablespoons** *plus* ¼ **cup NESTLÉ® TOLL HOUSE® Baking Cocoa,** *divided*

2 **teaspoons baking powder**

¼ **teaspoon salt**

1 **can (12 ounces) NESTLÉ® CARNATION® Evaporated Lowfat 2% Milk,** *divided*

1 **tablespoon vegetable oil**

1 **teaspoon vanilla extract**

2 **tablespoons water**

Lowfat whipped topping or ice cream (optional)

PREHEAT the oven to 350°F. Spray 8-inch-square baking pan or dish with nonstick cooking spray.

COMBINE flour, ¾ *cup* sugar, 3 *tablespoons* cocoa, baking powder and salt in medium bowl. Add ½ *cup* evaporated milk, oil and vanilla extract; whisk until just blended. Spread batter into prepared baking pan.

COMBINE *remaining* ½ *cup* sugar and ¼ *cup* cocoa in small bowl. Microwave *remaining 1 cup* evaporated milk and water in small, uncovered microwave-safe bowl on HIGH (100%) power for 1 minute. Whisk sugar-cocoa mixture into milk mixture until blended. Gently pour over chocolate batter in pan.

BAKE for 20 to 25 minutes (25 to 30 minutes if using glass dish) or until cake layer forms on top and edges are bubbly. Let stand for 10 minutes. Spoon into serving dishes, spooning chocolate sauce over cake. Top with whipped topping.

Makes 9 servings

Tip: *Individual servings can be reheated in microwave for 10 seconds.*

CLASSIC HOLIDAY FAVORITES

Pumpkin and Cranberry Risotto

2 cans (14.5 ounces *each*) reduced-sodium chicken broth, *divided*

1 tablespoon butter

1 tablespoon olive oil

½ cup chopped onion

1½ cups Arborio rice

½ cup dry white wine

1 cup LIBBY'S® 100% Pure Pumpkin

½ cup sweetened dried cranberries

¼ cup grated Parmesan Cheese

Salt and white pepper to taste

Additional grated Parmesan cheese (optional)

BRING chicken broth to a boil in medium saucepan. Reduce heat to low; keep warm.

MELT butter and oil in large saucepan over medium-high heat. Add onion; cook, stirring frequently, for 2 minutes. Add rice; cook, stirring frequently, for 2 minutes. Add wine; simmer, stirring frequently, until all liquid is absorbed. Stir in pumpkin.

ADD ¾ *cup* chicken broth to rice. Reduce heat; simmer, stirring frequently, until absorbed. Continue adding broth, ½ *cup* at a time, allowing each addition to be absorbed before adding more broth. Rice should be tender but still firm to the bite and mixture should be creamy. This should take about 20 to 25 minutes. Stir in sweetened dried cranberries and cheese. Add salt and pepper to taste. If desired, garnish with additional Parmesan Cheese.

Makes 6 servings

CLASSIC HOLIDAY FAVORITES

NESTLÉ® TOLL HOUSE® Chocolate Chip Pie

1 *unbaked* 9-inch (4-cup volume) deep-dish pie shell*

2 large eggs

½ cup all-purpose flour

½ cup granulated sugar

½ cup packed brown sugar

¾ cup (1½ sticks) butter, softened

1 cup (6 ounces) NESTLÉ® TOLL HOUSE® Semi-Sweet Chocolate Morsels

1 cup chopped nuts

Sweetened whipped cream or ice cream (optional)

*If using frozen pie shell, use deep-dish style, thawed completely. Bake on baking sheet; increase baking time slightly.

PREHEAT oven to 325°F.

BEAT eggs in large mixer bowl on high speed until foamy. Beat in flour, granulated sugar and brown sugar. Beat in butter. Stir in morsels and nuts. Spoon into pie shell.

BAKE for 55 to 60 minutes or until knife inserted halfway between outside edge and center comes out clean. Cool on wire rack. Serve warm with whipped cream.

Makes 8 servings

CLASSIC HOLIDAY FAVORITES

Creamy Cheesy Mashed Potatoes

6 medium (about 2 pounds *total*) potatoes, peeled and cut into 1-inch chunks

¾ cup NESTLÉ® CARNATION® Evaporated Milk

¼ cup (½ stick) butter or margarine

1 cup (4 ounces) shredded cheddar cheese

PLACE potatoes in large saucepan. Cover with water; bring to a boil. Cook over medium-high heat for 15 to 20 minutes or until tender; drain.

RETURN potatoes to saucepan; add evaporated milk and butter. Beat with hand-held mixer until smooth. Stir in cheese. Season with salt and ground black pepper.

Makes 6 servings

Note: *Chopped green onions, chopped parsley or cooked, crumbled bacon may be added to mashed potatoes.*

CLASSIC HOLIDAY FAVORITES

Shrimp Fettuccine

8 ounces dry fettuccine

1 tablespoon olive oil

2 cloves garlic, finely chopped

2 tablespoons all-purpose flour

⅛ teaspoon ground black pepper

1 cup NESTLÉ® CARNATION® Evaporated Lowfat 2% Milk

¾ cup vegetable or chicken broth

½ cup (1.5 ounces) plus 2 tablespoons shredded Parmesan cheese, *divided*

½ pound cooked medium shrimp

½ cup chopped red bell pepper

   Fresh whole or finely sliced basil leaves for garnish (optional)

PREPARE pasta according to package directions; drain.

MEANWHILE, HEAT oil and garlic in medium saucepan over medium heat until garlic is fragrant. Stir in flour and black pepper; cook, stirring constantly, for 30 seconds. Add evaporated milk and broth. Cook, stirring constantly, for about 8 minutes or until mixture comes to a gentle boil and thickens slightly. Stir in ½ cup cheese until melted. Add shrimp and bell pepper; heat for an additional minute or until shrimp are warm.

TOSS with pasta. Top with *remaining 2 tablespoons* cheese and basil. Serve immediately.

Makes 6 servings

CLASSIC HOLIDAY FAVORITES

Pumpkin Pecan Rum Cake

¾ **cup chopped pecans**

3 **cups all-purpose flour**

2 **tablespoons pumpkin pie spice**

2 **teaspoons baking soda**

1 **teaspoon salt**

1 **cup (2 sticks) butter or margarine, softened**

1 **cup packed brown sugar**

1 **cup granulated sugar**

4 **large eggs**

1 **can (15 ounces) LIBBY'S® 100% Pure Pumpkin**

1 **teaspoon vanilla extract**

Rum Butter Glaze (recipe follows)

PREHEAT oven to 325°F. Grease 12-cup Bundt pan. Sprinkle nuts over bottom.

COMBINE flour, pumpkin pie spice, baking soda and salt in medium bowl. Beat butter, brown sugar and granulated sugar in large mixer bowl until light and fluffy. Add eggs; beat well. Add pumpkin and vanilla extract; beat well. Add flour mixture to pumpkin mixture, ⅓ at a time, mixing well after each addition. Spoon batter into prepared pan.

BAKE for 60 to 70 minutes or until wooden pick inserted into center comes out clean. Cool 10 minutes. Make holes in cake with long pick; pour half of glaze over cake. Let stand 5 minutes and invert onto plate. Make holes in top of cake; pour remaining glaze over cake. Cool. Garnish as desired.

Makes 12 to 16 servings

Rum Butter Glaze

MELT ¼ cup butter or margarine in small saucepan; stir in ½ cup granulated sugar and 2 tablespoons water. Bring to a boil. Remove from heat; stir in 2 to 3 tablespoons dark rum or 1 teaspoon rum extract.

CLASSIC HOLIDAY FAVORITES

Pumpkin Confetti Rice

1 **tablespoon olive oil**

1 **small onion, chopped**

2 **cups frozen mixed vegetable blend**

1 **cup LIBBY'S® 100% Pure Pumpkin**

1 **can (14 fluid ounces) vegetable broth**

¼ **cup water**

1 **teaspoon dried thyme**

2 **cups uncooked instant brown rice**

¼ **teaspoon salt or more to taste**

¼ **teaspoon ground black pepper**

Pinch cayenne pepper (optional)

HEAT oil in large saucepan over medium heat. Add onion; cook, stirring occasionally, for 3 to 4 minutes or until soft. Add vegetables, pumpkin, broth, water and thyme. Bring to a boil, stirring occasionally. Stir in rice, salt, black pepper and cayenne pepper; bring to a boil. Cover; reduce heat to low. Cook for 5 minutes. Remove from heat; let stand for 10 minutes or until liquid is absorbed. Fluff with fork before serving.

Makes 10 servings (½ cup each)

Winter

Rich Peppermint Sipping Cocoa Mix

Share the warmth of your kitchen this holiday season with creative homemade gifts. Choose from a variety of sweet treats including gifts from a jar and sturdy goodies that can be shipped.

1½ cups NESTLÉ® TOLL HOUSE® Semi-Sweet Chocolate Morsels

¾ cup NESTLÉ® TOLL HOUSE® Premier White Morsels, *divided*

15 (about 6 tablespoons) hard peppermint candies, unwrapped and crushed into small pieces*

1 (3-cup) gifting jar with lid or 16-inch disposable plastic pastry bag with twist tie or ribbon

To crush peppermint candies, place unwrapped candies in heavy-duty plastic bag; seal. Crush using rolling pin or other heavy object.

LAYER semi-sweet morsels, white morsels and crushed peppermint candies in gifting jar or plastic pastry bag. Seal jar with lid or tie pastry bag closed with twist tie.

Makes 1 jar

Recipe to Attach: *COMBINE entire contents of cocoa mix with one can (12 fluid ounces) NESTLÉ® CARNATION® Evaporated Milk and 1½ cups water in medium saucepan. Cook over low heat, stirring occasionally, for 10 to 12 minutes or until peppermint candy is dissolved and chocolate is melted. Makes 8 (4-ounce) servings.*

Tip: *The cocoa mix can be divided in half to make two mix gifts. Place mix in two smaller jars with lids or two 12-inch disposable plastic pastry bags.*

Recipe to Attach: *COMBINE entire contents of cocoa mix with ⅔ cup (5 fluid-ounce can) NESTLÉ® CARNATION® Evaporated Milk and 1 cup water in medium saucepan. COOK over low heat, stirring occasionally, for 8 to 10 minutes or until peppermint candy is dissolved and chocolate is melted. Makes 4 (4-ounce) servings.*

GIFTABLE GOODIES

Mini Pumpkin Pecan Orange Soaked Cakes

½ cup chopped pecans

1 package (18.25 ounces) spice cake mix

1 can (15 ounces) LIBBY'S® 100% Pure Pumpkin

1 cup vegetable oil

4 large eggs

Orange Syrup (recipe follows)

PREHEAT oven to 350°F. Grease and flour two 6-cake mini Bundt pans. Sprinkle nuts over bottom.

COMBINE cake mix, pumpkin, vegetable oil and eggs in large mixer bowl. Beat on low speed for 30 seconds or until blended. Beat for 4 minutes on medium speed. Spoon about ½ cup into each mold.

BAKE for 20 to 25 minutes or until wooden picks inserted in cakes comes out clean. Remove from oven. With back of spoon, carefully pat down dome of each cake to flatten. Let cool in pans for 5 minutes. Invert cakes onto cooling rack(s). Poke holes in cakes with wooden pick. Spoon a tablespoon of Orange Syrup over each cake. Allow syrup to soak in. Cool completely before serving or wrapping for gifts.

Makes 12 cakes

Orange Syrup

PLACE ¼ cup (½ stick) butter, ½ cup granulated sugar, 2 tablespoons water and 2 teaspoons grated orange peel in small saucepan. Bring to a boil. Remove from heat. Stir in 2 tablespoons orange juice.

GIFTABLE GOODIES

'Tis the Season Gingerbread Bark

Parchment or wax paper

2 **bars (8 ounces) NESTLÉ® TOLL HOUSE® Dark Chocolate Baking Bar, finely chopped**

¼ **cup NESTLÉ® TOLL HOUSE® Premier White Morsels**

1 **teaspoon vegetable oil**

⅓ **to ½ cup chopped or crumbled gingersnap cookies**

You may substitute 1¼ cups NESTLÉ® TOLL HOUSE® Semi-Sweet Chocolate Morsels for the dark chocolate baking bars.

LINE baking sheet with parchment or wax paper.

MELT ⅔ of dark chocolate in uncovered, microwave-safe bowl on MEDIUM-HIGH (70%) power for 1 minute. STIR. If pieces retain some of their original shape, microwave at additional 10- to 15-second intervals, stirring just until melted. Add *remaining* dark chocolate and stir until melted. Spread chocolate into 10×8-inch rectangle on prepared baking sheet.

MICROWAVE white morsels in small, *heavy-duty* plastic food storage bag on MEDIUM-HIGH (70%) power for 30 seconds. Knead bag until morsels are smooth. Add oil; knead to combine. Cut tiny corner from bag; squeeze to drizzle over dark chocolate. Immediately sprinkle chopped cookies over bark.

REFRIGERATE for 30 minutes or until firm. Break bark into 24 pieces. Store in airtight container at room temperature for up to 1 week.

Makes 2 dozen pieces

GIFTABLE GOODIES

Easy Toffee Candy

1¼ cups (2½ sticks) butter, *divided*

35 to 40 soda crackers

1 cup packed dark brown sugar

1 can (14 ounces) NESTLÉ® CARNATION® Sweetened Condensed Milk

1½ cups (9 ounces) NESTLÉ® TOLL HOUSE® Semi-Sweet Chocolate Morsels

¾ cup finely chopped walnuts

PREHEAT oven to 425°F. Line 15×10-inch jelly-roll pan with *heavy-duty* foil.

MELT *¼ cup* butter in medium saucepan. Pour into prepared jelly-roll pan. Arrange crackers over butter, breaking crackers to fit empty spaces.

MELT *remaining* butter in same saucepan; add sugar. Bring to a boil over medium heat. Reduce heat to low; cook, stirring occasionally, for 2 minutes. Remove from heat; stir in sweetened condensed milk. Pour over crackers.

BAKE for 10 to 12 minutes or until mixture is bubbly and slightly darkened. Remove from oven; cool for 1 minute.

SPRINKLE with morsels. Let stand for 5 minutes or until morsels are shiny and soft; spread evenly. Sprinkle with nuts; press into chocolate. Cool in pan on wire rack for 30 minutes. Refrigerate for about 30 minutes or until chocolate is set. Remove foil; cut into pieces.

Makes about 50 pieces candy

Holiday Peppermint Bark

2 cups (12-ounce package) NESTLÉ® TOLL HOUSE® Premier White Morsels

24 hard peppermint candies, unwrapped

LINE baking sheet with wax paper.

MICROWAVE morsels in medium, uncovered, microwave-safe bowl on MEDIUM-HIGH (70%) power for 1 minute. STIR. Morsels may retain some of their original shape. If necessary, microwave at additional 10- to 15-second intervals, stirring just until morsels are melted.

PLACE peppermint candies in *heavy-duty* resealable plastic food storage bag. Crush candies using rolling pin or other heavy object. While holding strainer over melted morsels, pour crushed candy into strainer. Shake to release all small candy pieces; reserve larger candy pieces. Stir morsel-peppermint mixture.

SPREAD mixture to desired thickness on prepared baking sheet. Sprinkle with reserved candy pieces; press in lightly. Let stand for about 1 hour or until firm. Break into pieces. Store in airtight container at room temperature.

Makes about 1 pound candy

GIFTABLE GOODIES

Marshmallow Pops

20 **lollipop sticks (found at cake decorating or craft stores)**

20 **large marshmallows**

1 **cup (6 ounces) NESTLÉ® TOLL HOUSE® Premier White Morsels**

1 **cup (6 ounces) NESTLÉ® TOLL HOUSE® Milk Chocolate Morsels**

Decorating icing

Assorted NESTLÉ® Candies and Chocolate*

*NESTLÉ® RAISINETS®, NESTLÉ® SNO CAPS®, WONKA® NERDS®, WONKA® TART 'N TINYS® and/or SweeTARTS® Gummy Bugs

LINE baking sheet with wax paper.

PUSH each lollipop stick halfway through a large marshmallow; set aside.

MELT white morsels according to package directions. Immediately dip 10 marshmallow lollipops lightly in the melted morsels for a thin coating. Set stick-side-up on prepared baking sheet.

MELT milk chocolate morsels according to package directions. Repeat dipping process as above with remaining marshmallows.

REFRIGERATE marshmallow lollipops for 10 minutes or until hardened. Use decorating icing as glue to decorate with assorted candies.

Makes 20 marshmallow pops

GIFTABLE
GOODIES

White Fudge with Crystallized Ginger & Cranberries

1½ cups granulated sugar

1 teaspoon ground ginger

⅔ cup (5 fluid-ounce can) NESTLÉ® CARNATION® Evaporated Milk

2 tablespoons butter

2 cups miniature marshmallows

2 cups (12-ounce package) NESTLÉ® TOLL HOUSE® Premier White Morsels

1¼ cups (6-ounce package) sweetened dried cranberries, coarsely chopped

1 jar (2.5 ounces) or ½ cup crystallized ginger*

*Crystallized ginger can be found in the spice aisle of the grocery store.

LINE 8- or 9-inch-square baking pan with foil.

COMBINE sugar and ground ginger in medium, *heavy-duty* saucepan. Add evaporated milk and butter. Bring to a full rolling boil over medium heat, stirring constantly. Boil, stirring constantly, for 4 to 5 minutes (to 234°F). Remove from heat.

STIR in marshmallows, morsels, cranberries and crystallized ginger. Stir vigorously for 1 minute or until marshmallows are melted. Pour into prepared pan; refrigerate until firm, about 1½ hours. Lift from pan; remove foil. Cut into 48 pieces.

Makes 24 (2-piece) servings

CARNATION® Famous Fudge

1½ cups granulated sugar

⅔ cup (5 fluid-ounce can) NESTLÉ® CARNATION® Evaporated Milk

2 tablespoons butter or margarine

¼ teaspoon salt

2 cups miniature marshmallows

1½ cups (9 ounces) NESTLÉ® TOLL HOUSE® Semi-Sweet Chocolate Morsels

½ cup chopped pecans or walnuts (optional)

1 teaspoon vanilla extract

LINE 8-inch-square baking pan with foil.

COMBINE sugar, evaporated milk, butter and salt in medium, *heavy-duty* saucepan. Bring to a *full rolling boil* over medium heat, stirring constantly. Boil, stirring constantly, for 4 to 5 minutes. Remove from heat.

STIR in marshmallows, morsels, nuts and vanilla extract. Stir vigorously for 1 minute or until marshmallows are melted. Pour into prepared baking pan; refrigerate for 2 hours or until firm. Lift from pan; remove foil. Cut into 48 pieces.

Makes 24 (2-piece) servings

Milk Chocolate Fudge: *SUBSTITUTE 1¾ cups (11.5-ounce package) NESTLÉ® TOLL HOUSE® Milk Chocolate Morsels for Semi-Sweet Morsels.*

Butterscotch Fudge: *SUBSTITUTE 1⅔ cups (11-ounce package) NESTLÉ® TOLL HOUSE® Butterscotch Flavored Morsels for Semi-Sweet Morsels.*

Peanutty Chocolate Fudge: *SUBSTITUTE 1⅔ cups (11-ounce package) NESTLÉ® TOLL HOUSE® Peanut Butter & Milk Chocolate Morsels for Semi-Sweet Morsels and ½ cup chopped peanuts for pecans or walnuts.*

Gift-Giving Pumpkin Cranberry Breads

6 **cups all-purpose flour**

3 **tablespoons plus 1 teaspoon pumpkin pie spice**

1 **tablespoon plus 1 teaspoon baking soda**

1 **tablespoon salt**

6 **cups granulated sugar**

1 **can (29 ounces) LIBBY'S® 100% Pure Pumpkin**

8 **large eggs**

2 **cups vegetable oil**

1 **cup orange juice or water**

2 **cups sweetened dried, fresh or frozen cranberries**

PREHEAT oven to 350°F. Grease and flour four 9×5-inch disposable loaf pans.

COMBINE flour, pumpkin pie spice, baking soda and salt in extra large bowl. Combine sugar, pumpkin, eggs, oil and juice in large bowl with wire whisk; mix until just blended. Add pumpkin mixture to flour mixture; stir until just moistened. Fold in cranberries. Spoon 4 cups of batter in each prepared loaf pan.

BAKE for 75 to 80 minutes or until wooden pick inserted in center comes out clean. Cool in pans on wire racks. Once completely cooled, wrap pans with colored plastic wrap. Decorate with ribbon.

Makes 4 loaves (12 slices per loaf)

GIFTABLE GOODIES

Pumpkin Cranberry Bread Mix

1½ **cups all-purpose flour**

2½ **teaspoons pumpkin pie spice**

1 **teaspoon baking soda**

¾ **teaspoon salt**

1½ **cups granulated sugar**

½ **cup sweetened dried cranberries**

1 **can (15 ounces) LIBBY'S® 100% Pure Pumpkin**

COMBINE all ingredients, except pumpkin, in large bowl. Pour into 1-quart resealable plastic bag. Place in fabric bag. Place bread mix and can of pumpkin in 9×5-inch loaf pan.

Makes 1 loaf (12 slices)

Recipe to Attach: *BEAT together ¾ cup LIBBY'S® 100% Pure Pumpkin, ½ cup vegetable oil, 2 large eggs and ¼ cup orange juice or water in large mixer bowl until blended. Add contents of bag; stir until just moistened. Spoon batter into greased and floured 9×5-inch loaf pan. BAKE in preheated 350°F oven for 60 to 65 minutes or until wooden pick inserted in center comes out clean. Cool in pan for 10 minutes; remove to wire rack to cool completely. Makes 1 loaf (12 slices).*

GIFTABLE GOODIES

Lavender Chocolate Fudge

⅔ cup (5 fluid-ounce can) NESTLÉ® CARNATION® Evaporated Milk

1 tablespoon dried culinary lavender (use less if desired)

1½ cups granulated sugar

2 tablespoons butter or margarine

¼ teaspoon salt

2 cups miniature marshmallows

1½ cups (9 ounces) NESTLÉ® TOLL HOUSE® Semi-Sweet Chocolate Morsels

1 teaspoon vanilla extract

LINE 8-inch-square baking pan with foil.

PLACE evaporated milk and lavender in medium, microwave-safe bowl. Heat on HIGH (100%) power for 1 minute. Cover with plastic wrap; steep for 10 minutes. Strain into medium, *heavy-duty* saucepan; discard lavender. Add sugar, butter and salt to saucepan; bring to a *full rolling boil* over medium heat, stirring constantly. Boil, stirring constantly, for 4 to 5 minutes. Remove from heat.

ADD marshmallows; stir vigorously until almost melted. Stir in morsels and vanilla extract until melted. Pour into prepared baking pan; refrigerate for 2 hours or until firm. Lift from pan; remove foil. Cut into 48 pieces.

Makes 2 dozen servings

GIFTABLE GOODIES

Old-Fashioned Pumpkin Nut Loaf Bread

- 2 **cups all-purpose flour**
- 2 **teaspoons pumpkin pie spice**
- 2 **teaspoons baking powder**
- 1 **teaspoon salt**
- ½ **teaspoon baking soda**
- 1 **can (15 ounces) LIBBY'S® 100% Pure Pumpkin**
- ½ **cup granulated sugar**
- ½ **cup packed brown sugar**
- ½ **cup NESTLÉ® CARNATION® Evaporated Fat Free Milk**
- 1 **large egg**
- 1 **large egg white**
- 1 **tablespoon vegetable oil**
- ¾ **cup chopped nuts**

PREHEAT oven to 350°F. Grease 9×5-inch loaf pan.

COMBINE flour, pumpkin pie spice, baking powder, salt and baking soda in medium bowl. Blend pumpkin, granulated sugar, brown sugar, evaporated milk, egg, egg white and oil in large mixer bowl. Add flour mixture; mix just until moistened. Pour into prepared loaf pan; sprinkle with nuts.

BAKE for 60 to 65 minutes or until wooden pick inserted in center comes out clean. Cool in pan on wire rack for 10 minutes; remove to wire rack to cool completely.

Makes 12 servings

GIFTABLE GOODIES

Dipped Peppermint Spoons

¼ cup **NESTLÉ® TOLL HOUSE® Semi-Sweet Chocolate Morsels**

½ teaspoon **vegetable shortening**

2 tablespoons **NESTLÉ® TOLL HOUSE® Premier White Morsels**

3 (about 1 tablespoon) **hard peppermint candies, unwrapped and crushed into small pieces***

8 **plastic spoons (for dipping in chocolate)**

8 **cellophane bags and twist ties or ribbons for wrapping**

To crush peppermint candies, place unwrapped candies in heavy-duty plastic bag; seal. Crush using rolling pin or other heavy object.

LINE baking sheet with wax paper.

MICROWAVE semi-sweet morsels and vegetable shortening in small, uncovered, microwave-safe bowl on HIGH (100%) power for 20 seconds. STIR. Morsels may retain some of their original shape. If necessary, microwave at additional 10- to 15-second intervals, stirring just until morsels are melted.

DIP the end of *each* spoon in melted chocolate, tilting bowl to easily dip. Use side of bowl to remove excess. Place on prepared baking sheet. Refrigerate for 15 minutes or until set.

MICROWAVE white morsels in small, *heavy-duty* plastic bag on MEDIUM-HIGH (70%) power for 20 seconds; knead. Microwave at additional 10- to 15-second intervals, kneading until smooth. Cut tiny corner from each bag. Squeeze to drizzle over ends of already dipped spoons. Dip spoons in crushed peppermints; return to baking sheet. Let stand until set. Insert spoons into bags and secure with ties. Store at room temperature.

Makes 8 spoons

GIFTABLE GOODIES

Chocolate Indulgence Holiday Gifting Sauce

2 cups (12-ounce package) NESTLÉ® TOLL HOUSE® Semi-Sweet Chocolate Morsels

1 cup heavy whipping cream

2 tablespoons light corn syrup

2 to 3 tablespoons flavored liqueur or ½ teaspoon flavored extract (optional)

You may substitute 1¾ cups (11.5-ounce package) NESTLÉ® TOLL HOUSE® Milk Chocolate Morsels for the Semi-Sweet Chocolate Morsels.

COMBINE morsels, cream and corn syrup in large microwave-safe bowl.

MICROWAVE uncovered, on HIGH (100%) power for 1 minute. STIR. If necessary, microwave at additional 20- to 30-second intervals, stirring until morsels are melted and sauce is smooth. Add liqueur or extract; mix well.

SERVE warm as a dipping sauce for fresh fruit or spoon over ice cream or cake. Store remaining sauce tightly covered in refrigerator. Makes about 2 cups.

Makes 16 (2-tablespoon) servings

For Gifting: *TRANSFER sauce to clean gifting jars; seal well. Refrigerate up to 7 days.*

Serving Suggestion: *Serve with sliced pears and seasonal holiday fruits.*

GIFTABLE GOODIES

Chocolate Chip Cookie Mix in a Jar

1¾ **cups all-purpose flour**

¾ **teaspoon baking soda**

¾ **teaspoon salt**

1½ **cups (9 ounces) NESTLÉ®**
TOLL HOUSE® Semi-Sweet
Chocolate Morsels

¾ **cup packed brown sugar**

½ **cup granulated sugar**

COMBINE flour, baking soda and salt in small bowl. Place flour mixture in 1-quart jar. Layer remaining ingredients in order listed above, pressing firmly after each layer. Seal with lid and decorate with fabric and ribbon.

Makes 2 dozen cookies

Recipe to Attach: *PREHEAT oven to 375°F.* BEAT ¾ cup (1½ sticks) softened butter or margarine, 1 large egg and ¾ teaspoon vanilla extract in large mixer bowl until blended. Add cookie mix and ½ cup chopped nuts (optional); mix well, breaking up any clumps. Drop by rounded tablespoon onto ungreased baking sheets. BAKE for 9 to 11 minutes or until golden brown. Cool on baking sheets for 2 minutes; remove to wire racks to cool completely. Makes about 2 dozen cookies.

Winter

Dark Chocolate & Basil Truffles

Celebrate the winter holidays with scrumptious grown-up finger foods. Discover savory party recipes like Mexi-Meatball Kabobs or Smokin' Almond Blue Cheese Dip. For the sweeter bunch, try Dark Chocolate & Basil Truffles, Pumpkin Mousse in Cinnamon Pastry Shells, and so much more.

½ cup heavy whipping cream

2 bars (8 ounces) NESTLÉ® TOLL HOUSE® Dark Chocolate Baking Bar

1 tablespoon sour cream

1 teaspoon light corn syrup

½ teaspoon vanilla extract

3 tablespoons loosely packed fresh basil leaves (washed and patted dry), finely chopped

NESTLÉ® TOLL HOUSE® Baking Cocoa

LINE baking sheet with parchment or wax paper.

HEAT cream to a gentle boil in small, *heavy-duty* saucepan. Remove from heat. Add chocolate. Stir until mixture is smooth and chocolate is melted. Add sour cream, corn syrup, vanilla extract and basil; stir to combine. Refrigerate for 15 to 20 minutes or until slightly thickened.

DROP chocolate mixture by rounded measuring teaspoonful onto prepared baking sheet. Refrigerate for 1 hour. Shape or roll into balls. Dust truffles with cocoa.* Store in airtight container in refrigerator for up to 3 days.

Make 18 servings (2 pieces each)

To dust the truffles, place cocoa in a small, fine mesh strainer and tap over the rolled truffles.

Macaroon Butterscotch Tartlets

FILLING:

- ⅔ **cup (5 fluid-ounce can) NESTLÉ® CARNATION® Evaporated Milk**
- ¼ **cup water**
- 2 **tablespoons cornstarch**
- ⅛ **teaspoon salt**
- ⅔ **cup NESTLÉ® TOLL HOUSE® Butterscotch Flavored Morsels**
- 1 **tablespoon butter**
- 1 **teaspoon vanilla extract**

CRUSTS:

- 1½ **cups all-purpose flour**
- 1 **cup** *plus* **2 tablespoons sweetened flaked coconut,** *divided*
- 2 **tablespoons granulated sugar**

  Pinch salt
- ½ **cup (1 stick) butter, cut into small pieces**
- 1 **to 2 tablespoons water,** *divided*

FOR FILLING:

WHISK together evaporated milk, water, cornstarch and salt in small saucepan. Cook over medium heat, stirring constantly, until mixture begins to thicken. Remove from heat. Stir in morsels, butter and vanilla extract until smooth. For a smoother sauce, strain through metal strainer. Refrigerate for 1 hour.

FOR CRUSTS:

PREHEAT oven to 375°F. Grease 12 (2½-inch) muffin cups. Line small baking sheet with foil.

PLACE flour, *1 cup* coconut, sugar and salt in food processor fitted with metal blade. Process until finely chopped. Add butter and *1 tablespoon* water and pulse until fine crumbs are formed. Divide mixture evenly between muffin cups and press onto bottom and halfway up sides. Pierce bottom of each crust several times.

BAKE crusts for 15 minutes or until light brown around edges, repiercing bottoms of crusts after 8 minutes. While baking the crust, toast *remaining 2 tablespoons* coconut on prepared baking sheet in same oven for 8 minutes or until light golden brown. Cool coconut crusts in cups and toasted coconut completely on wire racks.

TO SERVE: Remove crusts from pans to serving platter with tip of knife. Spoon a heaping measuring tablespoon of Butterscotch Filling into each crust. Top with toasted coconut.

Makes 12 tartlets

FESTIVE FINGER FOODS

Mexi-Meatball Kabobs

Nonstick cooking spray

3 pounds lean ground beef

2 cups quick oats

1 can (12 fluid ounces) NESTLÉ® CARNATION® Evaporated Milk

2 large eggs

½ cup ketchup

2 packets (1¼ ounces *each*) taco seasoning mix

1 teaspoon ground black pepper

3 large bell peppers (any color), cut into 60, 1-inch pieces

60 (4-inch) wooden skewers

Salsa and sour cream (optional)

PREHEAT oven to 350°F. Foil-line 3 baking sheets and spray with nonstick cooking spray.

COMBINE ground beef, oats, evaporated milk, eggs, ketchup, taco seasoning and black pepper in large bowl until just mixed. Form mixture into 120 (1-inch) meatballs. Place on prepared baking sheets.

BAKE for 15 to 20 minutes or until no longer pink in center. Drain on paper towels, if needed.

THREAD two meatballs and one piece of pepper on *each* skewer. Place on large serving platter. Serve with salsa and sour cream.

Makes 30 servings (2 skewers each)

Tip: *Meatballs can be made and baked ahead of time, refrigerated for up to 3 days or frozen up to 3 months and heated prior to serving.*

Serving Suggestion: *Meatballs can also be served individually with toothpicks and dipping bowls of salsas.*

FESTIVE FINGER FOODS

Creamy Deviled Eggs

12 **large hard-cooked eggs, peeled**

¼ to ⅓ cup NESTLÉ® CARNATION® Evaporated Lowfat 2% Milk*

3½ tablespoons light mayonnaise

2 **teaspoons Dijon mustard**

    Salt

    Paprika

*Can also substitute with NESTLÉ® CARNATION® Evaporated Milk or NESTLÉ® CARNATION® Evaporated Fat Free Milk.

CUT eggs in half lengthwise. Remove yolks and place in medium bowl; mash well with fork or pastry blender. Add evaporated milk, mayonnaise and mustard. Stir until creamy. Season with salt.

SPOON or pipe into whites. Sprinkle with paprika.

Makes 12 appetizer servings

Dill Deviled Eggs: *Add 1½ teaspoons chopped fresh dill. Eliminate paprika.*

Curried Deviled Eggs: *Eliminate Dijon mustard, use ⅓ cup evaporated milk and add 1¼ teaspoons curry powder.*

Svelte Blue Cheese Dressing and Dip

½ cup plain fat free yogurt

¼ cup *dry* NESTLÉ® CARNATION® Instant Nonfat Dry Milk

½ cup chopped green onions

2 **ounces crumbled blue cheese**

1 **small clove garlic, finely chopped**

¼ teaspoon crushed dried basil

¼ teaspoon crushed dried rosemary

⅛ teaspoon salt

COMBINE yogurt and dry milk in small bowl. Add green onions, cheese, garlic, basil, rosemary and salt; mix well.

COVER; refrigerate for 30 minutes before serving.

Makes 8 servings

FESTIVE FINGER FOODS

Hint of Honey Pumpkin Spread

- **1 package (8 ounces) ⅓ less fat cream cheese (Neufchâtel), at room temperature**
- **½ cup LIBBY'S® 100% Pure Pumpkin**
- **2 tablespoons honey**
- **1 pinch ground cinnamon**

STIR cream cheese, pumpkin, honey and cinnamon in medium bowl for 1 minute or until smooth. Serve immediately or refrigerate in tightly covered container for up to 4 days.

SERVE with apple slices or whole wheat crackers.

Makes 10 servings (2 tablespoons each)

Nutty Dark Hot Chocolate

- **2 cups 1% milk**
- **½ cup NESTLÉ® TOLL HOUSE® Dark Chocolate Morsels**
- **1 tablespoon reduced-fat creamy peanut butter**
- **¼ teaspoon vanilla extract**

HEAT milk, morsels and peanut butter in small saucepan over medium-low heat, stirring frequently, until hot and morsels are melted. Do not boil. Stir in vanilla extract. Pour into mugs.

Makes 2 servings

FESTIVE FINGER FOODS

Smokin' Almond Blue Cheese Dip

- **1   cup sour cream**
- **¾   cup mayonnaise**
- **⅔   cup (5 fluid-ounce can) NESTLÉ® CARNATION® Evaporated Milk**
- **½   cup smoked almonds, chopped**
- **4   ounces blue or Gorgonzola cheese, crumbled**
- **1   tablespoon cider vinegar**
- **⅛   teaspoon ground black pepper**

COMBINE sour cream, mayonnaise, evaporated milk, almonds, cheese, vinegar and black pepper in medium bowl; cover. Refrigerate for 2 hours before serving.

SERVE with assorted cut-up vegetables or chicken wings.

Makes 20 servings (2 tablespoons each)

Variation: *To use as a salad dressing, increase evaporated milk to 1 cup.*

Chocolate Chip Cranberry Cheese Bars

- **1   cup (2 sticks) butter or margarine, softened**
- **1   cup packed brown sugar**
- **2   cups all-purpose flour**
- **1½ cups quick or old-fashioned oats**
- **2   teaspoons grated orange peel**
- **2   cups (12-ounce package) NESTLÉ® TOLL HOUSE® Semi-Sweet Chocolate Morsels**
- **1   cup sweetened dried cranberries**
- **1   package (8 ounces) cream cheese, softened**
- **1   can (14 ounces) NESTLÉ® CARNATION® Sweetened Condensed Milk**

PREHEAT oven to 350°F. Grease 13×9-inch baking pan.

BEAT butter and sugar in large mixer bowl until creamy. Gradually beat in flour, oats and orange peel until crumbly. Stir in morsels and cranberries; reserve 2 *cups* mixture. Press *remaining* mixture onto bottom of prepared baking pan.

BAKE for 15 minutes. Beat cream cheese in small mixer bowl until smooth. Gradually beat in sweetened condensed milk. Pour over hot crust; sprinkle with *reserved* mixture. Bake for 25 to 30 minutes or until center is set. Cool in pan on wire rack. Cut into bars.

Makes about 3 dozen bars

FESTIVE FINGER FOODS

Thai-Peanut Ginger Wings

1 **can (12 fluid ounces) NESTLÉ® CARNATION® Evaporated Milk**

1 **cup creamy or chunky peanut butter**

½ **cup soy sauce, *divided***

¼ **cup chopped green onions**

2½ **teaspoons ground ginger**

2 **teaspoons rice or cider vinegar**

½ **teaspoon red pepper flakes**

5 **pounds frozen chicken wings, thawed**

PLACE evaporated milk, peanut butter, 3 *tablespoons* soy sauce, green onions, ginger, vinegar and pepper flakes in blender; cover. Blend until smooth. Combine ½ *cup* peanut sauce, *remaining 5 tablespoons* soy sauce and chicken wings in large bowl; cover. Marinate chicken in refrigerator for 1 hour. Refrigerate remaining peanut sauce.

PREHEAT oven to 425°F. Foil-line and grease 2 baking sheets with sides.

PLACE chicken on prepared baking sheets. Discard any remaining marinade.

BAKE for 40 to 45 minutes, turning once, or until chicken is cooked through. Remove from baking sheets to serving platter. Stir *remaining* peanut sauce and spoon some over wings. If desired, serve remaining sauce with wings and assorted cut-up vegetables.

Makes 20 servings

Serving Suggestion: *Jazz up the presentation with a colorful array of fresh vegetables, such as peapods and red and yellow peppers.*

FESTIVE FINGER FOODS

Bolivian Quinoa Humintas (Tamales)

1 package (4 ounces) dried corn husks, *divided*

¼ cup (½ stick) butter

1 medium onion, finely chopped

2 cups cooked quinoa

⅔ cup (5 fluid-ounce can) NESTLÉ® CARNATION® Evaporated Milk

2 large eggs, lightly beaten

1 tablespoon sugar

1 teaspoon salt

½ teaspoon anise seeds, crushed

½ teaspoon ground cinnamon

1 tablespoon hot yellow pepper paste or purée

1 cup (4 ounces) shredded Chihuahua, mozzarella or Muenster cheese

¼ cup grated Parmesan cheese (optional)

SOAK 12 large or 24 small corn husks in warm water for at least 1 hour or until softened and easy to fold. (A plate placed on top of husks will help in keeping husks submerged.) Set aside *remaining* dry husks; they will be used later in recipe.

HEAT butter in small skillet over medium heat. Add onion; cook, stirring occasionally, for 3 minutes or until tender.

PLACE quinoa in a food processor; cover. Pulse a few times until coarsely ground. Add evaporated milk, cooked onion, quinoa, eggs, sugar, salt, anise, cinnamon, pepper paste and cheeses. Pulse until well blended. (The batter will be somewhat thick.)

PLACE one large or two small soaked corn husks overlapped on work surface. Spread ⅓ cup filling, using back of spoon, to form a square in the center of the lower half of husk(s). Fold left edge over filling. Fold pointy end of husk and tuck in while folding over right edge (one end will be open). Tie with strip of corn husk or twine. Repeat with *remaining* dry husks and filling.

PLACE vegetable steamer in large pot; add water to just below steamer. Arrange tamales upright in steamer rack. Cover top of tamales with *remaining* dry husks and a damp towel; cover with lid. Bring to a boil; reduce heat to low. Steam, adding water as needed, for about 30 to 45 minutes or until filling pulls away from the husks. Serve warm.

Makes 12 tamales

FESTIVE FINGER FOODS

Chocolate Mint Truffles

1¾ cups (11.5-ounce package) NESTLÉ® TOLL HOUSE® Milk Chocolate Morsels

1 cup (6 ounces) NESTLÉ® TOLL HOUSE® Semi-Sweet Chocolate Morsels

¾ cup heavy whipping cream

1 tablespoon peppermint extract

1½ cups finely chopped walnuts, toasted, or NESTLÉ® TOLL HOUSE® Baking Cocoa

LINE baking sheet with wax paper.

PLACE milk chocolate and semi-sweet morsels in large mixer bowl. Heat cream to a gentle boil in small saucepan; pour over morsels. Let stand for 1 minute; stir until smooth. Stir in peppermint extract. Cover with plastic wrap; refrigerate for 35 to 45 minutes or until slightly thickened. Stir just until color lightens slightly. (*Do not* overmix or truffles will be grainy.)

DROP by rounded teaspoonful onto prepared baking sheet; refrigerate for 10 to 15 minutes. Shape into balls; roll in walnuts or cocoa. Store in airtight container in refrigerator.

Makes about 48 truffles

Variation: *After rolling chocolate mixture into balls, freeze for 30 to 40 minutes. Microwave 1¾ cups (11.5-ounce package) NESTLÉ® TOLL HOUSE® Milk Chocolate Morsels and 3 tablespoons vegetable shortening in medium, uncovered, microwave-safe bowl on MEDIUM-HIGH (70%) power for 1 minute. STIR. Morsels may retain some of their original shape. If necessary, microwave at additional 10- to 15-second intervals, stirring just until morsels are melted. Dip truffles into chocolate mixture; shake off excess. Place on foil-lined baking sheets. Refrigerate for 15 to 20 minutes or until set. Store in airtight container in refrigerator.*

FESTIVE FINGER FOODS

Chunky Pecan Pie Bars

CRUST:

1½ cups all-purpose flour

½ cup (1 stick) butter or margarine, softened

¼ cup packed brown sugar

FILLING:

3 large eggs

¾ cup corn syrup

¾ cup granulated sugar

2 tablespoons butter or margarine, melted

1 teaspoon vanilla extract

1¾ cups (11.5-ounce package) NESTLÉ® TOLL HOUSE® Semi-Sweet Chocolate Chunks

1½ cups coarsely chopped pecans

PREHEAT oven to 350°F. Grease 13×9-inch baking pan.

FOR CRUST:

BEAT flour, butter and brown sugar in small mixer bowl until crumbly. Press into prepared baking pan.

BAKE for 12 to 15 minutes or until lightly browned.

FOR FILLING:

BEAT eggs, corn syrup, granulated sugar, butter and vanilla extract in medium bowl with wire whisk. Stir in chunks and nuts. Pour evenly over baked crust.

BAKE for 25 to 30 minutes or until set. Cool completely in pan on wire rack. Cut into bars.

*Makes
3 dozen bars*

Party-Perfect Mini Quiches

1 can (12 fluid ounces) NESTLÉ® CARNATION® Evaporated Milk

3 large eggs, beaten

2 tablespoons all-purpose flour

¼ teaspoon salt

¼ teaspoon ground black pepper

2 cups (8-ounce package) shredded mild or sharp cheddar cheese

2 cups frozen chopped broccoli, thawed and drained

½ cup chopped red bell pepper

PREHEAT oven to 350°F. Grease and lightly flour 12 (2½-inch) muffin cups.

WHISK evaporated milk, eggs, flour, salt and black pepper in medium bowl until blended. Stir in cheese, broccoli and bell pepper. Spoon ¼ to ⅓ cup of mixture into *each* prepared muffin cup, filling almost to rim. Stir mixture frequently to evenly distribute ingredients.

BAKE for 23 to 28 minutes or until knife inserted near centers comes out clean and tops are lightly browned. Cool in pans for 15 minutes. Run knife or small, flat spatula around inside edges of muffin cups. Carefully remove quiches.

Makes 12 servings

Tip: *Quiches can be made ahead and frozen. To reheat, place on baking sheet and bake in preheated 325°F oven for 25 to 30 minutes*  *or, place 2 to 4 quiches on microwave-safe plate and microwave on MEDIUM-HIGH (70%) power for 2½ to 5 minutes or until hot.*

FESTIVE FINGER FOODS

Thai Pumpkin Satay

1 cup LIBBY'S® 100% Pure Pumpkin

⅔ cup (5 fluid-ounce can) NESTLÉ® CARNATION® Evaporated Milk

⅓ cup creamy or chunky peanut butter

2 green onions, chopped

2 cloves garlic, peeled

2 tablespoons chopped fresh cilantro

2 tablespoons lime juice

1 tablespoon soy sauce

2 teaspoons granulated sugar

⅛ to ¼ teaspoon cayenne pepper

1 pound boneless, skinless chicken breast halves, cut into 1-inch pieces

2 large red bell peppers, cut into 1-inch pieces

2 bunches green onions, cut into 1-inch pieces (white parts only)

30 (4-inch) skewers*

*If using wooden skewers, soak in water for 30 minutes before threading.

PLACE pumpkin, milk, peanut butter, chopped green onions, garlic, cilantro, lime juice, soy sauce, sugar and cayenne pepper in blender or food processor; cover. Blend until smooth. Combine ½ *cup* pumpkin mixture and chicken in medium bowl; cover. Marinate in refrigerate, stirring occasionally, for 1 hour.

ALTERNATELY thread chicken, bell peppers and green onion pieces onto skewers. Discard any remaining marinade. Grill or broil, turning once, for 10 minutes or until chicken is no longer pink. Heat *remaining* pumpkin mixture; serve with satay.

Makes 10 servings (3 skewers each)

Winter

Roasted Vegetable Soup

Take away the winter chill with these simmering soups and stews, chunky chowders, and delicious chili recipes. They're simple to make and easy to enjoy!

- 1 **small (about 2 pounds) butternut squash, peeled, seeded and cut into 1½-inch pieces**
- 3 **cups (1 large) peeled and very coarsely chopped sweet potato**
- 1 **cup (1 large) peeled and thickly sliced parsnip**
- 1 **cup (1 medium) thickly sliced leek (white and pale green parts only)**
- 3 **large cloves garlic, peeled**
- 2 **tablespoons extra virgin olive oil**
- 2 **teaspoons MAGGI® Granulated Chicken Flavor Bouillon**
- 3 **cups water,** *divided*
- 1 **can (12 fluid ounces) NESTLÉ® CARNATION® Evaporated Fat Free Milk**
- ¼ **teaspoon crushed red pepper**
- ¼ **to ½ teaspoon finely chopped fresh sage**

  Roasted pepitas (optional)

PREHEAT oven to 425°F. Line shallow roasting pan with foil.

PLACE squash, sweet potato, parsnip, leek and garlic in pan; drizzle with oil. Sprinkle with bouillon; toss to coat.

BAKE for 15 minutes; stir. Bake for an additional 10 to 15 minutes or until tender.

PURÉE *half* of roasted vegetables with about *1½ cups* water in food processor or blender; cover and process until smooth or until desired consistency. Add more water as needed for processing. Pour into large saucepan. Repeat with *remaining* vegetables and *remaining* water.

STIR in evaporated milk, crushed red pepper and sage. Heat over medium-high heat until heated through. Serve with pepitas sprinkled over top.

Makes 4 main-dish or 8 side-dish servings

WINTER WARM-UPS

Ham-It-Up White Bean Soup

- **1 tablespoon olive oil**
- **½ small onion, chopped**
- **2 garlic cloves, finely chopped**
- **¼ cup all-purpose flour**
- **1 can (12 fluid ounces) NESTLÉ® CARNATION® Evaporated Milk**
- **1 can (14½ fluid ounces) reduced-sodium chicken broth**
- **1½ cups (about 6 ounces) cooked ham, cut into ½-inch pieces**
- **1 can (15½ ounces) cannellini (white kidney) beans, undrained**
- **½ cup frozen peas***
- **Ground black pepper (optional)**

You may substitute 1 cup coarsely chopped spinach leaves for the peas.

HEAT oil in medium saucepan over medium heat. Add onion and garlic; cook, stirring occasionally, for 1 to 2 minutes or until onion is tender. Stir in flour. Gradually stir in evaporated milk and broth. Cook, stirring constantly, until mixture comes to a boil. Add ham, beans and peas. Heat through. Season to taste with pepper.

Makes 6 servings (1 cup each)

Baked Potato Soup

- **2 large or 3 medium baking potatoes, baked or microwaved**
- **¼ cup (½ stick) butter or margarine**
- **¼ cup chopped onion**
- **¼ cup all-purpose flour**
- **1 can (14.5 fluid ounces) chicken broth**
- **1 can (12 fluid ounces) NESTLÉ® CARNATION® Evaporated Milk**
- **Cooked and crumbled bacon, shredded cheddar cheese and sliced green onions (optional)**

MELT butter in large saucepan over medium heat. Add onion; cook, stirring occasionally, for 1 to 2 minutes or until tender. Stir in flour. Gradually stir in broth and evaporated milk. Scoop potato pulp from 1 potato (reserve potato skin); mash. Add pulp to broth mixture. Cook over medium heat, stirring occasionally, until mixture comes to a boil. Dice *remaining* potato skin and potato(es); add to soup. Heat through. Season with salt and ground black pepper. Top each serving with bacon, cheese and green onions, if desired.

Makes 4 servings

Variation: *For a different twist to this recipe, omit the bacon, cheddar cheese and green onions. Cook 2 tablespoons shredded carrot with the onion and add ¼ teaspoon dried dill to the soup when adding the broth. Proceed as above.*

WINTER WARM-UPS

New England Clam Chowder

- 4 slices bacon, chopped
- 1 pound (about 3 medium) potatoes, peeled and cut into ½-inch chunks
- ¼ cup chopped carrot
- ¼ cup chopped onion
- ¼ cup finely chopped celery
- 2 cans (12 fluid ounces *each*) NESTLÉ® CARNATION® Evaporated Milk
- ¼ cup all-purpose flour
- 2 cans (6.5 ounces *each*) chopped or minced clams, undrained
- ½ teaspoon salt
- ½ teaspoon Worcestershire sauce
- ¼ teaspoon ground black pepper

COOK bacon in medium saucepan until crisp; drain. Reserve *2 tablespoons* bacon fat. Return *reserved* bacon fat to saucepan. Add potatoes, carrot, onion and celery. Cook, stirring frequently, for 6 to 7 minutes or until potatoes are tender.

COMBINE evaporated milk and flour in small bowl until blended; add to potato mixture. Stir in clams with juice, salt, bacon, Worcestershire sauce and pepper. Reduce heat to medium-low; cook, stirring frequently, for 15 to 20 minutes or until creamy and slightly thick.

Makes 4 servings

WINTER WARM-UPS

Pumpkin Peanut Soup

2 **tablespoons butter**

1¼ **cups chopped onion**

¼ **cup chopped shallots**

2 **cloves garlic, finely chopped**

½ **teaspoon crushed dried marjoram**

¼ **teaspoon crushed dried thyme**

3 **cups chicken broth**

1 **can (15 ounces) LIBBY'S® 100% Pure Pumpkin**

1 **can (12 ounces) NESTLÉ® CARNATION® Evaporated Lowfat 2% Milk**

⅓ **cup creamy peanut butter, (up to ½ cup)**

MELT butter in large saucepan over medium-high heat. Add onion, shallots and garlic; cook, stirring occasionally, for 3 to 5 minutes or until tender. Stir in marjoram and thyme; cook for 1 minute. Stir in broth and pumpkin; bring to a boil. Reduce heat to low; cover. Cook, stirring occasionally, for 15 to 20 minutes. Remove from heat; stir in milk and peanut butter.

TRANSFER mixture to blender or food processor (in batches, if necessary); cover. Blend until smooth. Return to saucepan. Cook over medium heat, stirring occasionally, for 5 minutes or until heated through.

Makes 6 servings

WINTER WARM-UPS

Cheddar Cheese Soup

- ¼ cup (½ stick) butter or margarine
- ¼ cup all-purpose flour
- 2 cans (12 fluid ounces *each*) NESTLÉ® CARNATION® Evaporated Milk
- 1 cup beer or water
- 2 teaspoons Worcestershire sauce
- ½ teaspoon dry mustard (optional)
- ¼ teaspoon cayenne pepper
- 2 cups (8 ounces) shredded sharp cheddar cheese

    Toppings: crumbled cooked bacon, sliced green onions, croutons

MELT butter in large saucepan. Add flour; cook, stirring constantly, until bubbly. Add evaporated milk; bring to a boil, stirring constantly. Reduce heat; stir in beer, Worcestershire sauce, mustard and cayenne pepper. Cook for 10 minutes. Remove from heat. Stir in cheese until melted. Season with salt. Serve with toppings.

Makes 4 servings

Creamy Roasted Red Pepper Soup

- ¼ cup (½ stick) butter or margarine, *divided*
- ½ cup chopped onion
- 1 clove garlic, finely chopped
- 1 jar (12 ounces) roasted red peppers, drained, seeds removed
- ¼ cup all-purpose flour
- 1 can (12 fluid ounces) NESTLÉ® CARNATION® Evaporated Milk
- 1 can (14.5 fluid ounces) vegetable broth
- ½ teaspoon salt
- ¼ teaspoon ground black pepper

MELT 2 *tablespoons* butter in medium saucepan over medium heat. Add onion and garlic; cook, stirring occasionally, for 1 to 2 minutes or until onion is tender. Transfer onion mixture to blender. Add red peppers; cover. Blend until smooth.

MELT remaining 2 *tablespoons* butter in same saucepan. Stir in flour. Gradually stir in evaporated milk and broth. Cook, stirring constantly, until mixture comes to a boil. Stir in red pepper mixture, salt and pepper. Heat through.

Makes 6 servings

All-Star Potato, Bacon & Corn Chowder

- **2 cans (14 fluid ounces *each*) reduced-sodium chicken broth**
- **2 cans (12 fluid ounces *each*) NESTLÉ® CARNATION® Evaporated Milk**
- **2 cups instant mashed potato flakes**
- **1 can (15¼ ounces) no-salt added whole-kernel corn, drained**
- **8 slices bacon, cooked and crumbled**
- **2 teaspoons onion powder**
- **¼ teaspoon ground black pepper**

    Shredded cheddar cheese, sliced green onions, additional cooked and/or crumbled bacon (optional)

COMBINE broth and evaporated milk in large saucepan. Bring mixture just to a boil over medium-high heat; reduce heat to low. Add potato flakes, corn, bacon, onion powder and pepper. Cook, stirring frequently, for 5 to 8 minutes until creamy and slightly thick. Top each serving with cheddar cheese, green onions and/or bacon.

Makes 8 servings

Cream of Chicken and Vegetable Soup

- **¼ cup (½ stick) butter or margarine**
- **¼ cup all-purpose flour**
- **1 can (12 fluid ounces) NESTLÉ® CARNATION® Evaporated Milk**
- **1 package (16 ounces) frozen mixed vegetables, prepared according to package directions**
- **2 (about 8 ounces *total*) boneless, skinless chicken breast halves, cooked and cubed**
- **1 can (14.5 fluid ounces) chicken broth**
- **¼ teaspoon onion salt**

MELT butter in medium saucepan over medium heat. Stir in flour. Gradually stir in evaporated milk. Cook, stirring constantly, until mixture comes to a boil. Add vegetables, chicken, broth and onion salt. Heat through.

Makes 6 servings

Lower-fat Version: *Substitute NESTLÉ® CARNATION® Evaporated Lowfat Milk and 1 can (14.5 fluid ounces) light or fat-free chicken broth. Proceed as above.*

Ham & Tater Corn Chowder

- 18 frozen potato puffs
- 2 cans (14 fluid ounces *each*) reduced sodium chicken broth
- 2 cans (12 fluid ounces *each*) NESTLÉ® CARNATION® Evaporated Milk
- 2 cups (8 ounces) cooked ham, cut into ½-inch pieces
- 1¾ cups instant mashed potato flakes
- 1 can (15¼ ounces) no-salt added whole-kernel corn, drained
- 2 teaspoons onion powder
- ¼ teaspoon ground black pepper

  Sliced green onions (optional)

PREPARE potato puffs according to package directions.

MEANWHILE, COMBINE broth and evaporated milk in large saucepan. Bring mixture just to a boil over medium-high heat; reduce heat to low. Add ham, potato flakes, corn, onion powder and black pepper. Cook, stirring frequently, for 5 to 8 minutes until creamy and slightly thick. Top each serving with three potato puffs and green onions, if desired.

Makes 6 servings

Broccoli Cheese Soup

- 3 cans (14½ fluid ounces *each*) reduced-sodium chicken broth
- 2 packages (16 ounces *each*) frozen cut broccoli
- 1 small onion, coarsely chopped
- 1 teaspoon bottled minced garlic
- 1½ cups *dry* NESTLÉ® CARNATION® Instant Nonfat Dry Milk
- ½ cup water
- ¼ cup all-purpose flour
- 1 cup (4 ounces) shredded cheddar cheese

  Shredded cheddar cheese (optional)

HEAT broth in large saucepan to boiling. Add broccoli, onion and garlic. Return to a boil. Reduce heat to low; cover. Cook for 5 to 7 minutes or until broccoli is tender. Remove from heat; cool slightly. Transfer half of vegetable-broth mixture to blender or food processor (in batches, if necessary); cover. Blend until desired consistency. Return to saucepan.

COMBINE dry milk, water and flour in medium bowl; mix well. Stir into soup; season with salt and ground black pepper, if desired. Heat through. Add 1 cup cheese. Stir over low heat until melted. Sprinkle with additional cheese.

Makes 6 servings

WINTER WARM-UPS

Calabaza Soup

2 tablespoons olive oil

3 pounds calabaza (can substitute Hubbard, butternut or acorn squash), seeded, peeled

1 medium ripe tomato, peeled, chopped (about 1½ cups)

½ cup finely chopped red onion

1 can (12 fluid ounces) NESTLÉ® CARNATION® Evaporated Milk

1 teaspoon granulated sugar

½ teaspoon ground nutmeg

½ teaspoon salt

¼ teaspoon ground white or black pepper

Ground cinnamon

Sour cream

CUT calabaza into chunks. Steam or boil in large saucepan on medium-high heat until tender, about 25 minutes. Drain; place back in saucepan and set aside.

HEAT olive oil in large skillet on medium heat. Add tomato and onion, cook until soft. Add cooked tomato mixture to calabaza. In two batches, place cooked calabaza and tomato mixture in blender container or food processor; cover. Blend until smooth.

PLACE mixture back into large saucepan. Stir in evaporated milk, sugar, nutmeg, salt and pepper; mix well. Cook over medium heat, stirring occasionally, until just boiling. Serve in soup bowls with a sprinkle of cinnamon and a dollop of sour cream.

Makes 6 servings

WINTER WARM-UPS

Creamy Pumpkin Soup

- ¼ cup (½ stick) butter or margarine
- 1 small onion, chopped
- 1 clove garlic, finely chopped
- 2 teaspoons packed brown sugar
- 1 can (14½ ounces) chicken broth
- ½ cup water
- ½ teaspoon salt (optional)
- ¼ teaspoon ground black pepper
- 1 can (15 ounces) LIBBY'S® 100% Pure Pumpkin
- 1 can (12 ounces) NESTLÉ® CARNATION® Evaporated Milk
- ⅛ teaspoon ground cinnamon

MELT butter in large saucepan over medium heat. Add onion, garlic and sugar; cook for 1 to 2 minutes or until soft. Add broth, water, salt and pepper; bring to a boil, stirring occasionally. Reduce heat to low; cook, stirring occasionally, for 15 minutes. Stir in pumpkin, evaporated milk and cinnamon. Cook, stirring occasionally, for 5 minutes. Remove from heat.

TRANSFER mixture to food processor or blender (in batches, if necessary); process until smooth. Return to saucepan. Serve warm.

Makes 5 servings

INDEX

INDEX

INDEX

INDEX

INDEX

INDEX

INDEX

INDEX

INDEX

METRIC CONVERSION CHART

VOLUME MEASUREMENTS (dry)

1/8 teaspoon = 0.5 mL
1/4 teaspoon = 1 mL
1/2 teaspoon = 2 mL
3/4 teaspoon = 4 mL
1 teaspoon = 5 mL
1 tablespoon = 15 mL
2 tablespoons = 30 mL
1/4 cup = 60 mL
1/3 cup = 75 mL
1/2 cup = 125 mL
2/3 cup = 150 mL
3/4 cup = 175 mL
1 cup = 250 mL
2 cups = 1 pint = 500 mL
3 cups = 750 mL
4 cups = 1 quart = 1 L

VOLUME MEASUREMENTS (fluid)

1 fluid ounce (2 tablespoons) = 30 mL
4 fluid ounces (1/2 cup) = 125 mL
8 fluid ounces (1 cup) = 250 mL
12 fluid ounces (1 1/2 cups) = 375 mL
16 fluid ounces (2 cups) = 500 mL

WEIGHTS (mass)

1/2 ounce = 15 g
1 ounce = 30 g
3 ounces = 90 g
4 ounces = 120 g
8 ounces = 225 g
10 ounces = 285 g
12 ounces = 360 g
16 ounces = 1 pound = 450 g

DIMENSIONS

1/16 inch = 2 mm
1/8 inch = 3 mm
1/4 inch = 6 mm
1/2 inch = 1.5 cm
3/4 inch = 2 cm
1 inch = 2.5 cm

OVEN TEMPERATURES

250°F = 120°C
275°F = 140°C
300°F = 150°C
325°F = 160°C
350°F = 180°C
375°F = 190°C
400°F = 200°C
425°F = 220°C
450°F = 230°C

BAKING PAN SIZES

Utensil	Size in Inches/Quarts	Metric Volume	Size in Centimeters
Baking or Cake Pan (square or rectangular)	8×8×2	2 L	20×20×5
	9×9×2	2.5 L	23×23×5
	12×8×2	3 L	30×20×5
	13×9×2	3.5 L	33×23×5
Loaf Pan	8×4×3	1.5 L	20×10×7
	9×5×3	2 L	23×13×7
Round Layer Cake Pan	8×1½	1.2 L	20×4
	9×1½	1.5 L	23×4
Pie Plate	8×1¼	750 mL	20×3
	9×1¼	1 L	23×3
Baking Dish or Casserole	1 quart	1 L	—
	1½ quarts	1.5 L	—
	2 quarts	2 L	—